*Between Earth
and Paradise*

Between Earth and Paradise

MIKE TOMKIES

*with photographs in black and white
and colour by the author*

HEINEMANN : LONDON

William Heinemann Ltd
10 Upper Grosvenor Street, London W1X 9PA

LONDON   MELBOURNE   TORONTO
JOHANNESBURG   AUCKLAND

First published 1981
Text and Illustrations © Mike Tomkies 1981

434 78800 7

Printed and bound in Great Britain by
Morrison & Gibb Ltd., London and Edinburgh

For Vin

"In the time of middle earth, timeless aeons before the fall from grace, there was a place where men could pass quite freely between earth and paradise. So that men's minds should not be dazed by the shocking beauty of paradise, the place was made in the celestial image, a high place of ethereal beauty, masked in soft mist, earthly yet shot through with a spirit beyond the range of men's minds. So perfect it could not be other than the roots of heaven."

(A legend told in the Allinson family of Westmorland.)

1

THE GALES WERE BLASTING over the island from the north-west, whipping off the tops of the Atlantic billows and from the mouth of the sea loch, three miles away, deep trough-like waves were roaring up to where I stood, their crests foaming and frothing, until they smashed themselves with elemental fury at the rocks below. It was as if the ocean had declared war on its ancient rival the earth. From the low, black clouds scudding across a sky shot with grey and violet, intermittent squalls of hail were being unleashed, the stones hitting the old, stone pier and my boat with such force that some of them bounced three feet back into the air. The afternoon passed slowly then I noticed that after each hailstorm, the wind lessened for a brief while. If I was to get across at all this day I would have to risk it during one of these slight lulls.

I had been waiting for twenty-two hours. The island's big boat had almost gone down in the previous day's storms and I had spent the night in my old Land Rover parked above the pier.

It was now 5 pm and would soon be dark. The tide had been on the ebb turn for two hours and if I left it much longer I wouldn't be able to clear the sandbank to the west. At low tide my boat, which had dragged its rear anchor in the gales, would be on the rocks below the pier. And the next high tide would occur in the dead of night, the pier would be covered again and the boat would be at the mercy of the rough seas. So I now had little choice but to go.

After the next hailstorm had hurled down its worst and a clearer patch was heading over, I hauled the boat into the pier, loaded in my backpack, sacks of supplies and the fuel tank, hauled up the anchor and set off. Even going slowly head-on into the foaming waves, the boat banged up and down in the troughs so violently it was hard to keep my seat. By the time I was above the sandbank another squall hurtled over the mountains and now that I was *moving* against the wind the hailstones were hitting me hard, as if thrown down by a vast angry hand. I had to shut my eyes for it was like being stoned by hundreds of small pebbles.

With one hand on the tiller and squinting through the barely opened fingers of the other held across my face, I thought I would perish in the roaring noise for I could hardly tell the difference between the hail and the lashing spray, the stormy grey of the air and the green of the icy water. For a time I virtually had to steer by the *feel* of the waves and the wind. I limped into the lee of the island, turned west for the last two miles, negotiated the narrow channel between two rocky islets where resting seals were reluctant to hump their way into the still-stormy water and after another brief blasting from the gales blowing down a valley, finally reached the shelter of my little bay.

As I hauled my boat into the special "cradle" of planks and rope I'd made to protect it from the rocky shore, knowing that yet again I'd have to come around 2 am and haul it above high-tide level, I felt only a surge of gratitude. In this wild remote place, just to reach home safely with some supplies was thankful deliverance.

As I puffed with loaded pack and hand-held provisions up the steep 300-yard slope to the old wooden croft, my trousers drenched beneath the cheap storm suit, I smiled ironically – to think I had imagined the Scottish Highlands would be a more benign environment than the Pacific coast cliff-top in Canada where I had spent three-and-a-half exciting years!

Indoors, I lit the paraffin lamp and as my room sprang into bright focus and the beam shone through the window upon the ash trees that lined the burn and shielded the croft from the worst of the Atlantic gales, I glanced at my calendar – October 20 reminded me that it was precisely a year since I had first arrived in Scotland in my old Land Rover as part of an odd pilgrimage – to take a second look at the islands of my birth and to meet author Gavin Maxwell whose *Ring Of Bright Water* had suggested to me a wilderness life in Britain was really possible. Not until I reached the Lake District, had I learned of Maxwell's early death so it was a year ago to this very day that I had descended the bleak lonely hill above his former home, Camusfearna, and found the cottage gone, with only a small, green wreath before the little rock under which his ashes then lay.

Now I lit the fire in the open hearth and sat back staring at the flickering flames, reflecting what an extraordinary year it had been for me. It seemed like a decade since I had watched the sunset from the drift log cabin I had built on the British Columbian coast wondering what to do with the rest of my life. I had gone to Canada four summers earlier seeking tranquillity in new surroundings to write a novel.

Although the book failed, during the years of working on it my youthful love of nature had been re-born, and I had known some thrilling experiences with wildlife, culminating in treks into one of the last true wildernesses in all North America. I had watched grizzlies, bald eagles, cougar and caribou in their remote fastnesses, both alone and in the company of an old Scots-Indian called Tihoni, who taught me more by example than word. To me those treks could not be repeated and when they were over a strange sense of anti-climax had pervaded the months that followed. I had learned to live with and to love the wilderness but for me the time had come to move on.

One morning I had woken up to a faint banging sound. At first I thought Booto, the wild stray dog that had come out of the woods during my first winter and had been my only companion for years, was playing at the foot of my bed. But through the window I saw a bulldozer clearing trees on the once-deserted northern spit of land over which the bald eagles flew to their nest. A speculator had bought the area and was building vacation chalets. That afternoon on the little island where I collected my small "ration" of oysters, I found a new notice board "Private Oyster Lease. No Trespassers". I rowed home, my little bag of shellfish beneath my seat, feeling like a thief.

On my next visit to the far store the forest road was unusually thick with traffic and there had been unprecedented queues a mile long at the ferry crossing from Vancouver that weekend. More city-bound folk had discovered the beauty of the coast and it was now becoming a major vacation area.

Early the next weekend Booto gave a warning growl and I heard voices outside the cabin. I went out – to greet a crowd of smiling new neighbours. A 160-foot strip of land next to mine was now owned by *five* Vancouver families. As we shook hands they told me I had put them to shame.

"We've been looking at your cabin," they said, "and now we've seen what one crazy Englishman can do on his own, we're all going to build summer cabins too." They seemed surprised when I told them it wasn't my *summer* cabin but my only home. For the rest of the week the woods rang with the joyful shouts of children, the ring of axes, whir of chain saws, grinding of winches and the thumps of falling trunks as some of the fathers ignored the good drift logs on the beaches and felled young, green trees for cabin bases. They borrowed my boat, drank cans of pop, and the air was filled with the smoke of their camp-fire barbecues, to which I was invited and assured that this was the life.

During the ensuing talk one of the men said, "Y'know, Canada is a great country and British Columbia is the best part of Canada. I've no wish to go anywhere else. We're so lucky in this country because we can *lean* on America and be protected." I stared at him sadly. The old pioneers who had opened up this vast country – men like Ed Louette, the old woodsman who'd helped me build my cabin, and Tihoni who'd guided me into real grizzly country, were slowly dying out. The new third or fourth generation urban dwellers had little desire to pioneer in *all* weathers in really wild country. To them the wilderness was merely a summer playground.

"That's right," broke in one of the other men as he cracked an alder branch across his knee with an extravagant gesture and threw it on to the fire. "You sure couldn't live like this back in the Old Country, eh?" I agreed it would be difficult.

"Yep," he added. "It sure must be sad living in a country that was once great, seeing it sink into the sea."

I sat in silence a few moments. This remark, which mirrored my own feelings on first leaving Britain, now oddly produced a surge of defensive patriotic pride in me – Britain, the country that had given a concept of free democratic government and jurisprudence, liberty under law, to all North America, who had opened most of it up, a land whose inventive genius had pioneered aviation, TV, jet engine, hover-craft, penicillin . . . that had given the world Shakespeare, Dickens, Tennyson, Keats, Wordsworth, Burns and a great naturalist tradition with men like Richard Jefferies, Charles Darwin, Julian Huxley, Henry Williamson. . . . That summer there had been paralyzing strikes among the BC telephone and mail workers, the coastal ferries, the logging companies, even among local teachers, a worse strike record than any I'd known in Britain.

"No worse than living in a country that's going down without *ever* being great," I said icily. I could be facetious too.

For long lonely nights now memories of the British Isles, my boyhood in the woods and fields of Sussex, came crowding back to my mind, and I think I managed to divorce some of them from mere nostalgia. To paraphrase Kipling: "What do they know of Britain, who only Britain know?" After the entire North American experience – for I had also taken time out to drive my old milk truck all round America and Mexico – I was now looking back at Britain with new eyes.

I drifted through the next weeks lost in indecision. I was dispirited, low in funds, and even Booto seemed bored with my company for he was spending as much time with other folk he knew on the coast as with me, mostly a retired construction man, Fred Johnston and his wife.

One morning I went on a hopeful visit for mail, for I'd been writing to old friends in London, but all that waited for me was a large buff envelope. I put it on the truck seat to open when I got back to the cabin, then went on to see if Booto was at the village refuse tip where he sometimes went to rendezvous with summer lady friends. He was not there but I found a tattered paperback book – *Ring of Bright Water* by Gavin Maxwell, which I'd heard of but had never read.

Back in the cabin I opened the envelope. Inside was a brochure of England's Lake District. There was no letter and I had no idea who could have sent it. But as I turned the pages I found myself staring enraptured at the beautiful photos. One, taken over Derwent Water, seemed an exact replica of the sublime Pacific view on which I had gazed so often and so long. How odd it now seemed that I had never even visited such places while actually *living* in Britain. Next to the picture were the words of an ancient Westmorland legend:

"In the time of middle earth, timeless aeons before the fall from grace, there was a place where men's minds could pass quite freely between earth and paradise. So that men's minds should not be dazed by the shocking beauty of paradise, the place was made in the celestial image, a high place of ethereal beauty, masked in soft mist, earthly yet shot through with a spirit beyond the range of men's minds. So perfect it could not be other than the roots of heaven."

Romantic though these words were, they reached into my heart, as if the sun were suddenly shining upon some long-buried seed. Nostalgia and love for my native islands hit me in a flood. I had an overpowering urge to go home, back to my roots. If Britain was "sinking into the sea" then maybe I should return and damn well sink with it. And as I read Gavin Maxwell's enchanting story about his life with otters at Camusfearna, I suddenly knew what I was going to do. If such places as these still existed in the crowded lands of my birth, I would return, raise some "stake" money, then somewhere in the length and breadth of the British Isles, I would find a remote and lovely place and re-create my little wilderness paradise.

There was no "drop-out" philosophy in my intent, for I had no wish to be a philosophizing parasite on social security. I had learned, as had the old pioneers, that the more you free yourself from conventional life, the harder you have to work to *earn* that freedom.

That same week, by surprising coincidence, a friend in London sent me an article in which Maxwell described how he had lost *his* paradise – Camusfearna had burned down and he had moved to a lighthouse, with little energy left to start again. I resolved to meet him and see if we might go into some wilderness venture together.

I decided to sell my land lease. Although replies flooded in from folks who thought they wanted to leave city life, asking questions like "What *shape* is the cabin? Where can we park the car? What cooking fuels are available? What furnishings are there?", the few that actually came to see it were portly middle-aged couples who'd spent time in the beer parlours. Blowing like whales along the trail, talking of their youthful fishing in the wilds, they would take one look at my unstately home, at the rugged terrain, the lack of mains water, gas, electricity, phone and road, and that was that. Most had no intention of buying, they were bored and just wanted somewhere to go while up on the coast.

I'd almost given up hope of selling when one afternoon I saw children stumbling along my beach, followed by a couple and a dog. The man was an English professor at a Vancouver university and he told me they had been looking at a piece of land similar to mine but with no beach or cabin. They were being asked $3,500 for it.

I saw his children looking up expectantly, their big eyes full of hunger for their very own outdoor place by the sea. These children might yet have some of the wonderful wildlife experience I had enjoyed. And I liked the quiet manner of the man himself.

"You can have this land, cabin, furniture, boat, slipway and this beach for a thousand less," I said.

The doctor was puzzled. "You mean a thousand more?"

"No. I mean a thousand *less*."

He came up the log staircase and introduced himself. It seemed more than another coincidence that his surname, Kendal, was exactly the same as that of a Lake District town, the largest in Westmorland (now Cumbria). And as he wrote out a deposit cheque there and then, I felt already a stranger. Among the goods inventory I bequeathed to the new owner, the following tell their own little story:

1 Cedar pole boat slipway.
1 Gin pole plus block and tackle.
1 Kidney-shaped fir desk.
1 Board bed on saw horses.
1 Driftwood chair with cushion.
1 Pair hand-made spruce oars.
1 20-gallon drum.
1 Twin tree log staircase (Safety not guaranteed). Etc.

The hardest part of all was leaving Booto. I desperately wanted to take him back to Britain with me but at his age – nine or ten (no-one knew) – it would have been cruel to sentence him, a wild, free animal, to a year (as it was then) in a cage in some British quarantine kennels. He would not have understood. He had lived on that wild coast all his life and to him it was home. But he himself had taught me not to be too possessive about him. In recent weeks, bored by my inactivity, he had spent much time with other friends and we had all been sharing his favours. The Johnstons and the family who ran the local café said they would gladly feed him, as they had done many times before.

When the last day came and I locked up the cabin, Booto made little mewing noises. He knew I was leaving and those last hours with him were heartbreaking. I sat awhile with him on the beach, holding his paw, stroking his head, telling him it was not goodbye for ever, that someday I would be back, trying to explain.

After the last load had been carried up the trail into the truck, I took Booto round to Fred Johnston's and watched him eat a plate of dog meat his wife had already bought for him.

"I've bullied Fred into letting Booto stay in our warm basement for the winter," she said as Fred, usually an unsentimental man, smiled sheepishly. We talked about Booto awhile as he made a fuss of Rubena Johnston, and I suppose I should have stayed longer but somehow I couldn't stand it. I gave Booto a final clumsy hug, buried my face in his soft chestnut ruff, was unable to say the word "goodbye" and ran to my truck. I drove blindly back to the clearing behind the cabin and spent my last, sleepless night there.

Next morning it was pouring with rain which made it easier to leave, the heavy drops bending even the leaves into attitudes of patient dejection. I turned south and drove away on the first leg of the 3,000-mile drive across Canada before catching a jet plane to London.

I felt a strange mixture of emotions on arriving back in Britain – the tiny roads, squashed soggy little houses of London's outskirts, the little cars, delayed luggage and frowning airport faces – so many people crushed together. But one thing that struck me as never before was that, despite her economic troubles, Britain had preserved an extraordinary outward-looking attitude. One could travel all over North America and never hear more than a few words about Britain on radio or TV, or read more than a paragraph or two in the papers, yet in Britain most of the news was about *other* countries. The first radio programme I heard was "Any Answers", ordinary enough, but hearing the well-balanced and quietly expressed views on a variety of topics from folk mainly from the small towns and villages throughout the land, not the overheated big cities, made me feel Britain's heart was beating as soundly as ever. A big heart that would yet absorb the extremes of Left and Right and the excesses of the modern age, and still beat stoutly for individual freedom. Like many a returning emigrant, I was feeling intensely patriotic.

Adopting the attitude of the Canadian logger after long spells in the wilds, I had promised myself three luxury days in a posh hotel with a heated swimming pool before I looked for cheap accommodation. But I never had them. One evening I visited an old friend, photographer and entrepreneur Alex Sterling, an extraordinary character who had toured Mexico and Spain with Pietro Annigoni to produce glossy books that contrasted the arts of painter and photographer, and was a pal of the Maharajah and Maharanee of Cooch Behar in India. Alex once talked showman Mike Todd into making a film using Elizabeth Taylor as a *model*! Alex also ran an exclusive supper club in South Kensington for theatrical stars and as we talked long into the evening, recapturing our experiences among the fast-living set I had abandoned for the wilderness years in Canada, I told Alex I would soon be looking for a cheap London base. He suddenly seized my arm and propelled me through a door into a thickly carpeted room, empty save for racks of wine bottles and a camp bed.

"It's yours," he said. "Free, for as long as you like. But tell me if you drink any of the wine so I can change the inventory!" What an unexpected windfall! Next day I bought a small camp cooker, axe, tools, sleeping bag and pots and pans for my safari into the "wilds" of Britain. Then I purchased a secondhand Land Rover, took out the rear seats and built in cupboards, shelves, a clothes cabinet and a folding, plywood bed.

In less than a week I was in the Lake District and after much searching, hired a caravan on the banks of Esthwaite Water, a small but serene lake. That first day I tried fishing but I had no luck. Sitting there in a little polystyrene boat I had bought cheaply, the low, soft-green hills of England around me, I suddenly felt strange, oddly dissociated from the real world, like a being from another planet. Where is "home" anyway, I wondered.

Several weeks were spent exploring for an isolated waterfront home, driving and camping rough round the lakes. At Derwentwater I found Friar's Crag and the vista which had helped me decide to return to Britain. What the photo had not shown was the whole town of Keswick!

Finally, after two months and some odd encounters, I decided the Lake District was too highly organized, too crowded and far too expensive for my slender finances.

I would go to Scotland, continue my search there and meet Gavin Maxwell. One October night in a Lake District pub, one of two young nurses started talking to me, asking if I was going up to Scotland. I said I was. She then asked if I was going to visit Camusfearna which seemed more than coincidence. I said I had planned precisely that and I also hoped to meet Maxwell himself, to see if we might partake in some worthwhile wilderness venture together, for I felt he had made many unnecessary mistakes.

"You know he's dead?"

Her question shocked me for I had not known, and I had not thought of checking. She told me that the writer had recently died of cancer in hospital at Inverness – during the week I'd made my decision to return to Britain. The nurse was a friend of a Highland couple who had been great friends of Maxwell's, and she now told me Camusfearna's real name.

I drove up through Cumbria and across Scotland, arriving at the area on a dingy, grey day. Parking by a Forestry Commission fence, I climbed over and pushed my way through the thick, young conifers on the hill behind where I thought Camusfearna lay. After half a mile I saw a telephone line. By following it I came to Maxwell's overgrown track through the trees. I was surprised that he had had a phone.

Camusfearna looked dark, lonely and bleak. The cottage had been destroyed by fire and razed to the ground. One rough stone lay over Maxwell's ashes, and a wreath of fading, green leaves and a wire cross with conifer leaves interwoven in it were the only signs of the man who had created a concept of paradise for so many. Nearby, its surface covered with the scarlet berries of the rowan tree on which Maxwell believed he had been cursed, stood the stone monument to Edal, his famous otter who had replaced Mijbil. And engraved on it Maxwell's inscription silently exhorted the dark sky and the rowan tree "Whatever joy she gave to you, give back to Nature".

At that moment I felt an impulse to try and breathe new life into the place, fill it with love, resurrect it. And when I saw another old croft on the site which Maxwell had not mentioned in his book, it seemed right for me to try and acquire it, so that I could restore Camusfearna to a new beauty. I knelt there silently, eyes closed, but no thoughts or inspiration came, only a sense of overwhelming sadness and desolation. Not for many years, until I had read Maxwell's later books and the biography by his friend Richard Frere, did I realize that superb lyrical writer though he was at his best, I would have little in common with Maxwell as a wild-animal keeper, wilderness dweller or as a man. But I did not know that day and I paid a visit to the titled owner, who seemed amused at my direct approach – thus began negotiations which ran into weeks.

Back in London I again met the girl I had loved before emigrating to Canada, who was still unattached. Then a leading popular magazine offered me a writing contract for six months. Flattered at being remembered after so long an absence, needing finance for my wilderness life in Britain, I accepted and moved into a flat in Knightsbridge – for that was what the lady wanted. But the renewed romance fared little better than before, and taking the job proved a mistake. I had been a free wilderness man too long. One can never go home again – not on the same terms. I felt like a man in a cage, sold the flat lease again – lucky to escape after only three months.

9

In early New Year I went back to Camusfearna to meet Frere, now one of Maxwell's executors, who had a small cottage for sale on the author's estate. We met at a lonely crossroads near Glenelg but the cottage was not what I wanted. It was half a mile from the beach and one of the ferry roads to Skye ran between it and the shore. It could never be the small wilderness paradise I sought to re-create.

I travelled the Highlands, living rough, finding places with names where there were no longer the places, feeling a growing empathy with the landscape itself, its misty, mystic beauty. its hidden wildlife. But I just missed a lonely seaside cottage which had stood empty for six years on the Inverness-shire coast. An aged couple said they might sell an old house four-and-a-half miles from the road on a sea peninsula when they were too old to reach it in the summers – they were in their 80s! After one night's camp by an ancient croft site at Port Luinge I woke to an almost identical view to my place in Canada and I half expected to see again the log staircase and cabin. But I had no luck with the absentee landlord of the 40,000-acre estate on which it stood. On another visit I badgered and tried to charm various factors who all gave non-committal replies and took several weeks to put me "on the files".

I began to feel I was on a hopeless chase, but decided I would try once more then go back to Canada. In March I visited the Forestry Commission office in Inverness – where I was shown a huge bundle of letters. all similar enquiries to mine, but this time I was given details of an isolated forestry cottage on a fresh-water loch in north Argyll, which was to be put out to public tender.

Half-heartedly I drove away, then decided to first cut across country to Arisaig where I'd heard vague stories about palm trees, silver sand beaches and warm waters from the Gulf Stream Drift. I arrived in the setting sun and, astonishingly, there was a palm tree – by the side of the road – and there *were* the silver beaches of pure shell sand, green crystal waters bathed in the dying sun's golden light. Travel weary, I dropped into the Arisaig Hotel bar.

The habitués were initially suspicious of this dishevelled stranger in their midst out of season, but the owner, Murdo Grant, listened patiently to my tale of woe. Next morning Murdo kindly put me on to Mrs Cameron Head of Lochailort who just as kindly gave me the names of two people who might help.

I found myself heading south to meet an estate manager who lived at Dorlin on Loch Moidart. As I drove along, a bend in the road suddenly opened out on to a view so magnificent, right down the sea loch and over the islands of Eigg and Rhum, its beauty hit me like a stroke in the soul. Entranced, I stopped the Land Rover and impulsively knelt down to kiss the ground, to touch the rocks on the shore. A strange excitement grew within me for I felt in some odd way that I was actually coming home. (Although I knew I had *some* Scots blood, I didn't know until a talk with my father over a year later that my mother, Adele MacKinlay Stewart, who died when I was four, was pure Highland, and that her father John Stewart was born on Islay).

When I met the estate manager it seemed I was doomed for more disappointment. Mr Phil Corcoran told me his estate had nothing suitable. I turned away and looked out to sea. A shimmering blue vista of myriad islets in the loch led out to the great Atlantic. To the north lay a three-mile-long island, partly covered with many different kinds of conifers – to anyone who loved trees and sea as I did it was clearly a paradise. The ruined shell of ancient Castle Tioram, stronghold of the Clanranald chiefs, stood silent sentinel over an idyllic scene.

The lovely island was called Eilean Shona and the other name Mrs Cameron Head had given me was of its owner, Mr Digby Vane, a retired economist and a one-time Olympic reserve sprinter. I prevailed on Mr Corcoran to telephone Mr Vane and the upshot was an appointment for me to ring him myself at 4 pm that day.

Feeling sure this lead would also not work out, I raced away to view the forestry cottage, realizing halfway I had insufficient time, and hurried back to explain my quest to Mr Vane over the phone. He agreed to meet me next day.

In blazing sunshine and a stiff, westerly breeze Digby Vane roared across the mile of sea from his home on the south-east edge of the island in a triple-hulled dory and pulled up with a grin. I think we liked each other on sight, and he invited me back to at least take a look and meet the family. We bounced over the seas at a terrifying speed and I had to cling with both hands under the thwart to stay in my seat.

We met his wife Kay and their partner, inventor and pioneer in radar monitoring systems, Reggie Rotheroe, and went to talk in their antique-filled lounge. The Vanes had bought Eilean Shona, whose literal translation from the Gaelic, Eilean Sean-ath, means Island of the Old Ford, from Lady Howard de Walden in 1962. As we talked, Kay told me that *Peter Pan*'s author, J. M. Barrie, had written the first film script of the book and part of his *Marie Rose* there in that very drawing room. (They still had Barrie's desk.) "And he called it the most beautiful island in the world," Kay added. If it was good enough for Barrie, it would be more than good enough for a two-failed-novels "author" like myself, I thought.

Later as we walked in the rhododendron-filled garden, by the lily pond flanked by large and rare meta sequoia and Japanese cedar trees, in which otters sported at dawn and dusk. Digby Vane told me there were seventy different types of conifer on the island. Many of them had been planted personally by a previous owner, seafarer Captain Swinburne, who had collected some of them on the China Trade runs. It was reputedly one of the most comprehensive collections of conifers in Britain.

We skimmed away in the dory along the island's superb coastline, then staggered over seaweed-covered rocks to look at an old cottage which nestled in a green dell. It had no doors or windows, the skylights were broken in, the wooden floors had perished and sheep were using it as a shelter. None of this bothered me but I said it wouldn't do because when I turned round I could *see* a single-track road and a couple of cottages on the mainland!

On the Atlantic edge of the island, two-and-a-half miles from the little mainland pier, we came to a secluded natural bay with high rocky walls on either side. Almost three hundred yards above the sandy beach stood a large dark wooden croft – broken windows, rotten boards hanging from rusty nails, and a corrugated-iron roof. We plugged our way up the steep bracken-covered hill to it and I turned to look at the view. I could see over the whole mouth of the sea loch and across the Atlantic, a vast 180-degree panorama and not a house, road or sign of human habitation in sight. From a hill to the west I could see straight over the Atlantic and, again, the mist-shrouded islands of Muck, Eigg and Rhum.

I stood there spellbound, feeling that pang almost of pain, of first love. A row of tall, ash trees protected the croft from the western blasts without spoiling the view. An agate-coloured burn gurgled past the croft, provider of the most valuable element for a wilderness living. Overhead a large, speckled buzzard soared, it too following its own lonely star.

"There's nothing between you and Canada here!" laughed Digby, regarding me quizzically. "You're not a *smuggler,* are you?" I laughed too, assured him I was no smuggler. Already Canada was becoming a dream.

"What's this place called?" I asked him.

"Ballindona," he answered.

"Ballindona?" I repeated. "Like Bella Donna. Beautiful woman. Well, I don't have the beautiful woman but this place would be paradise enough for me!"

Digby coughed quietly. "Well, you seem a reasonable sort of chap. If you're crazy enough to do the place up and live all the way out here alone, you're welcome to it."

We looked over the cottage. Much of its woodwork was rotten. There was no road, no electricity, gas, phone, bathroom, kitchen, toilet or even piped water. Sheep dung covered the floor five inches thick. A dead sheep's carcass propped up the shattered door. As I picked up the skull by a horn the hoofs rattled down from the tocsin skin, making my first entrance macabre. It was going to be hard work; all the building

First view of Ballindona, late winter.

materials, timber, tools and personal possessions would have to be ferried over two-and-a-half miles of uncertain seas, then carried up the steep near-300-yard slope. But nothing could have dissuaded me.

Over lunch at the big house the arrangement was made. I could have it for at least three years, unless they had to sell the island for economic reasons. I need pay no rent, just repair the place well enough to live in myself.

I'd only £297 left to start my new life in the Scottish wilds so back in London I lined up some writing work then hurried back to the Highlands. The Land Rover was now loaded down with the tiny polystyrene boat, window glass, axes, saws, pickaxe, sledgehammer, plastic loo (shipped from Canada), water carriers, clothes, books, bedding, fishing gear, paraffin heater (found on a London dump and the best I ever had), oars, gas canisters, tinned food and a portable cold box. At a saw mill near Fort William I strapped on three dozen heavy timbers and slowly groaned the last forty miles of single-track road to the little pier opposite the island.

Next day, regarding my tiny boat dancing like a feather on the choppy ocean, I hired the island's two workers and the big thirty-foot boat to take the heaviest gear and timber to Ballindona. As the two men conversed volubly in Gaelic, I felt more "foreign" than when I had first landed in Canada! Even at high tide we could not get into the beach, they said – so everything had to be left on a high hump-backed rock overnight.

In the morning I rowed the two-and-a-half miles to the croft in strong westerly winds. The little boat may have been adequate for the Lake District waters but on that wild sea I was dicing with death. By the time I arrived I felt ready for bed but I had to spend the day hauling up the timber, glass, cement, hardboard and other gear in case the tidal waves smashed the lot along the rocky beaches. Thirty-eight times up and down the steep slope which in places was one in two, added up to over 30,000 steep feet, and as half of it consisted of perspiring upward

A rare calm day but in blowy April my first craft was too flimsy.

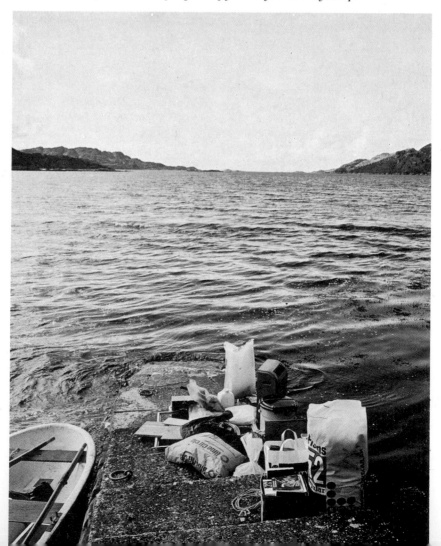

movement with heavy loads, I reckon I became a semi-fledged Scots hill walker that first day. Once, carrying sheets of hardboard on my back, a gust of wind sent me staggering across the burn. So I made a sled of two timbers and hauled them up four at a time, using a rope harness. My heart pounded, my legs gave out twice, and I knew the meaning of Scotch mist before the eyes.

During the week it took to make one room habitable I slept in an old caravan on the shore below the big house. It had a window missing, so was cold and as it poured nearly every day, I returned to it soaked with sweat and rain. With nowhere to dry clothes, I donned new gear the next morning and the following day had to put on the half-dry clothing from the previous day. One night I woke with the caravan being tossed around like a ship at sea. The island's six rams were using it as a rubbing post. On the third morning I borrowed a small, $1\frac{1}{2}$-hp outboard motor, a help to rowing against the wind but the beach presented problems. After clearing a channel through rocks with a crowbar, I found later that lots of small rocks had drifted in on their seaweed umbrellas, necessitating further clearing.

The fourth day was so stormy I had to walk in over the mountain trail, a sheep and deer "path" over quagmire, peat bog, spiky gneiss rocks, and over slippery stone causeways with two-foot gaps between many of the steps – which gave problems to a man with a full pack.

Shovelling out sheep dung, removing the window frame and re-glazing and painting it, fitting hardboard round the walls and rebuilding some rotten foundation sills, I finally had one room in fair shape. One afternoon I nearly lost the little boat when I underestimated the speed of the incoming tide – I just managed to reach it with a long pole, standing waist deep in the cold sea as it was about to depart for the open Atlantic.

But on the lonely walks over the hills I was continually rewarded – by the sight of three red stags moving so effortlessly over the rugged terrain that they seemed to float as if obeying the strings of an invisible puppeteer, by seeing a kestrel hovering in the wind like a tiny anchor in the sky as it scanned for mice or frogs below, and by seeing the buzzard again, soaring unconcernedly over my head.

On the eighth day Reggie Rotheroe came down to the caravan with a little radio he had made himself. "You'll be needing that up there," he said, plonking it down and leaving almost before I could thank him. Then the Vanes allowed me to borrow some items from a boatshed of furniture near the Shone pier. I picked an old single iron bedframe, a mattress, two rush mats, a kitchen chair and a superb mahogany 4-drawer desk. With the help of their chief man, Iain MacLellan, and the big boat, we shipped them over and lugged them up the hill. So I moved into my new wilderness home.

15

Moving on to the island – everything had to be left on a high rock overnight.

Even after the years in the Canadian wilds, the lonely wooden croft seemed a ghostly, isolated place that first night. A hundred years earlier a small settlement of crofters had lived there and the ruined stone walls of three of their primitive homes still showed above the bracken and rushes. I woke up after a few hours, scared because I was sure I could hear the distant skirling of ghostly bagpipes. But the noise was caused by the wind whistling through a knot hole on the window frame! Even so, now that I was some two miles from the nearest humans, the isolation seemed enormous.

Next day, as though welcomed by nature, the rain and storms had gone. I went out and stood on the green hill overlooking an ocean now beautiful and still. The early morning sun from the east now dazzled the myriad islets and upon the cerulean blue of the sea loch. Below me, down the path that followed the singing, winding burn, the waves broke gently emerald and crystalline over the white sand of the beach that now appeared to be lit from within, as if by some heavenly radiance. The feeling was strong upon me that I had indeed come home.

2

A MAY SHOWER HAD just passed over and the sweet smell of the
earth, after the benediction of the rain, mingled with the tang of
the sea air as I set out in goldpan sunlight for a walk to the
Atlantic edge of the island. As I trod the gleaming deer path I heard the
waves chuckling on the rocks below and lapping the small gravel bays,
the tiny burns tinkling as they etched their way through ancient granite
to their parent sea, the wind breathing through the heather. These
sounds were my only music — but a kind one could never hear in a
concert hall.

How different were the stunted trees and these open hills, still bare
with winter grey, from the mighty western Canadian forests, the
plunging torrents in the rivers when the winter snows began to melt,
from the long, tidal flats where the great grizzlies would now be grazing
on the first grass at dawn. Although I had studied English wildlife in
boyhood, I knew little about the Scottish Highlands. I felt filled with a
sense of discovery and open to new influences on my first exploratory
walk on the island. What wildlife would I find here?

Suddenly I heard a strident voice ahead. I peered through the heather
– there in a natural grotto of the grey, lichened rocks, perched on a fern,
was a tiny wren singing in stentorian tones far too loud for its size. With
the rocks reflecting his voice like an amplifier, he sounded like an
imitation canary, his whole body quivering with the effort of producing vibrant song. Another wren, presumably a female he was trying
to impress, for she was silent, flitted to a fern nearby. He flew to a little
domed nest below some heather on a rock and, spreading his short tail
feathers for support, flirted his wings in the sunshine, as if enticing her to
take a look. He succeeded for she flew straight in to the nest but a few

seconds later came out again and zipped back to her perch. He immediately flew towards her then veered off, whirring like a big, brown bee, towards a small waterfall into which he seemed to vanish. She followed but in less than a minute both flew out again and disappeared into some bushes in fast, dodging flight. I went over to take a look.

He had built a nest right beside the waterfall, so close that some drops of spray were falling on to its roof. But inside it was totally dry. No wonder early naturalists believed wrens used their saliva as gum to build waterproof domes on their nests.

Wrens, like their namesake Sir Christopher Wren, architect of St Paul's Cathedral, are master builders but only the males do the nest-making. Women's lib is a new concept in human life but in the wren world it has been the *status quo* for thousands of years. Perhaps they imported it from America for wrens are one of the few European birds who invaded the Old World from the New, crossing the then existing land bridge at the Bering Straits in the Pleistocene era! At any rate the little males build several intricate domed nests then have the task of enticing a female to use one and be a wife. So good an engineer is the male that he will gather wood fibres caught round fallen trees in rivers because when they dry out they bind the nest more strongly. A really vigorous male in his prime, in areas with plenty of sites and food, practises polygamy and can support several wives. But, I was to find out later, this almost never happens in the rugged Highlands of Scotland – just as the human divorce rate and extra-marital adventures increase in affluent or crowded city areas, in places where a living is harder to win, wrens have as much as they can do to support one wife and a large family.

As I walked on, the first, humble-bee queen of the year, sluggish from hibernation, zoomed past looking for a suitable site, like an old shrew hole, to make her nest and start her new colony. Suddenly I heard a strange sirening noise, a loud drawn-out "*Awhoo*" and at first I thought it came from the seals that hauled themselves out on the rocky islets at the loch's mouth. But surely only the grey seal makes such sounds? There was a commotion on the placid surface of the sea below – a splendid black-and-white eider duck drake was flap-chasing a dowdier brown female, his thick bandy legs thrashing the water as he seemed to be trying to grab her tail in aggressive courtship.

But the duck just swooshed into the water again and the drake went down too. Through my field glass I saw him swim urgently around her, like a hefty little tugboat, tossing his massive wedge-shaped beak skywards as if he was gulping. He really was a solid barge of a duck, decked out in superb evening dress, his black jacket a startling contrast to his white back and snowy velvet cheeks beneath his black-capped

Shoe Bay.

head. On his white breast was a patch of delicate peach, and overlaying each wing were long, white plumes, fine enough to grace the hat of the Laughing Cavalier. Occasionally he reared up, showing the female his black velvet belly, and flapped his wings. The lady, however, seemed unimpressed for she paddled stolidly along, though her bright eyes were shining like buttons. As I continued westwards into ever brighter light from the broad Atlantic, his gentle "*awhoos*" came like a soothing serenade from the sea.

Now three buzzards were circling overhead, lit bronze from the reflected light – a large female attended by two smaller birds whom I took to be males courting her, for birds of prey finish training their youngsters before winter is through. The two males showed no animosity towards each other, all three flying along together – if she was not already paired with one of them, she would choose soon.

I walked over two small ridges and found myself looking over a sublime natural lagoon. The tranquil, crystal water was the colour of jade near the rocky edges, deep as the blue of heaven out in the centre and light amethyst where it rippled gently on to a beach of white-shell sand. The whole floor of the shoe-shaped lagoon was also of this crisp sand, with just here and there a clump of green or brown tangleweed growing up like inverted chandeliers from the sea floor. It was now high tide and nowhere was this eighty-yard pool more than six feet deep. The little beach itself was protected on all sides by high rocks with a patch of green sward on its rear edge, like a preliminary carpet before you reached the sand. No South Sea island could boast anything better than this, I thought. It was as if the retreating glaciers had wanted to show they could fashion a bijou beauty too.

Now I saw something in the water, the broad head of an animal swimming, making an unusually wide V as it went. Not since boyhood on the river Adur in Sussex had I seen a British otter swimming but the huge V seemed too large. Through the field glass I saw it was indeed an otter but the illusion was caused by the otter having a little object, probably a butterfish, in its mouth as it swam along the surface. As it climbed out of the water, wet hair clumps dripping and began to eat, another otter a third of its size came up curiously. The mother otter stopped chewing as if to let the youngster have a piece itself, but apart from sniffing gingerly it showed no desire to eat. When the mother finished her meal she ran up and down a rock ledge less than a foot above the water. The youngster only followed her a few steps each way as she went past each time. Next thing I saw the mother seemed to be trying to nudge the baby into the water – but it didn't want to go. The adult then closed her forepaws against her sides and slid off the ledge. She dived, twisted, turned and rolled in the water with joyful abandon, as only an otter can, perhaps showing the youngster what a wonderful watery world there was to play in but her bairn showed no wish to follow. Out came the mother again and once more nudged her reluctant child – it seemed odd there was only one because otters usually have two or three – but it dug its little web-footed claws into the ledge for all it was worth. I wondered how long it would take for the mother to coax her baby into the sea. But suddenly she turned, squeaked so shrilly it was almost a whistle, and both she and the youngster went lolloping across the rocks and out of sight on the other side. I hadn't moved, the slight breeze had been from them to me, yet she had somehow sensed my presence.

As I passed the wrens' nests on the way back, the little male came darting fussily from one heather spray to another beside me, his wings making noisy "*brrrt brrrt brrrrt*" sounds. For all their $3\frac{3}{4}$-in size, male wrens are fiercely territorial and in the breeding season will frequently see you off, like a little suburban dog escorting the postman off the premises.

I cut down to the shore and after a few hundred yards came to a lovely secluded place, sheltered on both sides by high ridges covered with heather and rows of stunted trees. To my surprise there were six different kinds – oak, hazel, ash, rowan, birch and, nearest the shore, alder. None of them topped more than twenty feet yet they were old. They were also the last trees growing westwards on the island and seemed to have great characters of their own. Each had found a precarious foothold on the thin soil or, blown as seed into the rock crevices, had slowly thrust roots down every fissure to find a mite of sustenance.

They were dwarfed from surviving a harsh environment, bent from battling the prevailing south-westerly gales and crooked because every inch had adapted to slight variations in the passing seasons. Each tree was unique in its own way; the alder short and thick-trunked, the hazel bushes tight and canny, and the rowan like a witch's broom – they were small, but none had been defeated. As I stood in the little clearing, the alder buds the first to break and show the green of future leaves, the ash and oak still as tight as winter, I felt I could love them even more than the great forest trees of western Canada, growing tall and uniformly straight amid such protected abundance. These tough little characters, as honed as flyweights, had put up a brave fight to live, had earned the right to be there.

As I continued home again I was conscious that I had not yet earned that right. I didn't fool myself that because I was prepared to live alone on the remote edge of a Scottish island two miles from the nearest humans and slog over the stormy loch in a small boat, that was in itself a right.

To me living in the wilderness was a privilege. I felt these wild Highlands would help me only if I lived in them with reverence for their beauty. They might help me, as had Canada, to find a way of life in which I could avoid disturbances, temptations and social structurings of city life and be inspired, and gain time, to think and to write. Time was paramount for I was well into my forties and had proved I had no natural gifts as a writer. But once I had the old wooden croft in shape, renouncing all mod cons, I could get by on £7 a week, though I still had to earn *that*.

Bouts of work in a Sussex animal market, in a saw mill, as cook on a yacht, and in Canada as logger, salmon boat deckhand and assistant blaster had all been good experiences but had shown me nothing inspirational comes from low-paid labour in order to survive. I briefly considered usual Highland jobs like postman, road or forestry worker – and writing at night. But I had run out of youthful energy and living on an island made such jobs impractical anyway.

I walked on, feeling an interloper, but as I reached the green hill of the croft again, the little banks of wild daffodils, some broken off by recent gales, were all nodding in the breeze as if to greet me, the only gentle reminders that once a family had lived here. Not for thirty-three years had they heard the sounds of children's tears or laughter, the tired tread of father heavy from work after his walk across the dark island with an oil lantern in his hand. Now I had come, no part of the old crofter life, and yet the lonely flowers made me welcome. As I watched, their yellow heads nodded away and towards each other, as if they were whispering in the winds that stirred their green leaf skirts. I knew, no matter what men had been doing in the busy cities miles away over the sea, this brave little band of flowers had burst forth each spring, hoping perhaps that someone, some time, would come along again and be inspired by their own struggle when all had often seemed lost.

There had been no daffodils on the lonely cliff in Canada but these reminded me of the daffodils of my own country boyhood in Sussex where my first love of nature began. Suddenly they seemed an emotional link with those happy carefree days, and I felt oddly grateful to them. Then I smiled at a memory. Months earlier I had taken the girl I loved down to see my old nature haunts. "You'll never be happy unless you get back to that life for good," she had said. But an isolated life in the wild Highlands had no appeal for her whatever! One evening I had taken her to see the film *Paint Your Wagon* and when grizzled old timer Lee Marvin had grunted out "Wanderin' Star" with lines like "Do I know where hell is – hell is in hello. Heaven is goodbye for ever, it's time for me to go", she had nudged me. "That's you!" Lee Marvin! Unfair, I thought, for I *had* asked her to marry me. Yet she had a point – before the Canadian years I travelled and worked in eighteen countries.

I chuckled as I walked into the lonely croft. Well, I'd lost the lass for she was now married to someone else. But if I was to live alone for good, what an idyllic place in which to suffer.

Yet to earn even a small living I was still trapped in the trade for which I'd been known by publications in nine countries – writing about the movie world and the famous. But, to me, a great boring porridge of kitchen-sink concepts, the elevation of the moronic life into drama and the cult of the anti-hero, had pervaded much of literature and entertainment. After years of dreary digs over half of Britain as a struggling young reporter, it had taken me a long time to break away from all that, and I didn't want to write about it for a living. Nor about the new actors who had emerged, excellent craftsmen maybe but who were often boring off screen. The era of the colourful characters like Wayne, Gable, Mitchum, Bogart, Ava Gardner, Monroe, had passed, and prudent technicians had taken over. I had grown older too and it wasn't fun any more. The once "glamorous" theatre world now appeared to me to be only a few acres of grey buildings in various capitals where some folk were overpraised for pretending to be someone else; and so few films or plays had any real vision.

Yet for over a year I still had to dash down to London, where I retained a small bed-sitter for the purpose, race round studios, sell articles, then hurry back to the island and what to me was the last reality – the natural world. I dislike grants or subsidies, especially for writers or artists. I feel if you can't make your own way you don't deserve to do such work. Therefore, I had to overcome my new dislike of the work to which I'd been attracted in earlier naïveté. But the visits to London grew shorter and each time I returned to try to slowly immerse myself into Scottish wilderness life.

Slowly was the operative word for while the Canadian years had equipped me better than if I'd come straight from English city life in the first place, the animal life of these open hills and small forest was quite different. The contrast between overall "harmony" of nature and its "callousness" towards the individual life, was repeated here but on a more finely etched scale that was somehow more personal.

One March morning as missel-thrushes, robins and chaffinches filled the little glen with song, and the sheep around the croft, soon to have their first lambs, began to bleat more noisily, a racing pigeon with red, blue and green rings on its legs flew in, fluttered down weakly and began pecking at scraps. As I went down to the shore to fetch a gas container, a small tortoiseshell butterfly that had wintered in the croft's roof, flew out beside me into the spring sun. The racing pigeon flew a few yards then sat in a cranny between two rocks with its feathers fluffed out. It had flown a long way and was exhausted.

The first bracken shoots were coming through now, doubled over like snakes' heads as if afraid to show their faces to winds and rain until they had grown stronger. I had been told the area would be engulfed by this weed in summer, its underground roots poisoning the earth so that little else would grow, so each time I went down the slope I kicked the snake heads off. Later, when I went down to re-set the boat on the high night tide, I found the racing pigeon had been reduced to a pile of scattered feathers, with just part of the skeleton and one eye left. I doubted that a sparrowhawk, whose larger female is only fifteen inches long, could have killed and eaten it so fast, so it was probably a fox. It seemed oddly sinister that this little murder had taken place only forty yards from the croft when I had not seen or been aware of anything at all. Here was the wild law of indifference towards the weak individual. The pigeon could not rest until it had found good shelter first, and it had been too exhausted to do that. There was no rest, even for the hard-working innocent.

On calm days when I knew I'd be at my desk for hours, I sometimes rowed up the loch after dawn for exercise. One morning, trying to dip the silly little oars of the polystyrene boat silently in an out of the water, I had just passed the pine and larch forests on Deer Island when I saw a row of nine bluish dots in the bents and grasses of a tussocky meadow. I was surprised as I slid nearer – why on earth were nine herons, all neatly spaced some seven yards apart, sneaking along as if on tiptoe between the little mounds? In their blue-grey outfits, white epaulettes and black-and-white head plumes, they looked like a search party of little traffic cops from some South American state as they quartered the slopes. I pulled in below a small heathery ridge and looked over – just in time to see one heron apparently go berserk. Raising its wings halfway like an old lady lifting her skirts, it ran gawkily all over the place, spearing its fearsome five-inch beak into the earth.

It missed whatever it was after but then the heron next to it did the same – darted about crazily, digging its bill into the ground. Evidently it caught what the first heron had been chasing, a mouse or frog, for it leaped clumsily into the air and flapped, long neck still extended, to the banks of a small burn. There it dipped the mouse or frog into the water, elongated its neck straight upwards and swallowed the creature. I could see its neck feathers stick out then smooth down again as the lump went down its gullet.

I must have moved then for the whole line of herons bounded into the air as if of one mind and flew with their strong but deceptively slow-beating flight back to the trees on Deer Island. Why there? I soon found out when I rowed over and walked below the trees. High up in the pine, larch and firs on the island's easterly shore there was a huge heronry and I counted thirty-eight nests. White droppings splashed below told me that the big birds were now roosting in the nests and the breeding season was starting. Until that day I had always regarded the heron as a lonely figure, patiently standing hours in water to make one lightning dart with its beak at any luckless fish that came near. In mediaeval Britain it was believed herons could actually secrete a special oil from their feet which *attracted* fish! But after what I had seen it seemed they also occasionally worked as a *team*. An extraordinary sight and I resolved to watch them whenever I could.

A week later I rowed back in the pre-dawn twilight with some hazel switches to bend as hoops into the ground and some sacking to put over them to make a "hide". I would erect this on a high knoll which was almost on eye level with the top of one large nest, cover it with conifer branches and herbage and so watch the birds while out of sight. I landed on the west edge of the island, away from the heronry, but as I stole through the trees it seemed the nests were devoid of birds. But believing a few could be sitting close, for some of the older nests were about five feet across, I kept going slowly. Suddenly to my right I saw a large blue-grey gliding form as one of the birds cruised slowly a few yards above sea level, dropped lower then disappeared. Leaving the hide materials behind I slid silently forward – to see an extraordinary tableau.

Some flat rocks just off the shore were a riot of colour, ablaze with herons, for twenty-nine of the huge, gawky yet elegant birds were standing on them. This had to be a "dancing" or gathering ground which I'd heard about in boyhood but had never found, the social meeting area which herons sometimes use before the breeding season really gets under way. Each heron stood as if it believed itself to be alone, its long neck hunched back into its shoulders, looking like a disgruntled pelican that had swallowed a rotten fish. Presumably there were both males and females in the party but there was no courting behaviour, no aggression or pecking, nor any sudden running at each other that one sees in gull colonies. Occasionally a new heron glided silently, and as it landed it kept its huge wings aloft and did a clumsy hop, skip and a jump for a few yards before it folded them. Whether this was to help stop its forward impetus or a deliberate "dance" I wasn't sure but each standing heron it passed opened its wings halfway, then did a little awkward, long-legged, forward fandango of its own. There was nothing regular about this "dancing" – maybe they heard a different drummer or one beyond human ken – but it was comical to watch.

Herons are loners most of the year and this odd gathering with its truncated gavottes is said to stimulate their social instincts and their sex hormones before breeding. As I sneaked back to the knoll and quietly erected the hide I felt fascinated by the herons, and each time I watched them over the next few months they seemed more weird and wonderful.

It was about this time a new "neighbour" came to stay around the croft. Woken up early one morning by a loud "*Kaah kaah!*" I looked out of the window to see a hooded crow perched near an old and what I'd thought to be a disused nest of old, dry twigs in a birch tree just above my little bay. He kept calling noisily then suddenly another crow, smaller and more tattered looking, landed near him. I was sure this was a female, maybe his mate, for crows pair for life. But to my surprise he immediately flew at her, flapping his wings and extending his beak aggressively, and drove her away. A few minutes later she came back again but receiving the same unchivalrous treatment, finally flew off to the east in apparent disgust. I knew a little about crows, having studied them as a youngster when I'd had a pet crow I called Clark, and also a fairly tame one who'd come round my cabin in Canada. When it comes to mating, crows are no casanovas but complete pragmatists, and they choose their mates for largely practical factors. It seemed he had summed up this old female and her abilities to breed, help repair the nest and rear young at a glance. She was old, past her prime, and he didn't want a tired old lady as a wife.

He called loudly during the next two days, and one afternoon I looked out of the small rear room I used as a kitchen to see his raucous clamourings had either attracted a female crow more to his liking, or else she was his normal mate who had returned from elsewhere. As a few sheep stood round in apathetic audience, he crouched beside the new crow on the green grass of the hill, fanning his black tail downwards and half opening his wings, then suddenly made two great fifteen-foot leaps into the air, performed a few corkscrew flight gyrations, then landed back beside her as if saying "Look what a magnificent athletic fellow I am". And she, bent low, beak almost touching the earth, acted as if she was embarrassed and saying "Now then, laddie, no need to make a fool of yourself"!

Next morning both crows were in the birch tree, freshening up the old nest with twigs, beakfuls of dead leaves, and wool pulled from the carcase of a winter-dead ewe in the hills half a mile away. Hoping they would breed there, giving the place at least one bird family, I put out bacon rinds, bread and scraps for them each morning.

Just as in Canada with the crow I had named Charlie, it became a one-way friendship. Crows everywhere are opportunists, quick to divine if a human is friendly or antagonistic, and before long the young male took full advantage. He too came early every day, waking me up like an alarm clock at dawn with his harsh "*Kaahs*" from the ash trees near the croft. I always stamped my food tins flat so they would take up less room in the wooden box outside before I buried them. And like the Canadian crow, if he didn't find enough scraps on the grass, he would haul out the meat tins, peck them loudly or throw them about with loud clinks, some of them landing in the burn. I named him Charlie II and he soon became a court jester, or rather croft jester, about the place.

In Scotland the hoodie is persecuted by farmers, shepherds, keepers and stalkers for alleged crimes such as pecking out the eyes of dying lambs, joining forces with ravens and black-backed gulls to prey on sickly sheep in winter, stealing grouse eggs and chicks, hens' eggs laid wild, or raucously warning deer of the presence of a lurking stalker. But it's not surprising that the crow, which has no real song – just a big mouth – has learnt to use man to its own advantage. It is clever, arrogant, bossy and assumes the world belongs to itself – all such human qualities, no wonder it's disliked! But it trades man guile for guile, an optimistic knave who virtually thumbs its nose at attempts to eradicate it, and has even been known to spring the now-illegal gin traps for foxes by dropping stones on them so it can get safely to the bait. Several times in my first summer I saw hoodies sitting in rock shadows, patiently waiting for oystercatchers, ducks, meadow pipits and grouse to reveal their camouflaged nests, so saving themselves an energy-wasting search. They also acted as sentry for their mates, perching on high rocks while the other looked for the food. At first, of course, I knew none of this and felt strangely flattered that Charlie II found me trustworthy.

He was certainly a natty character in his jaunty, grey waistcoat, black wings and tail, and his black cap, he looked as respectable as an undertaker. Yet his Latin name gave a clue to his real character – *Corvus Corone Cornix* – has an oddly Mafia-like ring to it. It seemed odd that a bird which needs to be ultra cunning to survive should have such easily seen plumage, apparently totally lacking all camouflage qualities.

Charlie working over the seaweed for small marine creatures.

However, one old gamekeeper I met at the local village held no grudges against crows. "Years ago when we stalked stags the hoodies would gather high above us in the sky warning the deer but that's rare today, though ravens will do it. I see far more crows on the seashore now than I used to. Perhaps they're changing their habits. Och no, tis herring gulls are the menace now, and if crows are taking *their* food, tis maybe not a bad thing. I don't bother shooting hoodies now."

In later days Charlie II became tame enough to drink milk from a tobacco tin left outside, and it became his favourite tipple. He'd uptilt a few beakfuls, quibble his mandibles a few times, wipe his beak on some bracken, then fly to the big rock outside my window until he felt like some more, then call peremptorily for a refill. Crows are like that – give them an inch and they'll take a yard. Like Uriah Heep, they work their way into your confidence then take you for all you've got. He also had a sadistic sense of play. I had once caught my Canadian crow playing with a frog. Charlie II ate frogs but one afternoon I found him fooling about with a toad. Toads have poisonous secretions on their warty skins so Charlie II had no gastronomical interest in the creature – instead he was playing with it like a cat with a mouse. Every time the slow, stolid toad tried to hop or walk away, Charlie seized it by a leg and dragged it back, or else hopped round to block its escape. Pure horseplay. Toads would be useful about the garden I intended to plant and as I was certain it didn't share Charlie's sense of fun, I rescued it by popping it into the burn. Charlie looked most put out that I had spoiled his little game and flew off. He constantly reminded me of the pet crow I'd befriended as a boy after finding him alone, apparently orphaned, in a big field.

Clark had possessed a devilish sense of humour too. Sometimes when our pet tortoise Toby stretched his crusty old neck out for a bite of lettuce, Clark would ding sharply on his shell with his beak. Toby retracted his head like lightning and Clark stared with fascination at this curious creature, walking round the tortoise until it plucked up courage for another try at the lettuce – then Clark dinged on his shell again. But a well-shied acorn hitting him amidships, plus a spell of detention in his converted rabbit hutch, finally cured Clark of this little prank. Then there was our cat, a floppy good-natured, marmalade, neutered tom called Ginger. For want of nothing better to do, Clark would stage little fights with Ginger, usually when the cat was snoozing. Clark would spar about like a little black featherweight from the Bronx, bop the cat smartly on the nose with his beak – or tweak his tail. Then as the furious cat swiped hopelessly beneath his rapidly rising form, Clark would fly to the safety of the conservatory roof and give vent to hoarse croaks that sounded like guffaws.

Crows have long featured in human folklore. In the Faeroes an ancient belief was that if an unmarried girl went out on Candlemas morning and threw a bone, stone or a lump of turf at a hoodie she would know her future marital state. Depending on whether the crow flew over the sea, landed on a nearby house or stayed where it was, she would know if her husband would come from over the sea, from that house or else she would remain a spinster. As the hoodie is usually a very wary bird and would fly off as soon as she even made to throw anything at it, she was at least certain to be reassured on the most important point. If the olden-day Scots said a man was a "gone corbie" or looked like "he would make the crow a pudding", it meant he was at death's door.

It was in early May that my "friendship" with Charlie II really ended, for like many jokers he began to overstep the mark. For several mornings I was woken up by loud thuds from the back of the cottage. At first I thought it was just the usual sheep rubbing its head and horns on the slats of the wooden wall but, finally mystified, I crept into the rear room. I found Charlie was busily pecking out the new putty from the window I'd recently installed. He apparently liked the linseed oil in it. That was going a bit too far. I opened the window fast, clapped loudly and after a couple of mornings of this treatment, he got the message. He flew off and perched on a far-away rock, looking most pained at this uncharitable attitude of his new friend!

Charlie had provided some good laughs but the civilized side of island life had its amusing moments also. There was no bank for forty-five miles, but my branch sent a mobile van to the nearest village once a fortnight, where it stayed forty minutes from 1 pm for business. At first I tried to boat out to draw my shopping cash but once, delayed by bad weather, I reached the spot at 1.30 pm. No bank. I chased it to a wee hamlet, and honked and flashed it down with the Land Rover lights. The driver explained: "We waited twenty-five minutes but no-one came. But don't worry. We will bring the bank to *you* if you'll just tell us where to meet you every second Thursday!" Knowing the intransigent weather, I was never able to take advantage of this kind offer, and was finally able to cash my cheques with local traders.

This happened in late March and on my way home I decided to visit Deer Island and spend a few hours in the hide I'd put up for the herons. While other herons seemd to be paired off in many of the other nests, the huge structure at my eye level seemed occupied by only one bird, a large male I presumed, for the males usually commandeer the nests first. Overhead a few lone herons soared and I was sure they were mainly unmated females for as each one came nearer to his nest, he raised himself to his full three-foot height as if to make himself conspicuous, raised his head crest of black plumes and made two or three odd hooting or honking noises, while throwing his huge bill backwards in a kind of tossing motion. But when any of the flying birds landed in his tree, he lunged at them with his beak and flapped his vast wings as if to frighten them away. With herons the sexes look alike and as they are solitary birds most of the year this apparent driving away of the first females is an instinctive action. It is up to her to prove her desire to mate, her "love" so to speak, and persist. But not until I had spent three hours in the hide the following day did I see a female force herself upon him.

She flew first to two other lonely males, suffered herself to be driven away, then went back twice to the male I was watching. The second time his beak jabs seemed increasingly half-hearted; she evaded them coyly and he then appeared to accept her for he clapped the two parts of his great beak together noisily then gave hers a series of long gentle nibbles. Two days later he was courting her by bringing gifts of sticks, some about eighteen inches long, which he offered to her with an elegant display of his head plumes. And she raised her plumes as if in thanks, took the sticks from him and arranged them about the nest, pushing and tugging them through twigs already there. Sometimes after this the two birds mated, she clinging to the precariously swaying branches while he mounted, both birds flapping their huge wings to maintain their balance. It seemed odd they should mate on such a flimsy perch when their feet were so well adapted for walking on the ground and standing firm on the most slippery of surfaces, of rock, sand or plain old mud. I felt the female had a rather hard time of it for the male seized the back of her neck with his bill and held on to it while mating but at least it didn't last long – as with most birds a brief touch of the cloacae suffices to pass the seed and the moment is over.

By mid-April there were four large blue-green eggs in the nest, and it seemed that herons practise equality of the sexes for the male provided food for his wife, and for a month he seemed to take a fair share of incubating the eggs. Later each bird flew away after being relieved by its mate to find its own food on the seashore. Once on a hot, sunny afternoon I saw both birds standing on the nest edges, shading and gently fanning the eggs with their great wings. As I sweated in the close, dank atmosphere of the hide I felt somewhat envious.

Twice as I watched the heronry over the next few weeks, hooded crow couples flew close overhead. Once a hoodie flew near, as if trying to lure the herons off to attack, so that its mate following behind could dive in and purloin an egg. But the herons I observed were not taken in by this ruse. Instead the female sat tight while her mate, perched on a branch nearby, pointed his huge beak at the flying crows, staring at them, his whole posture one of threat and aggression.

But clever *Al Corone* knows what he's doing and when I returned in the sixth week and saw only three gawky, incredibly ugly, fledgelings in the nest, I could guess what had happened.

Sure enough, at the foot of the tree lay some smashed shell of the fourth egg. Probably a hoodie had swept down during a brief unguarded moment, had quickly flipped out the egg and had then had to quarrel with a crony or two for the privilege of gulping the contents. I felt that the herons had enough problems just then and decided to leave them alone for a while.

3

AFTER THE PACIFIC COAST years in Canada I had deluded myself that I knew enough about living with a small boat and the seas. But here I was on a long sea loch barely three-quarters of a mile across at its mouth, and as the big spring tides rose and fell as much as seventeen feet, the tidal flow was fast. To avoid the barely submerged rocks and gain a help to rowing too, I learnt to keep well into the centre when going out or coming in *with* the tides. But when I went against the high tides I kept well into shore, for the back flow from the little bays and promontories reduced their speeds. There were three huge rounded rocks right across the entrance of my own bay, easy to see at low tides, or to ride over on highs, but on medium tides their granite tops lurked just below the surface. Although I was advised to cut off the seaweed that grew on them, I decided not to. We clear too much of nature; seaweed is vital for oxygenating the oceans and as food and nurseries for many sea creatures, and I'd learned in Canada it can be useful as a cushion for a boat in rough waters. And as this weed always floated towards the surface it indicated the positions of the rocks anyway.

Nevertheless, it was on one of these boulders I lost my flimsy polystyrene boat. Coming back with a full load of paint, putty, nails, lumber and other bric-à-brac for the croft on a wet and windy May day, I was struggling to make headway with the oars when one of them snapped in half. A huge wave lifted me up – and down – *bouf*. The keel hit the top of the eastward rock and despite the seaweed the boat split almost in half. Hurling what would sink beachwards, I flopped out fully dressed, grabbing the bow rope as I went and with the split hull now floating as it was relieved of my weight, swam and towed it slowly ashore. Bedraggled and shivering in icy water I rounded up what was floating but had to go back at low tide for the gear that had sunk.

Although I repaired the oar a little by nailing the sides of a stout tin round it as a splint, I was reduced to walking over the mountains to collect my weekly groceries and mail which now had to be brought to the big house with the Vanes' main supplies. At times as I struggled over the slippery rocky trail with full pack, constantly transferring a heavy $2\frac{1}{2}$-gallon paraffin can from hand to hand, there were moments when my friends' admonitions that I was too old to live such a life seemed right. But above all I wanted to be totally independent, so on my next trip south I called on a boating company at Bowness in the Lake District and bought a pair of magnificent ten-foot-long sculling oars for £3. Then I invested in a 13 ft 9 in Norwegian-style fibreglass boat with a deep keel, and a 7-hp outboard engine.

My bank account now almost totally denuded, I paid a desperate call to a leading popular magazine in the hope of selling them a series on a major Hollywood star I had known well. At that time Walter Clapham, author of several fine works including *Night Be My Witness*, was serving as features editor. I knew Wallie well as he had been the film critic on a Brighton paper on which I'd been a cub reporter. We were discussing various ideas when he suddenly asked me why I was now living so far away in the wilds of Scotland. Feeling we were just wasting time I told him briefly of my years in Canada, of the grizzlies, cougars and the two old woodsmen I'd met, and how I'd returned to Britain to see if one could actually live a wilderness life in one's native isles. "I suppose I was looking for paradise," I laughed, then went on to talk about other famous folk I might write about. Wallie listened then suddenly pounded his desk so hard with his fist that his old pipe jumped out of the ashtray.

"Mike, you are a prize, if you don't mind my saying so, twit! You're *sitting* on a good story." I groaned inwardly, sure he was going to ask me to deliver *Sinatra* by Sinatra or something equally impossible like Brando *by* Brando, but I said meekly, "What's that?"

"Your story, you fool. Your own search for paradise. Everyone wants that but it seems you've actually *found* it."

I stared at him. "My story?" I repeated. "I'm a journalist. I only write about other people's lives. No-one would be interested." But we went to lunch and Wallie insisted I write him a synopsis.

I returned to the island, the Land Rover laden with the new boat, engine and enough planed boards to cover half the croft's front wall. As soon as I put the boat into the water I no longer begrudged its cost. The deep keel made it secure in the choppy seas and although without the engine it weighed 275 lbs it was steady to row. I have always loved rowing and now I could not only save fuel on calmer days but I had a good replacement for city methods of keeping fit like playing squash, exercising in gyms in artificial light, plodding round a park or flailing away on a rowing machine without water. From now on rowing would not only be good exercise but useful too.

It was low tide when I arrived back at my little bay so I grounded the boat on the soft sand, tied its bow rope to a big rock then began the usual heavily loaded walks up and down the steep slope. So busy was I for the next two hours I completely forgot the boat. At dusk I came down to haul it in on the high tide – to find the rock to which the rope was fixed to be now under ten feet of water! With a southerly gale springing up I had to stay awake until the early hours when the tide had ebbed again then haul the boat over constantly re-set planks so it would not be damaged on the rocks when the high tide returned. Next day I invented a special "cradle" for it from ropes and three planks so that when the tides came in – I couldn't watch it *all* the time – the planks would protect the hull from the rocky beach. I thought of putting out a permanent mooring but on such a shallow beach where the sea receded four hundred yards, and which was exposed to the prevailing south-westerly gales and heavy rains that would fill the boat up in a day, I realized that was out of the question.

Now I pounded away on the magazine synopsis. As memories of the Canadian cabin, old Booto, my backwoods helper Ed Louette and the hard treks in the lands of the grizzly, cougar and caribou came flooding back, the story seemed to write itself. I suddenly realized that if I kept the main wildlife experiences out of the article I might have enough material left for a whole book. I shall always be grateful to Walter Clapham for thus nudging me into what became my first wildlife writing.

So excited was I by this new work that I was oblivious to all else and I suddenly found myself running out of stores. With the synopsis ready to post too, I had to go out. By the time I'd fought my way to the little pier against strong easterlies, I realized the store would be shut for half day in twenty minutes. Dashing through a seemingly shallow pool, the water splashed up, doused the Land Rover engine which misfired and broke down. I had to walk $1\frac{1}{2}$ miles to put the synopsis into the nearest post box then back a further mile to the pier and boat home. Once again the tide was low, the pouring rain would fill the boat in a few hours so I had to haul it 350 yards over planks.

That day, unable to get stores, I began the first experiments with wild plant foods. All I knew then was that young stinging nettles were a nutritious substitute, if a little bitter, for spinach. But during that first summer I learnt what other plants were edible by two methods, neither of which I recommend to anyone else. First I watched what the sheep were eating – grass, wild sorrel, dock, dandelion and bramble leaves –

Half the front wall completed.

and reckoned that if such were all right for sheep they probably wouldn't poison a human. Secondly I ate only small amounts, then waited for signs of stomach trouble. If none, I increased my intake. In this way I found that in summer and autumn I could provide most of my vegetable needs from the land around me.

On fine days when the sun was so hot through the south-facing window I gave up writing and slaved outside on the croft, repairing other windows, slatting on the new front wallboards, then painting the exterior. One afternoon at the end of May I took a tin of red oxide and a brush and climbed up a heavy scaffold device I'd invented to paint the iron sheets of the roof when, just as my head came over the top, I saw a huge brown-and-buff speckled bird hovering over the burn a mere thirty yards behind the croft. At first I thought it was an eagle but eagles don't hover in still air, and its lighter plumage told me it was the big female buzzard that often flew overhead. Her great wings were winnowing the air like a huge kestrel, her body perfectly still as her large brown eyes glared at the ground below.

Suddenly she closed her wings, dropped with an audible thump, and stamped, making convulsive, griping clutches with the yellow talons of one foot as if killing something. Then she jumped into the air and seeing me for the first time, so intent had she been on what she was doing, she flapped her wings with a loud beating sound and flew up the hill with a large frog in her talons. I'd never known a buzzard could hover in that way and it was clear why falconers use heavy leather gauntlets when handling such big birds. Not once had it attempted to use its beak, the killing had been done with the powerful talons.

Later, covered with dust and paint specks, I washed in buckets of water from the burn. Not *in* the burn itself for I had no wish to pollute the pure waters. Instead I threw each bucketful of sudsy waste over the virulent bracken roots, so using it as a weed killer. By now the first deer flies, known in the Highlands as clegs, were vying with the little black midges to make outdoor periods a misery. If anything, the clegs were more irritating for they buzzed about slowly and noisily, landed right near the eye, in your mouth or more often on your back where you couldn't reach them. Often the first thing you noticed was a painful prick as they dug their hard mouth parts into your skin so they could suck some blood. But their slowness was deceptive for they often dodged your swatting hand, zoomed round in a tight two-foot circle, and landed back in the same spot for another try. While you might squash a few of them unpleasantly on yourself, a fair number got away with enough of your blood to help perpetuate their pestiferous kind. But they seemed to come in batches and, thankfully, there were periods when there were none at all.

I was sunbathing in one of these free periods when I was presented with a hilarious entertainment. As I looked at the stonework below the wall boards of the croft, I saw it was literally freckled with little dark spiders who had spent the winter in tiny crevices and now were out to catch the sun. They were jumping spiders who, while they can spin line to drop to the ground from danger, don't make webs to catch their prey. Instead they stalk and leap upon flies and other small insects like tiny tigers. But I soon realized they were not just out for the sun or to hunt – they were also looking for mates.

The small black males outnumbered the larger lighter coloured females by some six to one, and if some human bachelors think romancing the female they most desire is fraught with troubles, they can be thankful they don't belong to the jumping spider fraternity. I watched one male attract the female of his choice. He advanced in short cautious bursts then quivered his left front palp at her. Then he paused and quivered his right palp. He paused again then quivered both palps at her intensely. Five times he did this and it seemed each time she received the vibrations from both palps, she made rushes at him. But each time he dodged back slightly, showing submission or at least respect. She then ran off some four inches, stopped as if she had changed her mind and went back to what seemed his irresistible appeal. Again he went through his routine, moving nearer but just then another male with only seven legs came along and had a brief skirmish with the first. The fracas lasted less than half a second, a quick flurry, then both males fell off the wall, a mere two inches, the first one dashed into the grass and keeled over dead while the one with seven legs staggered about in two-inch circles looking very shaky on its pins. In that brief time it seemed poisonous bites had been delivered by each spider. Others were quick to take advantage, however, and one small male now made a direct approach to the female – to be literally heeled away by an irritated flick of one of her rear legs, like a fencer not even bothering to look where she was thrusting. It seemed she had no time at all for a potential beau that hadn't bothered to learn a true palp technique.

Two more males received the same treatment then, as if in disgust, the female ran down the wall and into the grass. Within five seconds a new female had occupied her former space. One male began to court her with his palps while another dropped down the wall from the boarding crevices attaching its line to the stonework as it went, then landed one-and-a-half inches from the female. Instantly she attacked it and retreated again, two inches to the left. This bitten male also fell to the ground and began to stagger in circles, his movements becoming slower and slower. But now the seven-legged one had apparently recovered from the bite by its male opponent and rapidly scaled the wall towards the new female. He was just in the middle of a new palp routine when the male the female had bitten, seemingly recovered, re-entered the arena. This time he too got the worst of it in a brief fight with Seven Legs and once more fell to the ground. Seven Legs now appeared to feel he had more than proved his valour and had no more time to waste. Minus a leg or not, he certainly knew his palp technique and he started making intensely violent movements at the now hyptonized female – left down, right down, left up, both down and quivering. Again and again he repeated this odd semaphore until the female, seemingly convinced he was a worthwhile mate, walked slowly towards him. But she did not present her rear. She didn't have to – with a great leap Seven Legs was upon her and, clasping her tightly, allowed her to hurry off with him into the grass below the wall. No battlefield Hector deserved more the spoils of war, I laughed to myself. But what impressed me most was how the spiders could leap four or five times their own length on a *vertical* wall. The acrobatic techniques for such a feat are mind-boggling for the spider has to leap out slightly and move forward, yet pull sufficiently hard with its upper legs so as not to lose height, stick in its legs while in "flight" then extend them again at the end of the leap at just the right moment to grab the wall again. Yet they could do this several times in a second and still attach the line before each jump. Astonishing feats indeed.

By now the seals who hauled themselves out at low tides on the rocky islets offshore to rest in the sun after hunting fish, were well used to my comings and goings, and one afternoon as I rowed back from the pier they started to follow the boat. They lifted their puppy-profiled faces from the surface, looking at me with lazy eye blinks, their nostrils opening and closing for a hissed breath, then somersaulted down again with violent rear flipper splashes close to the moving boat. I found when I sang a song to them like *If Ever I Would Leave You* they came even closer, and by the time I reached my bay there would be over a dozen wet, gleaming heads bobbing up and down a few yards away. Once I came back and a pair of beautiful black and white oystercatchers flew up from the beach and began diving close overhead, issuing shrill "*pleep pleep*" alarm calls from their bright-orange beaks. But as soon as I landed they became silent, just flicking by with shallow wingbeats reminding me of woodcocks in "roding" flight over their woodland territories. I felt sure they had a reason for this odd behaviour and walked over to where I'd seen one of them rise. I almost stepped on their nest. Instead of making it amid the small carpets of herbage above the beach they had scraped out a shallow depression in the shingle lower down, almost as if to deliberately camouflage their three, greenish, brown-blotched eggs, for at a few yards they were indistinguishable from the multi-coloured pebbles. Sheep often grazed along the shore line and no doubt this way the oystercatchers avoided their nests being trampled. It seemed they were wily birds for while their noisy "mobbing" had perhaps been to discourage me from landing too close, when I was actually very near their nest instead of showing its whereabouts by increased alarm, they had fallen silent. But from then on I pulled my boat up on the far side of the beach.

One afternoon I was working at my desk when I saw a flock of gulls spiralling over the shore hills to the west. Some were diving at a pair of buzzards and shearing away again at the last moment. They seemed to concentrate more on the bigger female and when I went out to look I found out why. The smaller male was more adroit in the air and seemed to finally become angry for it turned on one gull and chased it a few yards, forcing it to swerve wildly to escape. Well, gulls do not spiral for nothing so I hiked over to see if they had found a deer or sheep or lamb carcase but after a thorough search found nothing. I came back along the beach and once more found myself in the secluded little glen right on the shore. As I looked at the square formed by the six different kinds of trees, all now in full leaf, I thought what a wonderful place for a small cabin, a beach studio from where I could watch the nesting eiders, gulls and oystercathers on Eilean an t-Sabhail, a small islet just off shore.

I could probably build the whole thing behind a sheltering rock slab so it would be invisible except from directly in front, where few boats passed.

With my thoughts back in Canada now I was writing the first book outline about life there, I felt strangely nostalgic. There is something magically satisfying about building with logs, scribing the knotted, rounded, uneven timbers so each fits precisely into the other, about making a home from natural objects. It also suddenly seemed important that I prove to myself I still had some of the skills taught to me by old Ed Louette.

That day was my birthday and on my way to buy a celebratory bottle, I met Digby Vane – to be immediately invited back for drinks at the big house. As we talked I slipped in my request to build the little cabin. They had now decided I could stay as long as the island remained theirs. I could indeed build a cabin on the beach and what was more if I ever had to leave they would repay my costs, but my labour, being self therapy anyway, would be free. I determined to cut no trees down, to use only windfall logs which otherwise would rot. While there were a few in Shona forest they would be hard for one man to drag to the beach but I'd noticed there were many on Deer Island which I could cut and tip off the low cliffs right into the sea for towing. I contacted the island's owner who said I was welcome to take a few fallers for a cabin.

Working mainly on windy, midge-free days, I toiled at the cabin site, grubbing down to bedrock for the corner posts and digging a peaty-water well on slightly higher ground so I could siphon water down. When I boated to the pier to fetch cement, lumber and a pair of heavy oak doors – bought for fifty pence each from a demolition site on my last London trip – the easterly winds freshened to slight gales. But I was loath to have to unload and come back another day so, taking a chance, I set off.

As any boatman knows, every engine and boat combination is different and I was now running before heavy seas fully laden. The speed balance had to be constantly altered for if it went too slowly, I wallowed between the troughs with the waves threatening to break over the stern. If I went too fast I slid down the far sides of the troughs with a great rush, nearly ploughing the bow under the swell of the wave in front. So I had to keep a little faster than the waves when going up them, then throttle back when shooting down again. It was a rough trip, filled with sun and spray, but I reached the shelter of the cabin bay safely.

Leaving the boat out at anchor, the tide well down, I managed to haul the lumber and heavy doors up to the site, stumbling thigh deep in the slippery rocky pools, and after a further hour of work felt very tired.

Some fifty yards east of the site was a large, flat, sheltered boulder covered with thick moss, now dry from sun and wind, and I went to lie down there for a while. How wonderful that moss seemed, a thick, green carpet which softened the sharp contours, laying a curving, caressing touch to the tired body as if it were provided by nature for a man to rest from his labours, a lush, miniature forest in which few insects dwelt and cool to the touch. I lay there looking into the cobalt vault of heaven, softly combed by the light-green leaves of a hazel bush that shimmered above me in the breeze, and fell asleep.

4

SUDDENLY I WOKE UP to strange, bleating cries coming on the wind. I crawled, keeping as low as possible, to a small, heathery ridge some twenty yards away and peered through, to witness an extraordinary sight. A large, browny-red hill fox had cornered a young lamb and appeared to be playing with it. As the lamb bleated helplessly, the fox darted underneath it, forcing it upwards and off its legs, jumped over its head, pushed it down with two black-tipped paws – enjoying itself like a cat with a large, white mouse. But before it could do anything more I leaped up to scare it away and it ran, long brush streaming like a thick banner, and disappeared between the rocks. The lamb continued bleating and ran away. It seemed strange its mother was nowhere in view but I found a large ewe some forty yards away to the windward, placidly grazing behind a ruined wall that obviously had not allowed the lamb's cries to reach her.

Now the lamb ran to her with piteous bleats for a reassuring suck but the ewe became alarmed and at first tried to butt it away. Then she seemed unsure of what to do, whether to accept it or keep driving it off. Evidently the fox scent tainting the lamb was the trouble for she kept huffing and snorting, torn between maternal desire and fear. But when the little lamb persisted and she got the right scent too, she finally accepted it back, and soon trotted off like an animated mop with her youngster wobbly on its legs beside her.

To see a Highland fox in broad daylight was rare enough but to see it actually *playing* with a lamb, perhaps before the kill, must have been a thousand-to-one chance. Certainly I've never seen the like since.

One day, wondering if a huge fallen tree I'd once glimpsed in the Shona forest might be a red cedar, from which I could split "shakes"

39

(wooden tiles) for the cabin roof, I walked the hilly track – to find it was a silver fir, useless for splitting. But as I searched unavailingly for a fallen cedar there were compensations – a brown blur from a mossy crevice and a robin had left her nest, revealing four white and pale red-speckled eggs. Further on, a short-tailed vole chewing young grass suddenly became aware of my looming shape, zig-zagged about a rock then spying its hole, dived down it. Green-veined white and speckled wood butterflies were flitting in the clearings and I saw a first green hairstreak, sunning itself on a leaf, a jade jewel of the forest.

Next day, feeling like an old-time hand logger, I boated to Deer Island with a scaffold jack, a car jack, felling and hand axes, and my four-foot tree saw. To procure big logs from a forest on his own, the hand logger finds or cuts one on a slope above the sea or a river. He cleans off all the branches, then cranks the jacks under the high end to tip it downwards. With care and luck the log heads into the water but it also often gets hooked up so the process has to be repeated. I climbed the steep, treed cliff on the west side of the island and got out my first two fifteen-footers. One went down superbly, hitting the calm water with a great splash. But the thicker log hit a rock, somersaulted and landing amidships across another rock, split in two.

I "timber cruised" the edges of the island for more logs knowing I couldn't get any out from the centre on my own. The heronry was now in full spate, the great birds wafting above the tree tops like huge snowflakes. but I didn't want to disturb them and after checking the three fledgelings in the nest I'd observed earlier were now sprouting feathers, I went to the north-east edge of the island. There, bridging a wide, marshy ravine, was a fine, dry larch tree just over a foot thick. Using the quiet hand saw (I couldn't afford a chain saw anyway) I had to cut first one end, then half through the other, to drop a thirty-foot log down far enough so that I could cut through its centre without risking injury or death. As I dragged each fifteen-footer along the marsh's edge where the mud was not too deep and down to the sea, I was surprised by how heavy the logs were. Then I realized why. Western Canadian trees can grow to a foot thick at fifteen to twenty years old but these larch did not attain that thickness for about sixty years, hence the wood was denser and heavier at the same size. Cutting and dragging one more, I heaved them into the sea, rounded up the floating log and towed them all to my own beach four miles to the west.

As we laboured into the open loch past Riska Island, I saw a dull-brown eider duck shepherding a flock of eighteen ducklings. The little ones scattered, racing over the water with flailing feet, their flipper-like, featherless wings beating unavailingly, like little seaplanes trying to take off. But the mother fluttered before the boat, trailing her wings to decoy me away from the babes. Then she dived to emerge among them many yards away. They could not all have been her own brood, and this and later observations led me to conclude that an eider mother will sometimes take over another's brood for a time, perhaps allowing the second duck to feed at some choice place. It also seems old or unmated ducks will help shepherd ducklings. It is at this time the youngsters are most vulnerable, for they are preyed upon by the big, black-backed gulls, can be seized from beneath by seals or otters, and on land by foxes, wildcats or even rats. The great skuas also eat them, harrying the brood who dive and dive until exhausted when the skuas take them easily. But the skuas lived further north and there were none on Loch Moidart. That night I felt too tired to haul the logs up to the cabin site so I left them tied by a long rope on my own beach, going down in darkness later to haul them in on the high tide.

Next day in blazing sun and tidal calm I towed them to the cabin beach. Now wet, they were heavier than ever and I soon cut my hands trying to drag them with short heaves over the rocks. As I worked the image of old, retired carpenter Ed Louette, who'd helped me build the log cabin in Canada, came often to my mind. I recalled his patient, slogging perseverance, at work he'd performed free for many folk over the years, his favourite phrase "Professor, here there is room enough and time enough!" What an extraordinary old man he had been for sixty-seven. As I hauled the logs over the rocks I was assailed by midges but I foiled them by tying butter muslin round my face. I could hardly see through it, sweat poured down but anything was better than those continual bites. And the harsh, grey granite rocks themselves seemed to possess demoniac characters of their own. Timeless, enduring, mocking the puniness of a labouring man, still and dead on cold days, treacherously slippery in the rain, they now shimmered unendurable heat waves into the air, sapping my strength with their reflected heat, and baking and cracking as if biting back at the sun. Anchored motionless for ever as they seemed to be, they were yet able to destroy, as if harbouring malicious spirits who forced my feet to hit them the wrong way as I toiled uphill with the logs, and thrusting their spikes upwards, twisting my feet in their crevices as if they had planned it all for my hardest tasks. What a difference it makes to have a few inches of soil and soft grass beneath our feet.

As I de-barked the logs with the hand axe, cut the wooden corner blocks, and set the foundations with cement, sand and granite chips, I was soon in trouble. The cement was too crumbly from too much sea salt. I had to boat to Shoe Bay for fresh sand from well above high-tide level which had had all the salt leached out of it for years by the rains, then re-make the foundations.

One day after cutting and hauling three more logs from Deer Island I was busy heaving them over the rocks with the rope sling when I saw the boat floating away. Anxious to get them on to land while the tide was still high I'd forgotten to tie it up and had underestimated the speed and pull of the ebbing tide. Now the east wind was blowing the boat westwards. I tried to reach it with a pole, then by tying a rock on to the pole and swinging the rock over the bow but it was now too far out.

I raced over the beach to the last land point but again it was tantalizingly just out of reach. As I watched it heading beam-on for the great Atlantic I realized I was about to lose both boat and engine for good. Off came my clothes, I dived in from the rocks, got my underpants tangled round my feet, kicked them off, lost them, but managed to reach the boat in forty yards.

As I tried to clamber into it stark naked, I heard sudden shouts. A boatful of young Sea Cadets who were camping on the north shore of the island had chosen that moment to make their first and only boat trip across the mouth of the loch.

"Do you need any help?" they yelled.

"Nope," I growled back through chattering teeth, my nakedness modestly curled up under the keel. "I'm just trying to cool off beside my boat." I felt it was okay for them to think they'd met a madman but not a naked madman. Puritanism and fey madness abound in the Highlands in equal measure and I felt I made a slight contribution to legend that day.

I returned to the croft to discover that in my hurry to haul that day's logs and boat off the mudbanks at Deer Island before low tide immured them for twelve hours, and marooned myself there too, I'd forgotten my hand saw and thickest boat sweater, and had left them behind. But next morning rain was pouring down so I worked on the last chapter of my novel, finishing its third re-write. Joyful, I looked out of the window.

The rain had eased off and two chaffinches were searching for food on the big, mossy rock below the window. I quickly made a small bird table from a piece of plywood, with upraised edges so food would not blow off, put on a crust of bread and returned indoors. Within seconds the colourful pink-chested cock bird landed, took a beakful, swallowed it, then seemed so happy, with both feet firmly on the bread, burst into its little chippy song! As he chirped away, full of cocky health, the three white stripes on each wing blazed like chevrons, and I coined a name for him: Little Fat Sergeant. I'd never known a chaffinch sing from anything but a tree branch before. But this was a minor prelude to the wildlife experiences I had over the next two days.

After sudden overnight gales I woke next morning to a calm sea, the air hazy with occasional sunny patches. I boated to Deer Island with the usual nails, rope and axes, to recover my saw and sweater and fetch more logs. But before starting work I went to check the hide on the

42

Little Fat Sergeant the chaffinch, first customer to the bird table.

knoll and the nest of young herons.

As I tried to walk unobserved beneath the tall conifers and the vast nests, some of the birds were with their half-grown fledgelings. But with their acute senses – they can hear a twig snap on the forest floor and with their slightly forward-placed eyes incorporating almost the stereoscopic sight of falcons – they knew I was there. They froze like grey bitterns, heads and long beaks sticking straight into the air while dozens of yellow eyes, bright as tiny catherine wheels, glared down at me from their long stalky necks. I crept into the damp sacking of the hide and focused my field glasses.

There was only one cowed youngster still in the nest.

The overnight gales had uprooted a pine which in falling against the nest tree had dislodged the other two nestlings. Then something grey below caught my eye. On the ground under the tree a young heron lay dead. But hanging from the twigs of a thick bush by a large foot was the third nestling. At first I thought he too was dead but then I saw his neck slowly bunch up like a snake's, in agony. Then his half-grown wings flapped feebly as he dangled, looking like a dead bird on a keeper's gibbet. He was clearly not far from death.

I climbed up to release him but as I carried him down, weak and cold though he was, he raised his spiky head crest in terror, trying feebly to stab at my hands with his beak. Placing him in some sacking, I hurried to the boat where I had a small fish I'd caught by trolling on the way over. Although I knew herons feed their young on pre-digested food by regurgitation, I felt a little of its flesh would do him no harm, and after mashing it up with my fingers, I pushed a few morsels down his throat. Then I had a good look at him.

He was a ridiculous, misshapen, ragamuffin character, his huge feet, head and long beak completely out of proportion to the rest of him. Laughing at myself for feeling the need to give him a name, for I dislike anthropomorphism – bestowing human traits on wild creatures – I nicknamed him Harry and checked him over for injuries. All else seemed well but the outside toe of his left foot was completely broken and dangling loose. Luckily the important third toe of each foot was undamaged. These toes are vital to herons – the claws like serrated combs, and are used for cleaning slime from eels and other fish from the feathers, to clean off body pests and to help hold down a fish. The claws are also used for preening – when the heron takes waxy, whitish-blue

Harry the heron on his nest, a photograph taken two years after his rescue.

powder from six special tracts on its body and spreads it over its feathers to give them a waterproof sheen.

Harry's toes were not webbed like a duck's but adapted for both perching in trees and working in marsh or water; they had spongy, spreading under-surfaces, ideal for walking on soft mud, in shallows or over slippery rocks. His long beak had jagged edges for holding fish and his gullet seemed almost as elastic as a pelican's.

At first I was tempted to take Harry home but then I realized he would still be needing his parents' pre-digested food. Besides, it is better to leave fledged nestlings for usually their parents are still feeding them on the ground. When I saw a heron flying low near the trees, I placed Harry in a prominent spot, made a show of leaving, then crept back to the hide. For two hours I watched poor little Harry crouching there but the mother heron only landed by him once. She was clearly perplexed for she could not possibly get him back to the nest, and when he tried his nestling trick of grasping her bill to induce her to feed him, she leaped gawkily into the air and went back to her remaining fledgeling in the nest. Clearly if I left him there his parents would abandon him and he would die. There was only one thing to do – try and put him back in the nest myself.

With Harry tied in some sacking round my waist, I drove six-inch nails into the tree trunk where there were no branches and using a rope also, managed to work my way upwards. I was astonished to find myself struck by a severe attack of vertigo, something I had suffered from slightly since a fall from the cliff top in Canada. At times I had to cling to the trunk, shivering with dizziness and fight a strange desire to just let go and fall. But talking loudly to myself, I went on. Near the top climbing was easier because of the extra branches of the lodged tree. But it was hard to reach round the four-foot width of the nest and only after being covered in dust, decayed vegetation, heron pellets and smelly undigested fish bones, could I manage to push Harry into it. Climbing down again seemed even more hellish as I kept removing the hammer from my belt to pull out the nails as I descended.

Shivering with fatigue and fear, I was in no mood for more logging and after finding my lost saw and damp sweater near the muddy edge of the lagoon where I'd launched the first logs, I boated home.

A few days later I returned to camp out and do a two-day shift which would get me all the logs I needed for the cabin. As the boat putted past the island there was a commotion among the terns nesting on the islets off the north-eastern edge. As I drew nearer I was susprised to see a large, tawny-grey animal with a thick, dark, striped tail bound off the rocks into the water. As it swam rapidly towards the shore its pointed ears flattening down as if to ensure water would not get into them, I realized it was a wildcat. It swam strongly, head and shoulders well clear of the water, covered the fifteen yards in less than half a minute, sprang out and without bothering to shake itself, bounded over the rocky bank and vanished into the woods. I was sure it had been after the young terns. Leaving the birds to settle, I beached the boat and walked through the trees to check little Harry Heron. He was still there and after a short while in the hide the mother returned, and Harry started to compete lustily with the other nestling for the food from her bill. That was a relief after what had been for me a frightening climb.

That night, after cutting more logs in strong winds, I camped well away from the heronry. In the morning the first thing I saw was a tiny, brown wren suddenly emerge from a hole in a hollow larch snag. I thought little of it, probably it had wanted a warm berth from the night winds but then out popped another, then another. In the end thirteen wrens came out of that hole, rather like morning commuters emerging from a tube station in the city. Wrens often share holes in trees to keep warm in harsh winters but the bird is usually warlike towards its own species at other times of the year. It seemed odd for at least two families must have shared that hole during the summer night.

As I slid out of my sleeping bag beneath a staked-out plastic sheet, the wrens appeared to gang up on me, all lining up on the twigs of a bush and making their chirring alarm calls at this odd newcomer into their world. After a sandwich breakfast I crept around the island but failed to get another glimpse of the wildcat.

I was de-barking a log in the afternoon when I heard another commotion from the tern rocks. I hastened through the trees. Now four herring-gulls were showing interest in the nests and the smaller terns were swooping and diving at the wheeling gulls, crying out loudly. One tern was still on the rocks, its scarlet beak agape as it defended two tiny, grey youngsters from one of the gulls. I launched the boat and as I drew near one of the fledgelings tottered, half-blown by the wind, to a cleft on the edge of a high rock. I feared it would be dashed to death, or drown if it fell into the sea for as yet it had no flight feathers. I rowed in and rescued the little mite. As I restored it to its nest in some grass tufts on top of the rock, it showed no fear at all, the loud shrill screams of the adult birds hovering and swooping above seemed to die down a little, as if knowing I meant them no harm. As I rowed back to pick up my logs, they settled down on the islet again, folding their long, swallow-like wings and running to check their young ones.

As I boated home with the logs behind, I saw thousands of tiny elvers in the clear water below, all shimmering like sequins in the golden sunlight as they neared the end of their incredible three-year-long, 3,000-mile migration from the Sargasso Sea where they had been born. Now they were heading for the fresh-water burns, rivers, lochs and lochans up to 1,000 feet high where they would spend up to fifteen years before turning into mature silver eels. Then they would set out once more, their stomachs atrophied for they would never feed again, for their birthplace where they would breed and finally die.

Once again, as I reached open water, seal heads began popping up around the boat as they followed me home. I'm sure that with such animals who are so well adapted to catching their fish prey, they often feel bored. And when they become used to a harmless figure in a boat, they follow him just for fun. I felt I was upon a fully alive sea, that the height of summer was now approaching. As I lay in the sun by the croft to rest awhile in the last rays before it sank below the high hills, two grey wagtails with pristine yellow breasts appeared from nowhere and began running over the ground snapping up tiny insects. And a few yards to my right I heard a humble-bee drumming in a foxglove flower.

How good it would have been to share such moments with a beloved woman, yet it was often in such happy periods that a feeling of intense loneliness would come upon me and I'd wonder if beauty of landscape could really be sufficient recompense in a life without human love. Now an odd little thought came to me: "Love looked in my door once. I said, 'Not today thank you.' Love closed the door quietly and never returned." The thought made me sad, for love had looked in my door many times during the years I had been caught up in the international set in the cities of Europe and North America, and I had known some of the world's most beautiful women. Now, for the first time, it hit me that I was going to have to face the future totally alone.

As I lay there, head pillowed on my arms, I suddenly noticed an odd puckering of the skin between the muscles of my shoulder tops. I blinked, looked again. There was no doubt about it – *age* wrinkles, the kind I'd noticed on old folk's bodies on the beach when I had been in my twenties and thirties and had sworn "That will never happen to me". But it was. I felt a momentary panic. I too was getting old. And when I cut my hair later with the help of two mirrors I saw masses of grey hair at the nape of my neck I'd not noticed before. Now I recalled how a few days earlier when walking up the hills I had noticed that my pace had slowed, an increasing desire to zig-zag sideways up steep faces, flat-footed too, rather than take them straight and on the toes. On recent London work trips I'd also noticed a sudden loss of confidence when meeting an attractive young woman.

Suddenly the awful loneliness of the first winter in Canada came flooding back. Alone in the wilds a man's conscience and self-awareness increase, hang over him like a hawk. The psychological effect of one's opinion about oneself is devastating in its ability to preserve – or destroy. Self-respect is the only foundation upon which one can survive. The new realization that I was almost certainly going to face the rest of my life totally alone seemed frightening. Surely, there is someone for

47

everyone, if you can only find them!

The point is that one is not lonely for just *anyone,* but for that special person whose mind inspires respect, whose interest comes from similar experiences, whose physical being attracts, whose spirit is parallel to one's own. I knew many men caught in a mutual trap with women they no longer loved, with each dawning a new mourning and no chance or energy to start again. Loneliness for one seems better than a spiritual jail for two. Alone there is hope. So, on my next trip south, I just worked up a few small writing jobs, bought materials for the cabin – glass, window frames, plywood for the floor, and on my return added to the full load with rough-sawn lumber for the walls from a saw mill near Fort William. Hard labour has always been for me a therapeutic way of alleviating loneliness. I ferried most of the materials in one trip by towing the lumber.

As ever, wildlife watching provided compensations for the lack of human company. One afternoon I was jointing the floor joists into the foundation logs when I saw a tern dive straight into the sea after a fish. And it did not come up again. I waited, wondering what had happened, when there was a violent splashing – and a large sea trout leaped out of the water and grounded itself on a smooth rock, just as a seal's head emerged and turned with a swirl. Thinking I'd get some easy fish meals, I ran over the rocks but before I got there the flapping fish, the rock slippery from its spray, flopped back into the water and disappeared. Nor did I see the seal again. I wondered if it had caught the diving tern or if the bird had become caught up in some seaweed but when I boated over I could not see it anywhere in the clear water.

Occasionally I went to Deer Island to see how Harry Heron was getting along. By the time he was about seven weeks old he and his mate seemed as large as their parents. Harry now climbed to the outside branches well away from the nest and clutching desperately with his feet, using his long beak as a stabilizer, he exercised his wings with violent movements. At times he flapped so hard the branch shot up and down as if about to snap. He seemed to have an innate building instinct for occasionally he flapped and half ran over the foliage, as if afraid to trust his wings alone, snapped off a small twig then brought it back as if trying to help his parents repair their ancestral mansion.

When I went back in late June I found the nest empty but as I took the hide down and walked out of the trees, there was a great flurry as a whole mass of herons suddenly flew up from the rocks of their spring gathering ground. The sky was literally thick with herons and I counted thirty-one as they dispersed to the meadows and loch shores. It was an astonishing spectacle, exhilarating too, for it was obvious to me at that moment that if such a huge 'sedge' of the big birds ever decided to attack a lone intruder in a boat, he'd have a hard time against all those pickaxe bills. Some of the birds were flying awkwardly, certainly the year's young, and as I scanned the sky with my field glass I saw one of them, its legs stretched out flat under its tail, had a broken toe that stood out clearly. I was sure it was Harry.

I had doubts that he would survive for long. Only one out of every five herons who leave the nest ever reach breeding age. Harry had a broken toe and had nearly died after falling from the nest. And while some adults stay with their young for a time to show them how to catch prey, many young herons have to look out for themselves. Harsh winters, the chance of choking to death on furry prey that hasn't been dipped properly in water, colliding with overhead wires, having their huge wings broken in storms, falling victim to man's pollution and pesticides, or being shot by fishery bailiffs who regard them as poachers, all take their toll of herons. Another factor is that heronries can only absorb about 20% of their youngsters at breeding age – the rest have to find homes elsewhere. It seemed unlikely Harry would become the one heron in five who survived.

But one late summer day I was boating past a small, rocky islet near my bay when I saw a heron standing on one leg on the line of tide wrack. Remarkably it remained still until I was thirty yards away, then it rose with the usual gawky leap. And there, outlined against the mackerel sky as it folded its legs neatly below its tail, I saw the broken toe again.

I began to see him more often as he seemd to have adopted my own beach for hunting his fishy prey. Sometimes when I was leaving in the boat he would fly over quite low with hoarse and strident *"kraink kraink"* calls then glide to shore with soft chuckling noises, stick out his long gangly legs and land as lightly as a toy balsa-wood glider.

Like all herons he seemed to have two main hunting methods. The first was "stand and wait" which he would do with the utmost patience for as long as two hours until some unwary little flatfish, eel, shrimp, crab, frog or vole came within his reach. The second was "sneak along slowly", like a cat stalking but knock-kneed and with his head jerking back and forth like a ludicrous metronome. Whichever technique he used the end was usually the same. A lightning dart or two with his beak, then he uptilted the prey and swallowed. Once I saw him beat a small fish against a rock to kill it first.

One thing I liked was that he peaceably allowed other smaller birds to feed alongside him and he often worked the shallows along with curlews, ducks, gulls and oystercatchers. While I saw occasional large gulls torment him by swooping low after he had caught something, as if to try and make him drop it again, I never saw him harry them. It seemed his attitude was "There's room enough for us all."

49

5

To MANY A LIFE of isolation on a Scottish sea island would perhaps be a recipe for boredom, or worse. "What on earth do you *do* all the time?" I was often asked on supply trips. In fact, there weren't enough hours in the day or night for all my tasks and I never got around to piping water into the house from the burn. I remained a "three bucket" man through the years on Shona – one for washing water, another of sea water for cooking, and a bigger one for slops which were emptied over the bracken. A plastic two-gallon container held my drinking water. Two driftwood shelves carried my books, small battery record player, letters and wildlife files. My ornaments were abstract "art works" fashioned by the sea into weird shapes from the roots of trees. My old hair mattress rested on the bedframe on sea-scoured fish boxes found on the beaches. My bedside "cupboard" was also a fish box.

To save money until my garden was producing, I had to feed as much as possible from the land around me. Apart from using nettles for spinach, dock leaves for cabbage, dandelion and sorrel leaves for salads, and blackberries, hazel nuts and rose hips as fruits, I conserved finance in other small ways. I learned to always put one pan on top of another when cooking. Thus the steam from boiling cabbage, carrots or nettles would also cook the potatoes. Or if making a stew I also heated the washing-up water by putting it on top of the pan instead of the lid.

Many recipes were devised. Saving all water in which vegetables had cooked, I could add sliced onions, some lentils and stinging nettles, dock or sorrel for a first-class vegetable soup. Mince became my staple meat. Fried lightly in onions, mixed with quick-boiled cabbage and potatoes, it was delicious and cheap. So was a lamb's heart stuffed with sage and onions, tied up and simmered in a stew of onions, split peas, lentils, carrots and potatoes, or with any of the wild foods.

For a "fridge" I used a plastic box kept cool by the evaporation from a wet cloth when left in a draught, or a waterproof galvanized box placed in the cold waters of the burn. But this needed tethering with light rope. Once after a spate from heavy rains I went out to find my meat "fridge" a few hundred yards down the burn, where it had burst open on a flat rock. And Charlie Crow and his mate rose into the air with harsh "*Kaahs*" – from the last piece of meat!

For a bread- and cake-making oven I used a large biscuit tin inside an old cut-out petrol can which was placed on a wire grill above the open fire. In the can and around the tin I put a layer of flat stones for insulation from the direct heat of the flames, then set the dough in the biscuit tin on greaseproof paper. Then I covered the lidded tin and can with a curved, iron sheet, which threw the hot air back down around them. If I wanted a fruit loaf, I just threw sugar, raisins, lemon peel and some malt extract into the bread dough.

I also tried to feed from the sea and it was no great chore to take my rod and row out past the islets into the open Atlantic and sit fishing in the sun. It seemed ironic that by giving up the modern desire for luxury, comfort and social status, I could live healthily and happily on about five pounds a week (then) yet spent much of the time doing what I used to slave and save for during three weeks' holiday a year. I now fished, rowed, swam, sunbathed, walked the glens and mountains, fitting all indoor and outdoor work into the pattern of the weather – all part of a natural life rather than a hurried once-a-year "escape" into the outdoors when it took time to wind down, when city life had so blunted the senses one just could not see, feel or hear many of the inspiring subtleties of the wilderness and all its wild life.

But I soon found fishing in Scottish waters totally different from the fish-rich seas of Canada's Pacific coast. No Atlantic salmon would take a lure trolled behind the boat in the sea as they had back there. These fish were filled with stored energy after years of sea feeding and were now intent on going up the rivers and fresh-water lochs before spawning. For days I tried all I knew but finally gave it up as hopeless. Here the seas seemed emptier of fish and it took time to learn new techniques. But there were mussels by the thousands on my rocks so I had many *moules marinière* dinners, or I just steamed them open with thick mushroom or tomato soup as sauce. I had no need to boil them for three minutes as in a polluted area. I "farmed" them, selecting only a few big ones here and there so the colonies would propagate naturally. The little black winkles were common and there was usually a fair spattering of chubby cockles left on the sands after storms had stirred up the sea bed at low tides.

Then the big spring highs washed them up the beach, to be exposed on the next lows.

I used mussels and cockles, half cooked to make them firmer, as fishing baits, holding them on the sandy bottom of the sea with a sliding weight on the line. If it was stormy I would forget the boat and cast out from the shore rocks. But I often had a lengthy wait for the bottom-feeding plaice and dabs until I learned to "ground bait" the area with some crushed mussels. I discovered a phenomenon with the local crabs that had not happened in Canada. Here the bigger ones clung tenaciously to the bait with their claws once they found it, reluctant to let the easy food go! And I could haul them all the way up to the surface and into the boat before they dropped off, making me snatch my naked toes well out of reach of their tough pincers. I was glad now I had not cut the broad leaves of the tangleweed from the three main rocks for on the lowest tides – when four hundred yards of sand would be exposed – I found the biggest crabs used the weed to keep wet and as shelter. Although crabs can breathe under water or on land with equal ease, they do need to keep their gill chambers damp. Again, I took only a few of the largest, leaving any less than four inches across the shell. Herons, gulls, hooded crows and oystercatchers also used these weed shelters as a food source when the sea was right out.

I became almost as dependent on the tides for food as the wildlife about me, learning that the highest and lowest "spring" tides occur when the sun and moon are in line on the same side of the earth – so exerting a combined gravitational pull on the seas. And that the medium "neap" tides are when the sun and moon are on opposite sides of the earth, their separate pulls tending to cancel each other out. Both springs and neaps occur alternatively roughly every two weeks throughout the year, low tides follow highs roughly every $6\frac{1}{4}$ hours, and each occurs some fifty minutes later each day. Island life made it essential for one to adjust these natural rhythms.

Slowly I learned new tricks of coping with the boat in the winds and tides on the long, shallow beach. The Vanes gave me two, heavy-iron, disc anchors to set from the boat's stern. Instead of re-setting planks and laboriously heaving the boat over them to beyond high-tide reach, I could now leave the boat on the sand on her rope-and-plank "cradle", go down at high tide, give a few heaves and in she would come.

Leaving the boat at the little pier gave me problems at first because the flow from the river Shiel on an ebbing tide tended to push the boat into the stonework. I always dropped the rear anchor a few yards out, leaped out of the prow on to the pier with the bow rope, then walked up and round to the side on the land, thus swinging the boat outwards again before tying up so she would not foul the pier. One day the island's head worker, Iain MacLellan, watched me with a slight smile.

"Now then, Mr Tomkies. There's a better way than that. Do you not know how to flick the *cruaidh* off the prow?" I said I didn't and what was a *cruaidh* anyway?

Iain explained it was the Gaelic name the old-time crofters used for an anchor, usually a heavy stone tied to a rope. He agreed the new disc anchors were an improvement for with their centre holes they were easy to handle, and their rounded edges meant less wear on the rope from the sea bed. He now showed me how to "flick" them off the boat. Balancing them so they teetered on the edge of the prow, and holding the bow rope in loose coils, he gave the boat a long, steady push out to sea. When it had gone some thirty yards he gave a violent jerk on the rope, the anchor discs tipped over and dropped to the sea bed, holding the boat far further out than by my method.

"Well, I'll be . . .. That's a good trick!" I said, wondering how I'd got through the Canadian years without thinking of it myself. I looked at Iain MacLellan with new respect. He was not a tall man but nor was he short. He had quick, bright-blue eyes, a high sensitive forehead, and an urgent almost huffy way of speaking and was as much at home with the Gaelic as with the English tongue. Although at first he appeared slimly built, his shoulders were square and straight, and as he worked the big boat, loading stores and heavy equipment for the island with quick, sure movements that belied his fifty years, it was clear he was as tough as whipcord and as strong as an ox. Iain had been born on Eilean Shona and apart from a wartime spell in the Scots Guards, when he'd been a highly regarded piper, he had lived on it all his life. The fact that I had once been a guardsman too, a regular in the Coldstream Guards, gave us a little in common but with the Highlander's typical reserve, it was more than two years before he called me anything but "Mr Tomkies".

One August evening I was sitting alone writing about the Canadian years, thinking about my old companion, wild dog Booto, and the adventures we'd shared together in bear country, when I heard a familiar sound from the long-ago land. A soft padding on the wooden floor, pad, pad, scratch, scratch, the tired walk of Booto, home from a solo trek to the far fishing village. Any moment now there would be a flump as he flopped down and his mouth would open in that silly grin, his flanks panting in the heat. Then with a start I realized where I was, five thousand miles from Booto, alone in a croft on a Scottish island. What could it be? It just had to be a dog, no other image seemed right. I moved silently and opened the door gingerly – nothing there. I looked in the other rooms then outside. The air was still and nothing moved anywhere. Fright hit me momentarily and I felt the hairs rise on my neck. There seemed no rational explanation for the noise. Perhaps old Booto was dead and by concentrating on him so hard I had somehow induced his ghost to appear? It was an eerie thought.

53

But next day I had the answer. Iain suddenly appeared at my door. He had lost Queenie, a new border collie bitch he had bought for £6 from a mainland friend. She had slipped her collar at Shona Pier on the day of her arrival and was now roaming the island, probably trying to get back to her old home. "She just hadn't had enough time to get to know me," he explained. A good shepherd, Iain loved his collies. "They may not have the same sense towards people – you can't train them to run after a man who's stolen a hundred pounds like an Alsatian but their intelligence is unique for working sheep. My old bitch doesn't know how to skive like human beings and she works herself to death for me."

He took a sip from the cup of tea in his calloused hands as he sat on my bed and went on "It's terrible to see her working now. It's all right on the morning gatherings but if we have to go on all day she gets tired and can't run after sheep that are fresh. But she tries until she's ready to drop. She's just too old now, that's why I had to get another." He left me a bag of grouse remains and I promised to do my best to catch Queenie.

At dusk two nights later the collie came furtively sniffing between the bracken patches, ate a piece of grouse but fled tail down when I tried to call her in. That night I rigged up a trap. I threaded light rope through eye-hooks and tied it on to the porch doors, then set a trail of tiny meat scraps to the main bait in the hallway. As soon as I heard Queenie come in I would heave the rope and slam the doors behind her. The first night she did not appear. On the second I went out after two hours – to find all the bait gone. She had sneaked in without a sound!

Next day I had a rough supply trip. Coming back the south-westerly rain-filled blasts were so strong that even head-on to the waves I was in danger of capsizing and I had to beach the boat in a bay to the south-east because I couldn't take the heavy seas round the last land point. That night, worried about Queenie still out in such cold, wet weather, I tied some meat bait with light fishing line to a tobacco tin in my room. As soon as she took the meat the tin would fall loudly and I'd slam the doors on her. But sitting in the draughty room, eyes aching from the light of a single candle and tired from the hard trip, until 2 am, I fell asleep. Clink – I woke up, reactions slow, slammed the doors but when I dashed out Queenie had shot outside again, fast as a cat, and had escaped. Luckily, after two weeks of living wild, she must have forded the low-tide shallows at the island's north-east shore, and had found her way back to her old home up Glen Moidart. Iain collected her by car, kept her indoors a few days, treating her gently and feeding her well, and she eventually became one of the best sheepdogs he'd ever had.

Sometimes I saw Iain fishing in the big boat way out in the Atlantic and I wondered what he was catching for with my shellfish baits I only seemed able to attract an occasional pollack less than a foot long. One day at the pier I looked into Iain's boat, astonished to see a big, wooden box filled with huge pollack, saithe and mackerel he'd caught for the islanders.

"Ye need only the *drogha* (hand line) for the fish here," he explained. "And on that you set the darrows, the 'murderers' we call them because they catch so many!" Then he showed me one of his own lines on which some two dozen, brightly coloured feathers fluttered in the wind. These were the "darrows", just feathers dyed bright green, red, orange, yellow and white, each one tied to a large hook and fixed singly about a foot apart. "You tie a weight to the end of the line, throw it all overboard then jerk it up and down to attract the fish," said Iain. "They're irresistible to mackerel who come nearer to the shores and up these lochs in summer. If you get into a shoal of them it's impossible not to catch all you need."

So I bought and made some darrows and one gorgeous, late-August afternoon rowed way past the loch mouth and over a mile into the mighty expanse of the Atlantic and began to fish. It was idyllic sitting there, and with the lion couchant landscape of Eigg, the high mountains of Rhum and the small island of Muck shimmering out on the horizon, it seemed I was almost back in the first paradisical days among the sea islands of the British Columbian coast. The beauty was intense, blue gold, enough to make the soul quiver. The blazing colours of the wonderful seascape seemed to drench my retina, and I felt as if I was living in two time phases at once. As I had a perfectly good sea rod left over from Canada I was not using a hand line. Suddenly the rod tip shot under the water and was jerked first one way, then the other. What had I here? I played the fish, its movements quite unlike anything I'd ever known before, to find I had caught *two* mackerel. I was into a shoal now and every time I threw in I hauled out one, two and even three fish at a time.

That was more than enough to keep fresh without a proper fridge so as I rowed past the islets on which the common seals had hauled out to bask in the sun, and they started hunching and sliding into the water as usual, I cut a few of the fish into three and threw in the pieces. To my delight, although they kept about thirty yards away, the seals began diving and rolling at the surface after the easy food. I whistled and crooned to them and they seemed more curious than before. They popped their heads up and down, snorted, splashed their hind flippers on the surface, submerged and came up somewhere else blinking their dewy eyes, and again followed the boat all the way to my beach. As I glided between the marbled islets with their nefarious tribes of gulls, cormorants, ducks, vivid, darting terns and brilliant oystercatchers, the seals splashing about me, it was as if I was indeed in paradise.

After such glorious days I became increasingly reluctant to head down to London, even for short visits to rustle up work but for the first year and a half I had no other choice. They were long 1,140-mile return drives and to save hotel bills I often pulled into little natural "dormitories", usually in woods, gypsy fashion, to sleep in the truck.

On each trip there were odd occurrences that made me feel increasingly at odds with modern civilization. Often they were trivial and to recount them appears mere peevishness yet they mounted up. If I picked up hitch-hikers hoping for some light chat on the long journeys, I usually found myself chauffeuring recumbent bodies as they fell asleep. I found such blasé thankless expectation from the immature irritating. One lad with flowing blond locks told me he'd won a race at school that day – and to get the kids interested the teachers had allowed each runner to take puffs from cigarettes at each stage of the relay! Modern education. Once I forgot my cheque book when going back to a bank where I was known and had a small cash-drawing arrangement. No, I couldn't have the usual cheque form, I was told, the new computer could not process them. So off I had to walk for the book and back again. I thought computers made life easier! At stores I was now asked "Do you have a credit card?" Believing credit buying to be a pernicious influence, for it made being in debt honourable and meant enjoying now what you had not yet *earned,* I'd burned the first one sent to me. But I was soon forced into line, and had to get another. As I walked away from one Camden Town shop with a new axe handle I was called back. "You can't take it like that, guv'ner. It's illegal, classed as an offensive weapon in the streets. I have to wrap brown paper round it." How a thin sheet of brown paper *prevented* it being a weapon I could not see. Bureaucratic obtuseness. Once, hurrying to an appointment, I was pulled up by a red light with just one car, a huge limousine with thick, darkened windows, in front of me. The lights went green but the limousine refused to move. As horns tooted behind me I went to the driver's window. "The light's green," I shouted. "Would you mind letting us all go?" The four young men in the car were gyrating in their seats to some loud pop record on their stereo, waving arms like thin sticks and as pale as dead fishes' bellies, their faces white with night club pallor. I recognized them as one of Britain's richest pop groups. Then one of them turned, treated me to a long rude stare, put out his tongue, and resumed gyrating.

Occasionally I went to cocktail receptions connected with work but now felt totally bored by the small talk, where little was said, little was meant, and nothing was remembered save those two variations from the truth, compliment or insult. My hankering for the wilds was always there and one solace lay in hiring boats on the dark Serpentine or Regent's Park lake, where I rowed madly up and down until tired enough to sleep through the traffic din below my little bed sitter. Once I went to Richmond Park to see the fine herd of some seven hundred red deer. Stags with finer antlers than any I'd seen on the island, here stood placidly just a few yards away. I met an old man photographing one with a tripod who told me he'd won a prize that way. No long skilful stalk on the hill – it seemed dishonest for it wasn't really wildlife at all.

The few relationships with young women I met in the city were fractured. None I was attracted to showed any real interest in a wilderness life and disillusionment set in. One night I went to a singles club, a "Disco" with two bachelor pals, as we had done so often in the past. Nostalgia was brief – the days of taking a feminine girl in your arms to waltz and listened to each other, had long gone. They all danced apart, doing their "own thing". To me discos were places where those with nothing to say took those who didn't want to listen. I looked at the long-haired, "trendy" peacock males, , of the early 1970s, anxious, bustling, with their smart city quips. I looked at the newly emancipated girls on whose faces the "back to the Twenties make-up had usually a Guy Fawkes effect. Male chauvinist pigs – matched by female chauvinist sows, I thought.

Perhaps it was because I grew up in the early Fifties when you could actually tell which was man or woman at first sight, when the *difference* between the sexes was what was emphasized. To me true feminity and masculinity were both superb but belonged on separate pinnacles, the two fusing together, complementing each other, when love came. Women were never the "inferior" sex but just as "equal" and in many ways superior. If any woman can do my job better than I, let her have the greater reward. But how can the women's libbers do that *and* be good mothers to young children? Perhaps, to avoid the increasing number of disturbed children, women will evolve into two kinds – mums and career ladies. Doubtful. Perhaps men will swing towards the "woman's role". Even more doubtful. I clutched my drink at the bar and started moralizing to myself. Unisex, women's lib, gay lib, were not dynamic trends at all, for they sprang from a combination of increased affluence, overcrowding and more labour-saving machines that gave folk time on their hands, so helping create boredom which led to dissatisfaction, then to neurosis and, often, to nihilistic "protest". Their practitioners were not social pioneers but *victims* of nature, for the end result of such concepts was an increasing polarization of the sexes, higher divorce rates, greater use of contraception and ultimately, for a while at least, the birth rate dropped. Not social pioneers at all, I thought, but victims of nature's slow relentless power, now major depopulating wars in the nuclear age were, so far, unthinkable, of keeping numbers down! And sex, increasingly commercialized, in advertising and pornography had become more boring.

57

Suddenly, as the disco music thumped on and there was no pleasure any more for me in this unnatural selection under artificial light, I caught a glimpse of my two old friends and myself in the mirror over the bar. The plain truth was we were now just three morose middle-aged moose who weren't getting much share of the action! And these trends were bound to be transitory.

But my attitudes towards these old friends and others, well placed in public, literary or business life, *had* changed. I sensed an increasing unease as if some secretly felt their existences had become somehow futile, yet they were unable to take a chance to change their lifestyles. Several times I was told that a simple rural life of meaning no longer existed, or that it was "irrelevant". None of them was remotely interested in my life in Canada either, for it was beyond their experience. But when you have trekked and slept out in the wild where animals like grizzlies and cougars roam, nothing is ever quite the same again. The normal goals of "success', the spare-time enthusiasms of city life like movies, shows, sports – where most were merely telly spectators removed from the physical action, now seemed to me colourless and mundane. I felt I had little in common with my own past or the old friends any more and one by one they all fell away.

Placing my novel and Canadian book outline proved hilariously frustrating. I had near misses with the novel at three publishers, was finally called in by one editor and told if I rewrote it in parts he would be interested. I dashed back to Scotland, rewrote in two months, only to find the editor had gone to a firm not interested in fiction. One agent went into hospital with a breakdown three weeks after accepting the novel. Another agent lost the top copy. A North American publisher kept the Canadian outline five months, wrote 'It's good. We may well want to publish it'', then sent it back well thumbed and minus its cover. It too had to be re-typed, a month's payless work in itself. I describe such frustrations as hilarious because there are two things you can do when faced with constant failure in middle age – laugh and carry on, or kill yourself. Unfortunately, I imagine if there *is* a next world the ones who take their own lives are regarded as gatecrashers who have not paid their dues. Perhaps much depends on the adjustments we make individually with the universe.

Slowly, too, my initial euphoria about being back in Britain dampened, for the social problems that had helped inspire me to leave in the first place were still afflicting society. There were the paralyzing winter strikes, so the city dweller could seldom rely on transport, fuel, heating, light, refuse collection, or even working telephones; plus vandalism, increasing violent crime and aggressive union picketing. And now a new phenomenon – terrorism and bomb planting by anarchists and subversives. Even the dwindling, overworked city police forces seemed to be receiving less support from the public. Of course it does no good to sulk about the apparent degeneration of the industrialized world, but all these factors and a tendency among the overcrowded British at the time to allow deadening bureaucracy and militant unionism to take over – plus a welfare system that seemed to do too little for the genuinely sick and the aged yet cushioned the lazy and foolish and penalized the enterprising; all these reflected a weakening of moral purpose, and appeared to whittle away at individuality itself. Yet I realized also that it was useless to castigate "society" or look to it to provide the individual with a meaningful way of life. Ultimately, and healthily, one has to make one's own way.

Sometimes I came back to the little pier after London visits and driving through torrential rains in Glencoe, to be told by locals that gales had been raging for days and they hoped my roof was still on. Yet the clouds would miraculously clear as I set out in my boat – to arrive at the bay of my little paradise in blazing sunshine. Nature's gods seemed to be offering me special privileges.

So, stage by inexorable stage, the sounds of city life and humanity would die behind me and I would be alone again in paradise. Yet loneliness was always strongest after being in the towns again.

On the next trip to London my bed-sitter/office was surrounded by scaffolding, workmen called to each other all day, so even writing the articles needed for survival finance was impossible. When the popular magazine said they *did* want to run a story about my wilderness life but in interview form and they could only pay £200 – take it or leave it – I took it, feeling a man couldn't sink much lower than selling a story about himself.

My next visit in the autumn of my second year proved the final straw – and the end to this last uneasy adjustment between my former life and my new. I returned to my bed-sitter to find it had been burgled. My few belongings – typewriter, camera, two tape-recorders, battery record player, a fan heater – had all gone. I raced round the streets in rage looking for a "swarthy man in a brown hat" who had been seen leaving the building with a full plastic sack but, perhaps luckily, I saw no-one fitting that description.

I now felt strongly that these annoyances were more than coincidence, more than fate, almost as if I were being *told* to sever *all* city connections. Galvanized into desperate action, I secured contracts with British and American publishers to write a book about a top movie star whom I had often interviewed and liked.

The money from these, I determined, would be my last "patron" from my old life. In Canada I'd felt vaguely that my future lay somehow between man and the last wild places. Now it had taken well over a year to learn again, finally, that only a wilderness life close to nature really interested me. I had grown apart from the mainstream of human life. It saddened but failed to deter me.

To "opt out" or flee cities because one could no longer endure them would have been mere withdrawal, but I was just too old to believe the naïve and nihilistic philosophy of the hippy movement. Indeed I had succeeded in cities as diverse as Rome, Paris, London and Hollywood, and experienced travel and relationships with interesting folk beyond my wildest youthful dreams. Even on the brief trips from the island I had done well to earn a living so far, and if I had stayed in my old work full time, from the book offers now coming in, I could be earning an easy £10,000 a year. But my once cherished goals of success and material independence had long been won and had proved meaningless for their own sakes alone. It was now clear that tree, crag, sea and torrent had anchored themselves in my mind and heart and it was there in the wilderness that I must now make my final stand to be a writer. Above all, I had to make up for wasted time, for now I knew it was no longer time I was losing but life itself. Back in a natural life rhythm I would finish the movie book then write only about the things I truly felt. With care I could last out another year. In such determined mood I sold off my former-work files to a popular magazine, gave up the bed-sitter/office in London, and drove home.

As if to teach me for such effrontery when I arrived back at the little pier a wild September storm was blowing and with the gales blasting the loch from the west-north-west I had to wait out the night in the Land Rover. As I toiled up the steep slope with a heavy load next morning, the biting midges seemed even worse than in mid-summer. Literally blown into my hair they were much faster to reach the roots and start biting. It seemed to be inherited learning over thousands of years – as if knowing they died sooner in the stormier weather of early autumn and needed to work faster to take a mite of your blood to propagate their species into next year. Biting midges are an economic factor in the Highlands for they affect one's ability to work outdoors up to 1,800 feet, pester holidaymakers and affect movements of wildlife too. Many a time I saw deer restrict their grazing to the windiest parts of the high hills in summer to avoid midges and other biting flies. Unfortunately midges have proved impossible to control for their larvae can live in the tiniest water pools, even in sodden vegetation.

But as I came up the path with the last load I was rewarded by my first sight of a rare merlin falcon, too small, fast and dark slatey-blue for a sparrowhawk, arrowing like a tiny meteor between the rocks and stunted trees, ready to tackle bird prey as large as itself.

What a treat it was to be back, as the Tilley lamp hissed away in the darkness and I arranged my few letters, business ones on top, personal ones below, and read what others had taken the trouble to write to me, sipping a few glasses of wine as my stew bubbled. But a letter from an American publisher contained a blow. He had turned down my novel saying "The hero is a giant, too unbelievable", and my Canadian book too with "There is no market for wilderness books today". But he added a note that a leading American colour magazine was looking for "backwoods stories". I sent off a story I'd written about days as a deck hand on the salmon boats along the wild British Columbian coast. When it came out with elaborate artwork weeks later it seemed a breakthrough – the first article I had published about my personal experiences after twenty-one years of writing only the doings and opinions of others.

By now the contrasts of autumn were showing on the wild seascape, the leaves were swirling from the alders on shore, the bracken was turning yellow, and the first ash leaves were flapping against the croft windows. I went to work again on the cabin, nailing down the whole floor. Once I was moving a large rock beneath it to put in a centre support post when the rock crushed the abdomen of a coach-horse beetle. As it reared up in pain, jaws champing, feet clawing at dust as it fought for life, my eyes were only inches away and I felt its entire agony. There was nothing to do but end its torture with a swift knuckle. But I felt sad. How many creatures do we kill with a single step, without even knowing? But the world was made thus. There is an awful waste in nature. Many times I saw newly hatched moths, unlucky to emerge on a stormy day, dashed to pieces on rocks by winds, or pinned upside down by gales and rain, wings smashed, having made only one brief pointless flight. If we are only part of nature, I felt, we are doomed.

It often seemed to me that the western Christian intellectual has become too far divorced from nature, like most of mankind, preaching homilies about a god of love, seemingly unaware of the harsh reality in the kingdoms of the wild, that it is man's duty to protect and enhance the last of the natural world. Animals are innocent. We have creative intelligence and foresight but abuse our privilege, for short-term gain.

By late September I had framed the walls, cut the roof beams and only the side cladding and roof needed completion. But with the nights drawing in, the rains increasing, I decided to lay it all down and cover it for the winter. I would finish the cabin in early spring.

Coming back up the beach on a cold, drizzly day, I found two buff-tailed humble-bees helplessly dying as they clung to the last purple knapweed flowers. I'd never seen bees work harder, lurching until well into autumn from flower to sparse flower, even when in five minutes I'd seen other bees denude the same flower of all nectar. Now, defeated by the cold and rain, they were still in the act of doing their work, probing their thick tongues painfully into flowers in dying slow motion. Such blind tragic dedication, it seemed, yet if only *we* could work like that, preserve in our own lives this god-like creative impulse. Was it not the great Goethe who tried to write a final poem with a finger upon his quilt even as he died?

As I stacked the tools in the far room and lit the paraffin lamp, a robin suddenly began to sing in the ash trees. I wondered if he thought the light was a new dawn for he flew to the scraps table and began to feed.

Suddenly there was a loud buzzing in a far corner. A huge, female humble-bee had come in for winter hibernation. She flew below the roof, examined a small hole then with a last "*zizz*" of wings disappeared into it. She would survive there until the spring then emerge again on a warm day and find an earth hole, there to raise a new colony. It was the males, the workers, that I had seen dying.

Mid-October produced the kind of glorious, eight-day "Indian" summer which seems unique to the Highlands. From clear skies the sun burned with a fierce heat upon the deep cobalt ocean waters, a total contrast from the limpid greeny blues and hazy mists of summer. Then came three cloudy and ominously calm days, and on October 18 the first real storms of autumn began. In late afternoon as I worked at my desk 70 mph gales swept the land from the west, bending the trees until they seemed to be holding hands over their heads. The wooden walls bulged inwards and every slight gap in the boarding leaked spurts of draught. The place was "air conditioned" all right. Cold air forced its way up through the floorboards, my feet chilled for the first time, as if the old paraffin heater had not been lit at all. I forgot the gales as best I could – then suddenly remembered the boat. I hastened down in the darkness, struggling to keep my footing on the steep, windy path, with a torch. It was banging about in the rough seas, heightened two feet by the power of the gales, and amid the crashing waves it was now filled with shingle, seaweed and water. I struggled to empty it, to pull it higher, scooping half a bucketful out at a time with fast, flailing strokes of an oar and filling the air with spray, but the sea filled it faster and in the dark and rain I had to give up.

At dawn, the gales still raging, I hurried down. The tide was down but the boat was now covered in weed, shingle and sand, smashed up against the green grass of the bank like a wreck that had been there for years. With frozen fingers I tore the seaweed from the anchor and bow ropes, bailed the boat empty again then hauled it higher up the bank. It was holed at last, two jagged rents on the starboard chines, but luckily they were small. I made a rain screen from a sheet of plastic, melted pitch with a candle flame to block the holes, then painted all white again. What a fool I'd been for not buying a fibreglass repair kit. But really I had been lucky for if the boat had been smashed up completely it would have been a disaster in my island life, more significant than the loss of any city car.

6

NEVER MORE THAN DURING the autumn storms does the island dweller learn his life is totally controlled by the moods of the sea and its tides. Once, after a dinner invitation to discuss the lease of some land of my own further up the loch, I returned at midnight to find the boat had dragged its rear anchors in the gales. At low tide it was tipped sideways on weed-covered rocks, the engine down and completely submerged in the sea. I shivered through the night without bedding in the Land Rover and when the tide came in again had to row all the way home in the pre-dawn twilight. I only made it by rowing half *with* the winds until in the island's lee, then it took a further two hours to fight back against the choppy waves, making only a yard of headway for each hard stroke of the oars. Then I had to carry the engine up to the croft, dunk it into the fresh water of the burn to prevent salt corrosion of its innards, and spend the day drying it out. That was my first and last "night out" on the mainland for over two years. The land deal didn't work out either.

Every boat trip was a different battle according to wind direction. If going home and the gales were from the north-east, I had to slide along in the lee of the Clanranald castle and Riska island, dash over the open part before Shona's shore, huddle along in the lee until another blasting in the exposed area below Arean, avoid the two rocky islets which the seals used as haul-out beds in summer, be shoved at great speed by the waves through the narrow gap between the mainland rocks and a small island, then limp thankfully into my bay.

Going *out* on a north wind there was a three-way fight, firstly to keep ahead of the huge troughs until about half way, secondly to negotiate turbulent choppy waters where the two curving streams of wind round the island met, and I then had to fight *against* big waves as I reached the main blast of the wind curling round the east edge of the island. In south gales it was hard, sometimes impossible, to launch the boat from my beach at all. At best two strong kicks and thrusts with an oar against the bottom won a few yards but if the engine didn't start with the first two pulls, I had to leap out to physically prevent the boat being dashed on shore, keep its bow to the waves, and try again.

At least with the south-easterlies it was easier coming home for one was literally blown back and I came to call this "going downhill". But as November wore on the gales came mostly from the north and by mid month it was so cold I had to find a better way of keeping warm while writing at the desk. Some 37,000,000 working days are lost each year in Britain through rheumatism and arthritis alone, and I couldn't afford to lose even one.

Although I had now insulated the double wall boards with bunched up newspapers and set sheets behind the hardboard, the cold winds still penetrated every tiny crack like sharp knives. If I put the old paraffin heater near the window on my left these shafts were warmer but the fumes were blown directly into my face. If I put it on my right, my left

The plastic "tent" around the desk in winter,

half slowly froze. So I invented a plastic "tent", rigged right round the desk with wooden poles, complete with a roof just two feet above my head. And I placed the desk on little wooden blocks so I could slide the heater a few inches under it. This way the hot air hit the bottom of the desk, blew round in the space below, thus preventing legs and feet becoming frozen, and seeped up above the desk too. To stop the fumes coming directly up my nose I tacked a thick towel along the desk's front, arranging it tightly round my waist each time I sat down.

Eking out finance as I was, I refrained from buying a costly calor gas heater, and humping more heavy cylinders across the stormy loch in a small boat with the other provisions. When winter finally set in I even stopped using the rear room as a kitchen and moved the two-ring camp cooker on to the shelves behind me – for the extra warmth from the cooking flames! At night the paraffin lamp on the desk by the window also filled the little "tent" with more heat. With only a few small trees nearby and loath to cut any down, I had no firewood but the old boards torn from the croft, or what I fetched on treks to the forest over a mile away. Wood fires became a treat at weekends only.

Life in the wilds has enough problems from the isolation alone but living frugally also forced little self disciplines on my appetites. I not only rationed wood fires but also playing the radio – a little at lunch, two hours at night, looking forward to certain programmes. I could only get Radio 2, however, and rarely Radio 4 at night, which came through better in stormy weather than in clear. My only other treat from civilization, before I brewed my own, was a few glasses of wine before supper. But to reduce temptation I refused to stock up drink and if kept from boating to the store in gales, this often had to be cut to one or even half a glass of tiny sips a night. "He died for a bottle of wine in a storm" would have been a shabby epitaph! I also rationed musical concerts on the small battery record player to Saturday nights, or after I'd fought home with stores and a handful of mail, the big day of the fortnight. Then I'd have a few wee sips, listen to the music, linger for an hour over the letters, teasing myself with quick readings so I could pore over it *fully* later, or leave the last page unread, so I'd have something to look forward to next evening. I began to read more books, choosing carefully. Re-reading Henry Williamson's *Salar The Salmon* and *Tarka The Otter*, I gained far more from them than I had as an unaware, untravelled youth. To discover that George Orwell wrote his essays in isolation too, on the island of Jura, seemed a small source of strength. So did my discovery of Thoreau's *Walden* where thoughts similar to mine, so well expressed, made me feel less alone. To find I'd already spent more than twice as long in the wilds as he had in his cabin in the woods of Concord renewed my resolve to carry on.

I now used the shortening daylight hours to pound away on my books. For exercise I'd go out and dash four hundred yards up the hill and back, my probably foolish recipe for keeping fit – get the heart pounding at least once a day.

By late November it was dark until 9 am and dusk again at 4 pm. Chaffinches and blackbirds had now moved to the easier pickings on the mainland for the winter. Only the friendly little robin stayed around for company. One afternoon, the bird table empty, he had been ticking his silvery notes on the big rock when suddenly he launched himself straight at the window, bounced off it and fluttered weakly back to the rock. I opened it. "Do you want some food?" I said, feeling ludicrous for talking to a wild bird. It dipped its head up and down expectantly, rocking on its thin knock-kneed legs, waiting for me to throw bread, then it dived upon it before I'd withdrawn my hand. It could certainly make its wishes known.

One misty morning, leaving early in calmer weather to shop so I'd still have some daylight left for work, I boated fast to the pier – and almost ran down a huge stag in the sea. It was taking a short cut from the peninsula to the mainland, probably to avoid crossing the little road near the ruined castle. Spurts of breath were blasting sideways from its nostrils, condensing in the cold air, like from a tramp steamer, its eyes showing white with fear as it tried to get away from the boat. Then its feet touched bottom and with powerful surges it came out of the water and galloped out of sight. For the first time I missed the loss of my camera though I'd seldom taken it anywhere for I did not think of myself as a photographer. But I realized that stag would have made a superbly dramatic picture.

On November 21, in a brief sunny period, I trekked to Shona House for my mail which I now had sent there with the island's post to force myself into taking exercise on foot. As I walked the rough track between the great oaks and conifers, feeling the enchantment of the still and ancient silences of the forest, I was overtaken by a flock of bullfinches, their snow-white rumps flashing like tiny lights as they dodged through the hazel wands of the under storey. Then some of the rosy-breasted males came back, de-budding twigs and making mournful little "*Tui tui*" peeps, like little sprites of the forest. Suddenly there was a thump at my feet as a large, brightly red-brown bird with barred plumage shot upwards. It was a woodcock and it winged powerfully but silently away, staying low with fast-dodging flight through the densest bushes and trees as if it knew that way it stood less chance of being shot. Woodcock have increased since protection during its breeding season, and in Scotland through the planting of new forests. When the woodcock floats high with quivering wings on its "roding" display and to beat the bounds of its territory in spring, few birds are more beautiful in flight. I laughed to myself as I recalled Sir Noël

Coward's remark to a hotel waiter when he thought the bird he was eating rather tough. In his fruity but measured voice he had said "The trouble is, young man, there is too much wood and not enough cock!" Before I reached the house I was overtaken by sleety snow, making a hissing noise as it fell through the tree foliage and hit the leaf-strewn forest floor. Among my mail I saw with delight a letter from a pal in Hollywood and from a girl I'd met and liked in London whom I had invited to visit. Was she really coming up for Christmas? As I left with the mail and two gallons of paraffin in my pack, I paused for a brief chat with Iain MacLellan. Dusk was now falling and a strong wind had started to blow in the trees. He looked up at the black, leaden sky with practised eyes and suggested I stay in the caravan overnight. But I was anxious to return to the little croft and enjoy my mail alone.

In the forest it was not too bad but when I came out into the high, open hills, the steep, stone causeway treacherous now with slippery snow, black snags of granite sticking up here and there, I walked into a totally different world. The rushing wind drove the sleet and snow-flakes, grey as ash against the sky, directly into my face in the dark.

I cursed myself for not putting new batteries into my pocket torch which was only just strong enough to show the sleet cascading like flashing icicles. I could not find even the little deer and sheep path but had to deduce where it was from the lie of the snow over the land. The blizzard did not let up for a second, the gale shrieked about my ears and my sweater was soon soaked through the thin, worn-out shower jacket. It was impossible to hurry as I was top-heavy with the pack and the wind nearly blew me off several small cliffs. When the torch batteries gave out I went low, floundering in peat bogs and snow drifts and I began to feel I might not make it home. But to stop in that wet cold would have been folly and, using the wind and sounds of the crashing seas as direction indicators, I kept going.

At last I came to the dell where the croft stood and I staggered through the door, my feet soaked, body sweaty yet shivering in the wet clothes. Snow fell from me in icy lumps. It was the worst walk I'd ever had on Shona. But I lit the lamp, prepared my vegetables and with keen anticipation opened my mail. The letter from my pal was amusing, reminding me of a life that now seemed to have belonged to someone else. But the letter from the girl said she had been to Portugal on holiday, and she had met this young fellow. . . . Next day the radio told me the same blizzards had caused the deaths of six walkers in the Cairngorms.

In mid-December I went across the stormy loch for a brief trip to London to see the publisher of the movie book and to pick up final oddments left in my former landlady's garage – TV set, files, clothes, books, etc. Offered a small rubber boat at wholesale price, I bought it for towing behind and easing the load in my main boat. And in calm weather it would be lighter and faster, thus saving on petrol bills. But I arrived back at the little pier at dusk to find raging squalls of hail raking the sea loch. As I was blowing up the rubber boat, estate foreman Phil Corcoran, who had been helping me try to find my own piece of land, drove by. He said the bad weather had not let up once during my absence, a boat going the short mile to the island had lost its engine to the sea the previous night, and that very morning a cottage near his had lost its roof. I knew I couldn't get across to Ballindona that night and as I unloaded, stacking the heaviest gear under a plastic tarp until morning, I saw him smile when he saw the TV set, for he knew I had no electricity.

'I'll not be having any more need for that,'' I said on impulse. "Here, have a TV set!'' And I shoved it into the back of his van.

As I spent the night in the truck, buffeted by the winds and noisy hail, trying to stem the drops of condensation plopping on to the plastic sheet over my sleeping bag with strategically placed rags, I felt like heading back south for Christmas. In truth, though, I had nowhere really to go. And nothing saddened me more than for the sake of not being alone, to accept a well-meant invitation and sit in another man's house, see his happy family around him, and feel a failure in that I did not have all that too.

But before dawn the wind dropped slightly and the hail ceased. I loaded both boats until low in the water and set off through choppy but not dangerous waves. Once again at the rocky islets the seals used in summer, cormorants flew near, veering off at the last moment to pinion away to the horizon. Several herons rose with gawky leaps and I knew the last one to be Harry for I saw his broken toe clearly. So the sounds of civilization died behind me and once more in now blazing sunshine I arrived. As I carried up three heavy boxes of books I felt they were now becoming my best friends – one can really *converse* with books for one reads *considered* thoughts.

It took eleven hard trips to carry all the gear up to the croft. I had nothing at all left in civilization now. It was the final commitment. But the sun shone all the time and when the last tin was carried in I went out again into the dying sunlight. The horizon was now blue and violet with purple-grey clouds racing in, icing the air. The burn gurgled its pure waters and the city world I had just left now seemed as remote as Hades. I laid out all the books for sorting, stacked everything in place and lit a wood fire to dry out the damp croft. Only when all was shipshape, fire crackling, the lamp hissing its golden light, did the storms break again, the sleet sliding down the windows as if reluctant to melt. As I felt the icy stabs of wind through tiny apertures, I realized I had struck the only patch of sun in three weeks. It was hard *not* to believe in some god watching over me, that I was *meant* to be there. I was home. I was alone and I was free – for nothing but work. My euphoria dampened when I found mice had gnawed a hole in the door and broken into the food packets above the cooker and stuffed rice and pearl barley into a shoe and inside the rolled-up door mat. And when I went to air my blankets by the fire I found they had fouled the centre of my bed. I nailed a strip of wood to the door to try and stop their little nuisances.

But at night it was hard to sleep for they pounded noisily round inside the double walls. In vain I banged a stick on the bedside wall hoping to drive them out but after a short silence they started again. One morning I found they had come in through a small hole near the chimney and had stuffed one of my socks with barley – like a peace offering. So I compromised, tipping a small pile of pearl barley in the porch each night with some boxes and rags for shelter. I worked – for a time.

Three days before Christmas the sleet and hail were replaced by rain, then the rain stopped and the winds veered to the south-west. During this brief lull I went for a walk westwards along the shore, saw no bird or animal life at all, then began climbing north over the hills.

As I ascended higher the wind increased once more making the climb-walking easier. But as I turned east heading back far above the croft again, the force of the renewed gales was so great my cheeks were blown out and I had to fight downwards through the heather and over the rock faces, actually leaning *on* the wind as it tore at my clothing. Rounding one knoll I saw what looked like a piece of cardboard bouncing up over the faces towards me but as it came nearer I realized it was a large sheet of corrugated iron. It was coming straight towards me and I suddenly felt as you do when you dream as a child that an aeroplane is crashing and no matter which way you run, you know it's going to hit you.

I dodged behind a rock and the sheet wafted past where I had been moments before. I forced my way down until I came to the side of the old croft ruin behind my home which still had two walls standing and some of its roof on. All the scrub oak, birch and alder trees were bending on the hill, as if tossing their heads in rage, and I saw the old ruin was systematically being destroyed by the raging gale. It bulged and then burst as if someone had put a bomb inside. Great sheets of its roof iron, eight feet by three, were being ripped off one by one and sent shooting up over the hill. If anyone had been up there in the way now they would have been sliced in half. It was quite terrifying for I was afraid my own roof would go too.

Then I saw the bricks, stones and mortar of the old ruin were also being destroyed by the wind, bricks were actually being shifted and pushed out before my eyes as if someone had put an invisible hawser round each and was pulling them out one by one. When I stumbled back into the cottage, the door was smashed open noisily by the gale and I struggled to push it shut again. I heard a crash and tinkle in the far room – one of the old panes of glass left in the window had split and one half had smashed on to the floor. The wooden walls of the croft were bulging inwards, the roof chattering madly. My thought that I should go out and nail half a sheet of plywood over the living-room window to prevent it being blown in too, was brief – there was no way a man could have held such a piece of flat wood steady enough to nail it down in such a tempest. As I stood in the corner away from the window in my little shelter in that wild place, I was most conscious of my own mortality, a man's puniness alone in nature. And yet the reality of it was somehow exhilarating.

As usual I dreaded Christmas Day and when I woke to torrential rain I at first took refuge from my isolation by turning on the radio – to hear there had been a record spending spree in Britain, holiday flights to the Mediterranean were double the previous year. A Force Nine gale "imminent" in my area and nowhere else, was announced. It just fitted my initial mood, I thought. Maybe the roof *will* blow off today!

Then followed one of those interminable pop music programmes where banal jingling double-entendre lyrics of "lerv" were interspersed with folks requesting DJs they didn't know to "wish" love to husband, sister, wife, aunt or Fanny Fannakapants next door, and names and addresses were reeled off as from a phone directory. Bleating, nasal, reedy or cat-strangle-voiced singers followed one another in dreary succession, each one being called "great" or "wonderful" or "superb" by the hosts who had more than a vested interest in perpetuating the slop. From one came a lyric "People who need people are the luckiest people in the world".

Not if they don't have anyone, they're not, I thought bitterly. In fact to me the precise opposite seemed to be the truth. Then for the first time I heard a song from a new rock musical about the life of Christ! The strange line "Who do you think you are . . ." was bawled out by a crying female voice, presumably referring to Christ himself. Later some church minister was saying such musicals would lead to a revival of Christianity. What they *will* be is just more linchpins in further reducing the recorded life and *example* of the man-Christ, the truth he had lived unto death – that only love and creation-in-love redeem – to the level of another mere folk tale. To sheer away the superstitious symbols, props and dogmatic assertions clapped on later by the many often-profiteering churches was one thing, but to replace the brave subtle philosophy with slick sentimentality, to appeal to those who were too moronic to examine for themselves, was no whit better. Just as the illiterate modern version of the Bible had eclipsed the sagacious

71

simple style of the James I version. I turned the radio off for good that day. We seem to be becoming a more and more trivial-minded society, using words like "great" to describe our contemporary "heroes" – football kickers, pop singers, ersatz composers, telly stars who found a career on a few catchy phrases, and the like. In such ways do the real meaning of such words become perverted to common dross and slang.

In the silence that followed I felt increasingly lonely but I wrote until near dark then cooked a usual lunch, adding chips and lighting a few candles as my only concession to Christmas. As the chips crackled away I realized I'd been unconsciously preparing myself for the year-end holiday – refraining from drinking for a few days so I'd have a little treat in store for Christmas itself. But as I now sipped sherry and wine before eating I realized I was acting from mere habit, forcing myself to enjoy in the traditional manner. After two half bottles had gone I knew there was no point in drinking alone and put them away. Another little discipline had been to refuse to play my battery record player for two weeks – hoarding the treat for the actual day, so I had something held in promise, in thrall as it were, and not under value.

I smiled as I recalled the comments of a well-heeled colleague in my old profession who had an elegant home in north London with four huge speakers dotted about his large living room. "You miss all the nuances of the music if you only have a battery player," he'd said. Some folk prattle like this to hear themselves use words like "nuances".

You can hear well enough, not pop maybe, but really fine music survived the test. I could play favourites like the stirring Carmina Burana, enjoy the blend of woodwind and piano in the "Clock" symphony of Haydn, the stately "Le Quattro Stagioni" of Vivaldi in perfect peace – without parking problems, hearing coughs, sniggers and sniffs, or being accidentally kicked up the console in the arpeggio, as it were. Music took on its real meaning in such a landscape.

So after lunch I wiped my sweatered arm over my records and played my favourite Berlioz, Haydn, Mozart and Beethoven. Had not the great pianist Vladimir Horowitz been a recluse for twelve years too?

So I was alone, with no loved woman at my side, but as the Eroica boomed through the croft from the wooden box in which I'd set the tiny speaker, I recalled many fine creators had been lonely men and often unsuccessful in their own lifetimes. Beethoven had never married. Haydn's great love went off to a convent. Berlioz had disastrous love affairs, trying to drown himself after his first fiancée married someone else. Bizet died before Carmen came out, never knowing of its success. Rembrandt died in poverty. Schubert made a mere £600 from his work during his lifetime. Van Gogh, the misunderstood Nietzsche and the exquisite nature poet John Clare died in asylums. The rural morons about him called the great Richard Jefferies "Loony Dick". Even

Thoreau had died a failure at forty-four, having himself had to pay for some of his work to be published. But none of this now seemed to me to be tragedy for I realized all true creators have a reward which is denied to most – the joy of creation itself. Approval by others is merely the seal upon the treasure chest. It seemed to me the only real truth for an artist of any kind is to smile ironically at misfortune – and to keep trying.

Quite suddenly a memory of the actress Brigitte Bardot came into my mind. We had been talking for hours in her flat in the Avenue Paul Doumer in Paris in the early 1960s and I had asked her if, in spite of her numerous romances, she ever felt lonely? She had replied at length but I now recalled the sad and serious expression on that dramatic face as she ended with "Everybody is really alone. You are always alone. You are alone when you are born and you are alone when you die. All your life you are alone. To me it is normal."

As I mused thus, consoling myself with other memories too, a small, white moth suddenly leaped from a niche in the woodwork, flew wildly around, then with a brief "whoff" burnt itself in the flame of the candle, and fell to the table beside me. It stayed there a moment, rearing up on its front legs as if beseeching forgiveness, then it flew up again, hit the flame and sank on to its tail, its wings drawn back like an archangel's, its feet praying against the wick. Its long proboscis glowed red like coals and the whole body went dark as the wax spread up it. Then suddenly, with a little pop, it burst into flame and became part of the wick, flames now springing from its head. Poor moth – it could not resist the flame and so it had died before its time.

As the rain sounded softly on the tin roof, almost in harmony with the fine music now filling the little room, I found I needed to occupy my mind from negative musings and self-pity, and I selected two new books I had bought by the writer I admired more than most, Henry Williamson. As I picked up the first I felt startled by its title, *The Dream Of Fair Women,* for to me *that* dream had lasted far too long in several big cities of the western world. In the book Williamson's mystic, pantheistic, sensitive hero Willie Maddison retires from the horrors of human war to a lonely Devon cottage to be at one with nature, and as I read Williamson's prose I found myself transfixed by his clear vision of beauty, of man and nature. Even out of context I felt thrilled by passage after passage. For instance, he had Maddison write:

"I can sympathize with all men because I am a man who wants natural happiness, someone to love, and someone to love me, to live with me in my cottage, to guard the well of my spirit where I draw Truth which is also my life. The day after I met you I sat here and loved the sun, the sea and the sky. Suddenly I was afraid; for I can love all these things but they do not respond. I realized that I should grow old, that I should die, and still the wind would shake the poppy, the blue butterfly seek the harebell, and trefoil be yellow on the hillside. I shall be gone, dead, and nothing I can do now can avert that . . . ."

Then:

"And certain idealists, whom men call fanatics and lunatics and criminals, try to break down the old civilization, hoping to re-create a better world of men but all is foredoomed to failure until the extra wisdom has come into men's minds. They neglect the secret of the woods and fields and how they expand man's spirit if he knows them when little. . . . ."

Wonderingly I turned to the second book, *The Pathway*, realizing that his story of young Maddison was really confession on the part of one of Britain's greatest writers, yet one who has often been written off by effete intellectuals who do not understand what man has lost by severing himself too far from the natural world, who call him a mere "nature writer". I turned the pages again, finding more gems for my own heart:

". . . I realized that all the world was built up of thought; that the ideals which animated the world were but thought, mostly mediocre and selfish thought. Change thought and you change the world."

I read on, surprised such words had been written in the early Thirties, finding more passages that were so beautiful, so close to my own feelings and unpublished writings, I felt profoundly moved. It was as if Williamson was there with me, talking to me, his words giving me new strength. Suddenly I felt lonely no longer and it seemed there could be nothing more wonderful in the world than to sit there alone, a fire of gathered, dead wood crackling behind me, reading such words and feel my own suppressed but highest dreams realized in a great writer's thoughts, his dreams, and to know, alone or not, I might be about to tread some ancient, right, fine and crowdless path. I was no longer unhappy for now I *knew* in my heart, really for the first time, that I was not withdrawing from reality, that loneliness was often the spiritual state of one who wished to create, successful or not. It *was* time to be insular, to look back, to allow the past to reveal its significant side, if there was one. I made a sudden resolve – I would finish the commercial book before the old year was over and that would be farewell for ever to that kind of writing. As I rose to prepare supper I realized my real, truly felt, work was really all I had left, and an odd thought came. "In work I trust – all else is therapy."

Boxing Day dawned in a radiantly clear sky. I slaved on the book but when the sun streamed through the window after midday I felt uncomfortable and went to look at the old ruined croft above. The storms had scattered the rotting boards over the ground, providing a fine source of new firewood, and I carried armfuls down to the croft.

I typed an average of 5,000 words of the book for the next four days, then ran out of carbons. But by running the old ones over the top of the paraffin heater, so the remaining ink melted and spread itself over the surfaces, I was able to make ten more copies from each! On New Year's Eve, desperate to finish in time, I typed 14,000 words, an all-time personal record of sheer slogging work. I told myself I was just sitting there and tapping keys after all. It *had* to be done, no-one was going to help, and in the end sheer anger took me through. My stomach and back ached, my fingers felt weak across their backs but by midnight I had the book beaten.

As I typed the last words Big Ben on the radio tolled the New Year in. As my pot of stew simmered away, I started flicking through the pages of a general British nature book I'd bought on my last trip. To my surprise I could identify almost as many indigenous birds and butterflies as I could when a nature-loving boy. My glance fell upon the walnut sparrowhawk I'd lovingly carved in a year and a half of woodwork lessons and spare time at boarding school, which had somehow stayed with me through all my travels and was now standing on the window shelf. Then I remembered something else, began to search among my boxes of forgotten books until I came to one wrapped carefully in plastic bags. It was a book about birds and butterflies I had written and painted in Sussex at the age of fifteen, and as I now looked at the pictures again my heart surged and for the first time in over twenty-five years everything seemed to fall into place in my mind.

Nature had been my solace as a child. I had fled to the natural world, but in a new environment in Canada, to find peace and inspiration to write what was to have been the big novel. There I had fallen in love with wilderness life itself. Now, in middle age, I had turned to the natural world yet again, this time in the Highlands, in the isles of my birth. Suddenly the pattern had become crystal clear. Nature had been my one constant love throughout life. But it was no longer enough to merely enjoy the wilderness, use it as a retreat or for inspiration, but to try and *pay it back*. It was then I made my one New Year resolution. From henceforth I would write only about nature and the last wild places and man's place in and influence upon them. I would finally abandon the novel, re-write the Canadian wilderness book until it was the best I could possibly make it. That would be the indoor work while outside I would now actively study the natural world in which I now found myself, the Scottish Highlands, one of the last truly wild areas left in Europe. Perhaps after twenty-two years of journalism, meeting man at his best and worst in half the western world, I could avoid the narrow, specialized naturalist's view. I knew now that only by giving myself totally to this new life, by trying to understand the magnificent Highland wilderness deeply, factually, and writing about it with reverence and love, had I the faintest chance of succeeding.

The decision made, I suddenly remembered my wise old Indian tracker in grizzly country, Pappy Tihoni, and how each New Year he slept out under the open skies in a symbolic act of spiritual renewal with nature. I took a double sleeping bag outside, into a world of violent indigo, the colour of ink, and there beneath the ash trees waving their heads in the wind as if drowning, I slept peacefully until dawn.

7

THE EDGES OF THE sleeping bag crackled with the ice-frost from my breath as I climbed out into New Year's Day and a sky as bright as a metal sheet from the light of the sun which was still skulking behind the hills. I had been invited for lunch at Shona house but unable to face my desk again that morning I set off on a trek along the high path to Shoe Bay and back along the shore to take a look at the cabin.

It was good to be out in the sharp, clear air, boots cracking the ice of small pools along the rocky track, the sweet tang of the sea filling my lungs. From the ridge above the blue lagoon I saw an otter leap from a rock, skewer down and turn to swim round a bend out of sight. Damn, I should have gone slower.

On the way back to the cabin, the sun now lighting the sea to amethyst blue, a fish leaped from the mill pond surface and fell back with a noisy splash. A bunch of black winter gnats danced above the high rock, up and down, up and down, as if with glee. Overhead the tiny kestrel swooped down to mob the huge female buzzard who sailed serenely on, taking absolutely no notice. As I crept near the little trees that surrounded the cabin, I was suddenly aware of a tiny head in the crushed brown bracken, like a miniature tank turret with two black, beady eyes set high up. Those eyes had seen me too, of course, and now the woodcock winged away like a bronze arrow. This bird can literally see all round itself at any time, has better binocular vision to the rear than to the front. And I realized it was the first time I'd been able to spot a *sitting* woodcock, before it flew away, since boyhood in the Sussex woods.

As I stood silently amid the leafless trees, noting that the coverings of the cabin floor and framed walls were still in place, the smaller male buzzard, probably following its mate, beat its way west overhead, saw me and immediately veered away with a noisy woofing of wings. It had not expected a human to be standing there.

Now I saw a female eider duck, her thick bandy legs wide apart, her profile Roman-nosed like a fighter's, staring at me from the shore. She sploshed into the water and paddled away. Then an eider drake in resplendent black-and-white evening dress came swimming along, did not see me, and went as if to peck the duck's tail. She pattered over the surface with fast-beating wings, closely followed by the male. The bright sunny day had perhaps aroused his courtship instincts early. Then a female merganser popped up to the surface with a small, red shore rockling in her saw-bill which she had caught by diving. Next moment the brightly coloured drake came up beside her – with nothing. With his chestnut breast, white neck band and double spiky crests on his bottle-green head he looked like a duck masquerading as Woody Woodpecker. Just then both birds saw me and began to run across the water. As they became airborne their creamy wing patches flickered like candle flames. Now little brown wrens were flitting around me, sounding their alarm notes like clock springs unwinding in the bracken.

Suddenly I felt an intruder and an unquieting thought came. What if the woodcock, eider ducks, mergansers or even the little wrens normally nested near the cabin site? Why was I intruding into what had hitherto been a wild area, when I had my own croft but half a mile away? Surely, if I cared about the beauty of wild, untouched places, it was selfish of me to build in one. I, claiming to be a wildlife lover, also needed to get my attitudes straight! All enthusiasm to complete the cabin waned right then. And when over lunch at the big house the Vanes gently hinted there might be problems with the planning authorities anyway, they were surprised when I agreed with them, I decided to leave the area undisturbed during the nesting season, take the cabin to pieces in the summer and use the timber for more repairs to the croft. That was the end of the cabin project.

Such fine days as there had been were now rare and December and January were the most depressing months. The low sun hid behind the hills to the south, barely illuminating the landscape so it was dark until 10 am and I had to light the lamp again before 4 pm. Squalls of sleet and hail were often replaced only by rain-filled gales for day after grey day and I now saw some of the problems wildlife faces in winter.

Harry and other herons were fishing in nearly every sea bay now and I'd often see him standing for an hour or more, head hunched into shoulders, peering into the water with nothing at all coming within range of his darting beak. Just how a hard winter can decimate heron numbers was shown by the icy spell of 1947 when nearly half Britain's heron population perished. They have even been found with water frozen round their legs. After the long, cold winter of 1962/63, when more snow fell in Britain than at any time in the previous 150 years, occupied nests fell from 3,700 to 2,200. I discovered the red deer now had to forage over a wider range. In summer when growth was lush they kept mostly to the cool high tops, away from midges, tabanids and other fly pests, only coming lower at dusk. But now they were coming close to the croft for mosses, lichens, heather, dead nettles, grass and to clip the tops off young bushes and trees, the twigs of lower branches and to eat all the bramble leaves they could find. Brambles keep many of their leaves until well into January and sprout them again before most bushes, and once I woke up to find a young stag cropping the leaves from my blackberry bushes that lined parts of the burn.

Sheep also eat bramble leaves but twice that winter I found these bushes had drawbacks for these animals. After heavy rains I went down the path on January 8 to find a large ewe had been caught by the incurved thorns on two thick bramble leaders. She was sitting down on a rock right in the raging icy water of the burn, her head lolling weakly, stoically ready for death by cold and starvation or perhaps drowning once her front legs could no longer support her. The ground was splashed along the banks where she had tried to break free.

As I stepped into the pool to pull the brambles from her wool she stuggled so my hands were soon gashed and bleeding, but bit by bit I freed her, put my hands under her soft bloated belly and lifted her up on to the grass. She could hardly totter away but after a few yards she began to graze weakly. A thick woolly coat may look warm to us but it clearly has its drawbacks when you only have a domestic sheep's brain.

Only five days later I started on a trek up the hills behind the croft when I found an older ewe, caught up on a briar out in the open. This one had stumbled in constant circles, tying the thick bramble tighter round her neck until she now just stood, unable to move, her head bowed awaiting death. This time, remembering my gashed hands, I went back for gloves and a knife and cut her free. How stupid they seemed for all they had to do was gnaw through the brambles. I recalled the wild sheep I'd seen in Canada, the mighty bighorn, now rarer from over-hunting and the loss of its habitat from man's interests, whose rams could hurl a wolf from a mountain ledge. These man-bred creatures seemed considerably different.

My battles with the noisy woodmice were still a nightly exercise for my soft-hearted porch feeding had merely increased their numbers. One night I was woken by a rustling noise. When I shone the torch I found a *shrew* beside the cooker, and it was chewing away at greaseproof paper on which I'd left some batter mixture and butter.

79

What a racket! It froze for a second but as I got out of bed it leaped three feet to the ground and vanished behind a tiny hole by the fireplace. Until then I'd always believed the shrew, our smallest mammal, to be a complete insectivore, feeding on insects, beetles, larvae and worms. If it was interesting to discover it would eat such kitchen food, I was more fascinated later when I found shrews will feed from the fresh carrion of deer carcases.

Normally I wrote on stormy days but now I became so engrossed in the Canadian wilderness book I hated to lose momentum. After a two-week spell of this, my movie book unposted, my stores were so depleted I just had to go out when the westerly gales were tearing off the wave tops. I managed to ride them "downhill" but had to leave the boat in the lee of the ruined castle because the sea round the pier was raging against the sea wall. On the way back I had a real battle, boat banging in the troughs, almost capsizing and water spewing over the bows. The sleet was blinding, my back and neck soaked in icy spray, my free hand clutched below my knee for warmth, and I felt a sudden rage at the storm for making an already hard life more difficult. I cursed the waves aloud. "Damn you, I'm *going* to get there and you won't stop me!" as I struggled to keep the boat on course and actually stay in it. But I immediately felt foolish, muttered an apology to whatever god was listening, felt I was being forgiven and reached the bay safely. By now the gales had piled huge banks of slippery weed on shore and at high tide I just hauled the boat on to it, no need for the protector cradle.

As I walked through my door I felt victorious, all feelings of loneliness gone. What a pleasure it was to reach the little sanctuary, knowing I'd posted off the movie book, a year's work, the end of all commercial writing, and to sit and sip a few glasses of wine knowing a large pile of mail awaited my pleasure. I prepared my supper, sang noisily and badly my favourite musical roles, banged about at will, held loud, imaginary, victorious arguments with those who constantly turned down my writings – all without fear of disturbing my neigh-bours, human or animal. While silence is important for a man trying to live close to wildlife I realized there are plenty of noises in nature too – stags roar, owls hoot, seals bark, gales howl, and thunder imposes its awesome tympani upon the hills and glens. As long as I kept my little celebration inside four walls I was doing no harm. What, after all, were the important things – doing work one really loves, reading a good book, eating a simple meal, saving one's boat from a storm, one's life from the sea, animals from death, reaching out to contact others, if only in letters or books. How meaningful life suddenly seemed, as if I'd switched away from a trivial dream. I soon felt happy again. Loneliness in the wilds, if only for a spell, should be compulsory for everyone! Later I read my mail listening to Bach's magnificent Toccata and Fugue in D Minor. I had no need to imagine the cathedral, made by man to the glory of God, in which it was played. Was I not hearing it in God's *own* cathedral, the wilderness, the natural world built *by* god?

By now even the friendly robin seemed to have gone and my only "pal" was a large spider I called Sarah who had made a web on the window in the west room. Patiently she sat in a corner, seemingly able to go without food for weeks. After a sunny day when a large fly buzzed into the lamp and dropped to the desk with singed wings, I put it into her web. She came down in a flash, wrapped it in silk, sucked all the juices, then two hours later cut the fly free and retired to her top corner without bothering to repair her web first. So if she woke up hungry she had less chance of a new meal. Just another lazy modern craftsman, I said to myself. But a week later I took pity on her again and put a lighted candle near her web. The few flies roused by brief sunny periods flew towards the flame at night and some hit into her web, thus she got her meals with no effort from me.

By mid-January I had a way of taking hard and useful exercise to offset the spreading waist that afflicts the writer: I started a garden, clearing over a ton of rocks from a ten-foot-by-eight-foot patch below my window, carrying up sacks of seaweed from the beach to fertilize the ground for spring planting, then taking the fine earth from mole hills over a wide area to replace the rocks with useful soil!

One day with slight snow falling I took a long walk along the high track to Shona House for my mail then returned along the lower path through the wild enchanted forest. The snow just could not settle and I felt I was at Camelot where it always blew away – at night of course! I walked up a lovely green dell which the islanders called "Lover's Walk" though it had been a long time since any young lovers had walked up there. Nor did any fine lassie emerge from the trees to play Guenevere to my jaded Lancelot. But deer trails there were aplenty, the deep twin slots showing in muddy patches, and a flock of woodpigeons had moved on to colonize new roosts in the conifers. I had seldom been in that wood without seeing something new and that day was no exception. Suddenly a huge bird, deep russet in colour, went up about thirty yards ahead and with rapid wingbeats, interspersed with short glides with its wings curved downwards like hooks, disappeared between the trees. It went too fast for me to get the field glass on to it but it was too large to be a grouse, more like a small turkey and for so heavy a bird it flew with unusual silence. It had to be a female capercaillie, an exciting sight for it was rare in the western Highlands.

There were so many windfalls in the forest at one point I had to keep re-crossing a deep burn gorge, like a miniature version of the grizzly forests of British Columbia, but this seemed even more beautiful, in a spiritual way. Being less common after years of felling in the Highlands, such woods are more precious – jewels among the hills to be preserved at any cost.

I had just left the gorge and emerged on to a small woodland plateau when I saw the flat, green surfaces covered in moss of an ancient rockfall just below me. Suddenly there was a flurry, a scuttering sound, and a large, tawny animal with pointed ears and a thick, black-banded tail dived off one of the rocks and disappeared between them. Again I had no time to get out my field glass. Had I been in Canada I would have sworn it was a raccoon but here it just had to be a big cat, almost certainly a wildcat and this was only my second glimpse of one. I went below the rocks searching for tracks and there in the mud I found two unmistakable four-toed prints without traces of the claws.

On the way home just after leaving the forest, I saw the kestrel being blown like a matchstick over the hills, its wings sharp pointed in the wind so it looked like a tiny cross against the sky. I gave a high piercing *"wheeoo"* whistle and it actually turned round in the air and came towards me for a few yards, its wings bending supply before reverting to its original course. Now I could use the field glass and I watched it flying and hovering, its wings making extraordinary, flickering adjustments to the winds. Suddenly it went down, hovered, lower, hovered again, then it dropped. It flew up in a few seconds with something small and black in its talons, probably a beetle. It must have had a hard time hunting with snow still falling.

For some nights I tried setting out night lines with a dozen hooks on each baited with bacon scraps and mussels but it seemed most of the fish had deserted the winter cold of the shores for the deeper, warmer waters of the Atlantic, and apart from an occasional ten-inch saithe, I caught nothing at all. The rough seas also frayed and drifted loose weed against my lines. Shellfish too were rarer and after one long search all I could find was a few winkles and *one* cockle under some seaweed. Even the mussels seemed to have halved their populations, and I discovered many had half buried themselves in the gravel and sand as if seeking a more stable bed in the rough waters from the wind-blown tides. Although I searched through abstruse biological literature about mussels on a later trip south, I found nothing to explain this phenomenon.

By late January flocks of curlews flying with oddly slow wingbeats were working the tidal sand flats near the pier and castle. They can use their uniquely long curved beads to probe for worms, molluscs and other small marine fauna deeper than any other wader finds it possible. Often I just drifted in the boat to hear their haunting *"kourlee"* calls, the very musical embodiment of the melancholy winter scene. Occasionally small groups of winter-visiting golden eye ducks from northern Europe came over the boat, wings whistling creakily from their squat bodies, then they glided down to the river mouth, stretching out their ludicrous, webbed feet, like air brakes before landing in the water. Then the white-breasted, black-backed drakes swam fussily round the browner females, flashing their circular white cheek patches as if they were silver dollars for the ladies to take.

Although snow had fallen heavily in the last few days, the westerly winds off the ocean kept the island ground just above freezing point, and it melted again each day. In a rare, sunny period on February 8 which made me feel maybe spring was on the way, I saw the male buzzard, a feather missing from its right wing, flying over the shore, being plagued again by the cheeky kestrel. The small falcon swooped down past it from above then looped up again from below like a yo-yo on invisible strings, as if showing off its greater agility in the air. Too small and light coloured for a peregrine it was moving exceptionally fast for a kestrel, and it clearly regarded the bigger buzzard as a poacher on its territory. This time the buzzard put on speed to escape its tiny tormentor looking like a dignified schoolmaster forced to put up with the shenanigans of a cocky student because of lax punitive laws yet still trying to retain his dignity. "Why doesn't the little pest push off!" I had been making notes on both birds' movements and it seemed the buzzard worked the area once every four days while the kestrel, covering a much smaller territory, was hunting over it every two.

But that brief, sunny period proved a mere glimpse of spring because overnight the wind changed to the north and new hail had frozen to the grass and plant stems and in tiny hillocks along my wooden sills. Even the water supply in the buckets *inside* the room had frozen on top. Because my boat engine was now often misfiring I brought it up to the croft but my hand melted the ice on its handle, and it slipped through my grasp and fell, smashing its lid upon a rock. But I repaired it as best I could with wire and cleaned the points and plugs.

On February 12 I had to go out to post urgent mail, right into the hailstorms that had swept the land for three days and which the Highland winters seem to shriek upon the coasts as a final gesture before giving way to spring. Hoping the engine wouldn't conk out I used the slight lee of every rock and islet for a brief, bucking pause before dashing for the next, then went across the main water. The skies were grey and violet, the winds most violent when they preceded the hail clouds that looked like great jellyfish dangling grey curtains of stingers. I could see the squalls coming because the wave tips a few hundred yards away would be torn off first, then the hail and dark was upon me, the boat bucking like a bronco as I tried to keep it straight, the stones, some half an inch across, rattling, bouncing and hissing upon and around me. Then the squall was past and in a brief glimpse of blue sky and blinding light the sea turned a frothing bright green and white. Coming back was even worse and I had to shelter in a small horseshoe bay below

Shona forest and wait until the next brief lull. At times I had to slide
rapidly into the centre of the boat, my arm stretched out to the throttle,
to keep my weight off the stern in the deep, following waves. I don't
mind admitting I prayed a little on such trips. This was no country for
atheists.

It must have been instinct that made me go out that day despite the
gales for I woke up to a wild blizzard and a world of white. Sleet among
the snow came down the chimney and tickled the paper in the fireplace,
like mice rustling for food. Vortexes of air in miniature whirlwinds tore
in from nowhere, blasting between the high rocks and across the ash
trees, tearing off the last old, brown leaves from the scrub oaks and
sending them soaring into the sky. The gusts ripped at the roof so the
iron sheets chattered like false teeth, the gutterings rattled and the doors
creaked, swelling inwards slightly like the windward, wooden walls
themselves. Sheep wandered, staring perplexed at a land they had not

The croft and its surrounds at dusk.

seen before, going *"mairr mairr"* in bewilderment and frustration. The sea mashed angrily below, white percherons romping against the rocky teeth and scrabbling over the granite, up, back and down into itself again. The great boomings and roarings of the surf followed by smashings and seethings and the clacking grind of stones. All around me the mountains crouched and hid in their blinding cocoons of snow.

Yet later in the morning small, white clouds like fleece scudded across a deep blue sky and the sun burned with a fierce primeval heat, and I sat in the porchway, sheltered from the north-west winds a fish box for a chair, stripped to the waist with sweaters tucked round the cold parts in shadow, and roasted with the heat. Minutes later it was so dark I could not see the beach or my boat and the storm was back, driving the flakes of snow against a grey-green sky. Looking up into that sky now was like looking into the jaws of hell, with the smoky smuts from the hell fires coming into the eyes, and the hail so bad it smashed through eyelashes. I went indoors, my whole face smarting and glowing rosily after the natural hot-cold sauna and skin massage no city masseur could have given.

Snow fell again all night and after the winds switched round the clock, from north-west to south-west to south-east and to north-east, they lessened to almost total calm. Now the waves that had fallen ferociously, dying on to my beach the day before, came in caressingly to fall with soft chuckles in the sunlight between the snow showers. I went for a walk along the south shore into a magnificent tableau. The birch and alder groves were now a fairyland, with every branch, twig and even delicate bud carrying two or three inches of snow because it was falling softly without wind, drifting down in a white and silent world. Sheep again stood about disconsolately, with one large ram appearing completely baffled. Some were trying to find food, thrusting their heads into the middle of rush clumps and bent grass tussocks. I cleared some open patches with a shovel, only to find the grass and ground now frozen hard underneath and the sheep took no notice of my handiwork.

Before lunch I stumbled through two-feet-thick drifts to the westward shores. I was just rounding a small rocky knoll when I saw a young red deer stag with six-point antlers ahead. It was scraping snow from heather tufts with a forefoot. The wind was in the wrong direction, from behind me, and it was too late to go back and in again from a different angle. It got my scent in seconds, looked round briefly, then bounded away, not as light on its feet as usual because of the drifts. Just then the big female buzzard flew from a tree where she had been sitting motionless. She had been watching the deer.

In the afternoon I boated out for supplies then, although the engine now seemed better, I rowed back against slight winds, sticking at it, for one never knows when one will *need* rowing fitness in a wilderness life. I picked up four fish boxes that had been washed ashore by the gales always useful for furniture.

As I rowed quietly along, a lone, black-throated diver, known as "loons" in North America, appeared to be the only other moving life in the silent, white land and seascape and flew overhead towards a freshwater loch on the mainland. It seemed a highly competent flier, its pointed wings beating like twanged steel. There was no wastage about it, like a snake flying, very sharp everywhere, a beautiful flying and diving machine.

That day some of the locals told me we were having the worst winter for years, and I was glad to be there to enjoy it, in a primitive life style, for somehow it made one feel closer to the vital animal state. At dusk all the hills looked different, white while the sky was black, the reverse of the normal, like living in a photo negative, and before the dark finally fell the sea shone with a beautiful turquoise colour.

8

BEFORE THE END OF February many small birds were coming to the bird table. Little Fat Sergeant, the colourful, cock chaffinch with three white stripes on his wing, was back with his demure, grey-green hen, waking me each morning with loud *"pink pinks"*. Three blackbirds had arrived, a cock with black plumage and bright yellow beak, and two brown hen birds who announced their presence by worried *"kip kips"* as they approached the table in fits and starts. A hedge-sparrow also came flitting through the old bracken stubs threw its bread to the ground where it felt more secure. Missel-thrushes were now singing their stormcock dawn songs in the highest trees, one atop a little spruce that yet reared its tip against the sky because it was rooted on a high ledge behind the croft.

By the end of the first week in March the daffodils had grown to ten inches, ready to flower. In the grottos along the south shore burn pussy willows were silvering the bushes with shimmering light. Each morning down on the shore brilliant oystercatchers bathed at low tide, flinging water everywhere with their black-and-white wings and orange beaks, preferring where the fresh waters of the burn mingled with the sea. A pair of pied wagtails came in from the east calling *"tisit tisit"* with each loop of their undulating flight, like a pair of noisy flying scissors, then flitted about the croft with tilting tails. In glorious sunshine on March 8, my paraffin heater off for the first time, I was startled when walking down to the beach when the first queen humble-bee of the year tried to go down my ear as she searched for nest sites, suddenly filling my world with loud, buzzing sound. Three days later as I boated out in a dead calm, a great spotted woodpecker drummed loudly on an old tree snag on the Shona woods, and there were small mating flocks of eiders on the sea, the males now sirening their mates with soft *"awhoos"*, a sweet music to usher in the warmer days of spring.

But on March 12 there was trouble on the bird table. A new cock chaffinch arrived, his upper wing chevron blazing white and thick, with a new hen who was fatter than the first one. Now he and Little Fat Sergeant were engaged in fights, flying straight up into the air, clawing and pecking at each other so hard that the feathers flew. The new cock seemed to win most of them and to be in charge of the table. Of Sergeant's little mate there now seemed no sign, and I wondered if she had perished in a hailstorm two days earlier.

At dusk now seven hinds, two yearlings and the young stag came behind the croft, so close I could hear them cropping the green sward. There is a theory in the Highlands that old hinds and stags *know* when the stalking season is over – for hinds it ends on February 16 and they then come closer to habitations! One evening, the wind from the south-east, I moved silently, a few inches at a time, straight towards them in a straight stalk from the west corner of the croft. I was within eight yards of the nearest before she saw me, then she barked loudly like the *"hoff"* of a black bear, and they all took off. And when next morning I saw one of the oystercatchers standing atop his mate while she held herself prone, I began to wish my camera had not been stolen in the burglary.

By March 15 the first primroses were out in warm, sheltered nooks along the burn but such emerging beauty had no peaceful effect on the chaffinches for they were still scrapping each day. But now I saw Little Fat Sergeant make a determined attack on the younger cock, driving it to the ground where he won the clawing, pecking brawl, for the new cock suddenly flew away. Sergeant, back in charge of the table again, also chased the new female off the bread as if saying "And take her with you!" Then he began to peep joyfully as if he'd enjoyed it all.

Three days later, the daffodils now breaking out their yellow petals, I heard a loud *"pink pink"* then the full chipping song of the courting chaffinch. I looked out. Sergeant was in the centre of the table and with him was his slimmer demure mate. He was in fine voice for he kept *"pink"*ing with his mouth stuffed full of crumbs, his little throat bulging to express joy at victory, his wife's return and oodles of free grub, but it sounded from far away, as if from a ventriloquist. There was now no sign of the other pair.

Sometimes when I went out with scraps in the early morning, Sergeant flew with his mate behind in great looping swoops up the hill from the shore trees a quarter mile away. "Grub up" he was probably saying to his missus. He was now in full song about the croft, vying for first place on the springtime stage with the thrushes, willow-warblers, wrens and robins.

One day as I dug and sieved the garden soil, the seaweed rotting down nicely, I saw the kestrel over the croft. By now I carried the field glass nearly everywhere and I trained it on the bird. It was hanging in the sky like a fulcrum of flashing copper light. Its small head had amazing mobility, looking round like a capuchin monkey's as it hunted by sight, glaring down at the earth. Not much would miss those eyes.

By the third week in March Charlie Crow and a mate were back at their old nest in the birch tree down by the shore, sheep were baahing noisily round the croft in the early hours, the lambing season about to start. I was looking at the daffodils when both hooded crows suddenly winged away shorewards. I'd just counted the flowers – fifty-three, and four more than last year – when shepherd Iain appeared, checking for new-born lambs. Busy treks on "The Hill" as Highlanders call mountains in the plural, now lay ahead for him.

On these rare, early-spring visits I came to know Iain MacLellan better. He said the island had been his idea of a Highland paradise when he was a youngster, with a crofter in every cottage, each with a couple of cows and about six sheep. They cut hay in the hills, peat for winter fires from the high bogs, ran small vegetable gardens and grew potatoes in fertile patches which they dug by hand labour into undulating "lazy beds". But even then the rising costs of food and distribution, the depopulation of the region as more people moved to better-paid jobs in the industrial cities, were changing the old ways and most crofters then also worked as employees on the estates for the lairds.

"We were taught to serve our masters well and not to waste his money," Iain said. "We learned about God and moral life at our mother's knee and that stayed with us through all our lives." His father James MacLellan had built the fine mahogany desk on which I now worked. "I used to walk here every Saturday morning, pick up stores left on the beach by the big boat, carry them up to the old croft behind you, then sit listening to the old stories of my father and uncle. Life was simple but I'm sure people were happier then. There was no television and we did not crave what others had or a richer life for we hardly knew there was one."

I showed him how the old ruin behind had finally blown down that winter, wondering if he was not pleased that I was there but he said 'Ay, it's gone now. And this would probably have gone too if you'd not put the new front on." He also liked my garden and promised me some fencing. "One day you may wake and find deer have had all your vegetables. You'll need a high fence and to roof it over."

Iain and his co-worker, apart from running the island's boat and other estate work, looked after the sheep flocks. It was hard work, far removed from the popular notion of shepherding. There were six gatherings a year when he, his wife Morag, and two or three other men, if they could get them, made several walking swathes over the hard hills to herd the sheep into the fanks on the east side of the island: in February for oral dosing against fluke and worm; in March, ten days before lambing, to dip them against ticks, lice, flies and other insect pests; June for shearing the yelds, castrating male lambs and marking the sheep; July for shearing the milk ewes; late August to September for selling surplus lambs, castrated males, some tups (rams) and the old ewes up to ten or twelve years old that probably would not survive the next winter, for mutton; and in October for winter dipping.

I had already found out from the Vanes that it then cost £700 for one man's yearly wages, yet the sheep only brought in some £800 a year, which included hefty government subsidies. These, in Shona's case, were paid on about 250 breeding ewes and in the early 1970s varied from £2 to £3.50 each ewe per year. The island also kept from forty to sixty ewe lambs plus eight to twelve tups for breeding. The truth is sheep cannot be successfully raised in the Highlands today without these subsidies, which are paid by all British taxpayers – who, of course, can benefit from the wool and meat.

At first it seemed strange to me, an incoming layman, that there should be such a deep attachment to sheep here when so many Highland lairds sold off their land to incoming southern sheep farmers, which led to the notorious Highland Clearances between 1782 and 1854 when thousands of crofters were thrown out, often having their homes burned, and were compelled to move to subsistence areas on the coast, or emigrate to Canada and Australia.

Yet it seemed that there could be few more effective ways for man to utilize such harsh hill grazings. Could it only be done by heavy subsidies? It seemed an odd economy to me at the time. In later talks the Vanes told me several reasons for keeping sheep, the least of which was profit. They were now a traditional industry, they caused the employment of a second man as well as occasional helpers, so helping the area's unemployment problem and they prevented the island from becoming too overgrown. Another reason was because Iain himself was a keen shepherd. While he was boatman, ran the island's little saw mill, large vegetable garden and poultry, stalked the deer and tackled most jobs as handyman-carpenter, he liked nothing more than to be on "the hill" tending his sheep. Thus if the sheep had gone they may well have lost an essential, possibly irreplaceable, worker too.

I wondered if Iain thought I felt that wildlife suffered from the grazings of sheep but I had as yet no real opinions on this though from Canadian experience and from finding several dead sheep on the island hills in winter, it was obvious such carcases provide valuable winter carrion for golden eagles, buzzards, ravens, crows, wildcats, gulls and even foxes. And as far as grazing competition went, red deer had been increasing in recent years in the Highlands.

Iain disclosed his co-worker wanted to leave the island. "We have a hard task keeping workers here," he said. "We've had fourteen in the last ten years, mostly married men. I get tired of ferrying them and all their furniture over and back. They don't like the isolation – or their wives don't."

Isolation? I thought. What would any married man or woman with other families near by on that end of the island know about true isolation! With a loving wife who felt as I did about the wilderness, I could imagine no finer place to be. But I could see if there *were* problems in a relationship, even such comparative isolation would increase them. I knew many city, working couples who survived together because they only took each other in short evening doses!

Then Iain told me his problems at lambing time, of young lambs falling into crevices, ewes with difficult births, and foxes taking the lambs.

"Often a ewe walks miles from her usual grazing area to give birth. I once found one from this area at Shoe Bay. The pain had made her move and seek cover – I found her dead with her front half wedged under a rock. The lamb was out but dead. Yet the previous morning after an eight-mile walk I'd seen nothing at that spot.

"Once I was up on the highest hill, Beinn a Brailidhe, and saw a ewe lying down. She got up and dashed away fast, then went round in circles. Something was very wrong as I could see a lamb hanging out. One foot was out below the lamb's chin, as both should be, but the other one was bent back behind its head. And when the pain was really bad the ewe charged off like a bullet. I ran down, caught her with my collies and holding her between my knees, pushed the lamb back and got the other leg out with my fingers. Then she gave birth normally."

Just then one of the hooded crows flew above the window. I remarked they had been back at their old nest.

"Ay," said Iain, "And the best thing to do with them is put a charge of shot right through it! I'd heard of hoodies preying on sick lambs but I asked if he'd not leave even *one* egg in the nest?

"No, Mr Tomkies, I would not. Hoodies – and ravens – will attack a ewe that's having trouble with her lamb. She tries to stand but because of the pressure and pain she sometimes topples onto her side or back. And she can't get up again if she's in a little dip in the ground. Then the hoodies and ravens come and peck out her eyes, at her tongue and kill the lamb."

"Ay, it's cruel if it's true." I agreed. "Yet animals evolved this way, it's part of nature's system, created by God." Iain, a religious man, deigned to answer the blasphemous doubt, that God had perhaps created an imperfect system. Such reasoning was hardly for man. His job was to protect his flocks as best he could.

"I came over to Shoe Bay once ," Iain continued, "And I found a ewe trying to give birth but she had rolled into a hole and couldn't get up. I found her because of the big black-backed gulls, hoodies, ravens and a buzzard circling over her. When I got there she had both eyes out yet was still alive and giving birth. I had no gun with me so I ran all the way home for a knive and back again. It's the best death – as the blood comes out she feels nothing, just fades away until her heart stops."

Iain reckoned the hoodies had flown off because they saw *him* coming. They knew him as an individual enemy. My befriending of Charlie had probably made them know I was harmless. He felt hoodies could tell the difference between individual human beings.

"Two years ago when it was my week on the lambing my co-worker was working the garden near the hen run – but he had nothing to do with the hens himself. He saw this hoodie coming and going but paid no attention as it wasn't in the run itself. Now, when hens get broody, they like to have their nests wild, where no-one can find them. What was happening was one of the hens was getting through the wire and laying her eggs near a stream a good way from the run. And that crow was coming to the tree directly above the hen while she was laying. As soon as the hen left the nest to go back to the run for food, down she came and took the egg. This went on for a whole week. But when I was in the garden the next week, the crow knew me as a personal enemy and never showed up once!"

Iain had work to do, set down his empty tea cup and as he left I said I'd do what I could to check the lambs in my area. While I understood his viewpoint, after returning from parts of North America where the predators were still wolves, coyotes, lynx and occasional cougars and bears, little mention had ever been made of smaller "varmints" like foxes and crows. It seemed ironic that in Britain where predatory man had long exterminated such large carnivores, his focus had now come down to the remaining little foxes, stoats and crows.

The handsome hoodie is a relatively rare bird on a world-wide scale, far more than the raven which *is* protected in Britain (except in Argyll and Skye). The hoodie only survives (mainly as winter migrants) in small numbers in England, on the north-east coast, and does not exist in Wales. While fairly common in Ireland and a few in Ayrshire, its main strongholds today are in the north-west Highlands, Europe and Scandinavia. In Russia it is limited to the western edge. Small wonder perhaps that the hoodie, known in Gaelic as "An t-eun g'un duileachan" (the bird without compassion) has evolved such great cunning to outwit his main enemy.

The day after Iain's visit I had some hilarious entertainment from the bird table. Little Fat Sergeant came back with *two* hens, his own and the fatter one that had been with the other cock, who had not reappeared. As I watched from the window Sergeant's wife chased the other hen off the bread then pursued her into the bushes for good measure. This battle between the hens was repeated several times while Sergeant went on nonchalantly stuffing himself with crumbs as if saying "Sort it out yourselves, ladies!"

April 1 certainly made fools of some flies who had hatched out in the far room. It was a cold day with heavy hailstorms and they walked about bedraggled, wings closed limply over their backs, unable to fly in the new hostile world into which they had emerged. But a day later after a period of sun the year's first emperor moth appeared on my window, drawn by the effusion of light rather than my playing Rachmaninoff's 2nd.

I was slaving hard on the Canadian book on April 6 when Iain appeared for a quick cup of tea. They were gathering in the sheep before the local foxhounds came on the morrow to try and clear out the foxes before lambing. We talked about foxes and I said I felt it wrong to hunt as a sport, to gain pleasure from "the chase" and the death of a far-outnumbered animal.

"We don't get pleasure," he explained. "We aren't sitting dainty on horseback. No horse could hunt these hills. We're on foot and it's hard work. I don't like killing anything really but foxes kill many lambs. I know they're not "evil". They have their instincts and you have to pit your instincts against theirs because they undermine your livelihood.

"From the first you look after your sheep the best you can. After the first lamb comes you have your hardest time. You have to try and visit them every day, cover the whole island. If you have a hundred ewes you may have a crop of eighty lambs. Then one day you walk the hills and find maybe six lambs, their heads torn off and the rest left to rot. It's waste. When wanton killing occurs like that you just have to go after the foxes.

"When foxes have cubs they often slit lambs and just take the stomach, which is full of its mother's milk, home for the cubs and leave the rest. Later they may kill and just take the tail, ears or head for the growing cubs to play with. I once found nineteen dead lambs in and around a fox's den, a terrible sight."

He had had many experiences of the fox's cunning. On one hunt with den terriers the vixen had come out and deliberately run close between two men before vanishing behind the rocks, as if knowing that way no-one would dare shoot! When in 1969 an act was passed banning the "gin" trap in Scotland, a four-year gap was left before it became law for the invention of a more humane trap to control foxes. One such was the "drowning set" – it is set in a pool at least fifteen inches deep but on a small peninsula from which a chunk has been removed, so making an islet, and the bait buried, so making it more selective for foxes. When the fox is caught it struggles, leaps and is quickly drowned by the weight of the trap which is tied to a heavy, underwater stone. But such pools and peninsulas are not easy to find. Iain made such a pool once – and the fox walked round it then dug a canal with its paws, so draining the pool!

I heard the hounds baying in the hills next day but all I saw of the hunt was a sudden, whitish shape outside my window. It was an old bitch hound, ribs sticking through her coat, who had broken away from the pack. She put her paws up, calmly stole the bread from the bird table, then sneaked off down to the south shore. It seemed she was not keen on hunting foxes any more and was just looking for grub and a quiet life. All that day the two hoodies were absent from my bay but just before dusk Iain's co-worker stood outside the croft, his shotgun upside down on his foot, and flourished a blind, dead fox cub, blackish-brown as they are at that age, with great pride from his pocket. The terriers had gone down one of the dens and had brought out two cubs. The vixen, no doubt trying to stay alive so she could raise whatever cubs might be left, had escaped.

At the time it appeared to me rather cruel and that much fuss, time and manpower were being expended for fairly minimal results. I wondered too if the relatively few foxes killed this way did not mainly result in the death of the old, diseased and less wary young that had not escaped into crevices from the terriers, so perhaps even *helping* to maintain vital fox-breeding populations by weeding out the less fit. Such killing was sporadic and it seemed likely other surplus foxes would come in from outlying areas to take the place of those killed anyway. But I was not a sheep farmer relying on it for a living and I could understand the feeling that *something* had to be done. It just seemed a lot of trouble for an industry that could not survive without subsidies. Indeed, the foxhounds themselves were also subsidised at the time by a £1,000-a-year grant from the Highlands and Islands Development Board.

It is general policy in the Highlands to try to control foxes most when they are feeding cubs, though despite some wanton killing by individuals it is not yet certain how many lambs taken are already dead from various causes, including never getting a suck of their mother's milk. Foxes can't eat lambs all the year round but the war against them continues all the year – yet they eat many voles which not only compete with sheep and deer for green grass but also act as hosts for a tick which transmits the serious "louping ill" disease to sheep. Foxes, weasels, stoats, owls and wildcats, against which gamekeepers and some farmers have waged war for years, keep vole numbers down. Foxes especially eat large numbers. In one Highland study by Dr James Lockie and W.

N. Charles it was shown that in winter foxes, owls and weasels between them reduced voles from 90 to 45 an acre.

Next morning Charlie Crow and his mate were back on my beach and gave me an exhibition of how they feed on shellfish. One hoodie suddenly flew up in the air with a cockle and dropped it on to the largest rock on the shore. The other bird flew in but the first dived down faster, picked it up, flew further, dropped it again and was down on to it and away with the succulent titbit from the smashed shell in a flash. I wondered if crows had worked out such methods by watching the herring-gulls who often smashed shellfish open this way.

When Iain next came by I told him about it. He felt the hoodie was as cunning as a fox. "Do you know it knows the difference between a rifle and a fishing rod?" he asked. "If you want to shoot a hoodie, disguise your gun like a rod and you'll fool them. Once I saw one sneaking along like a duck through a corrie to avoid me, keeping a large rock between us, so as not to be shot at. Then it flew from a peak further away. Some of them *know* the range of a shotgun."

Now April was doling out two more weeks of winter weather and hailstorms still beset my boat trips. Once the engine handle came right off and I had to hold the throttle with a pair of pliers, my hands frozen. The upper cylinder was showing wear, the plug oiling up frequently so I had to limp back on one cylinder while flailing away at the oars. Once I had to shelter at the south-east bay until the tide was high enough to go through the gap between the mainland rocks and the seals' islet to reach my own shore rather than face the rough, open sea with a faulty plug. But I used the two-hour delay to gather loose cockles on that beach. As I climbed from the boat I startled what seemed to be a huge hind who shot to the skyline then stopped and looked back. It would have been easy to shoot. As I trained my field glass on it and saw its massive body more clearly I thought it was a stag that had dropped its antlers. But I could see no sign of the white, blood-streaked pedicles on its head which would have been normal. It was certainly a "hummel," a permanently antlerless beast. The growth of the large antlers in red deer stags, which are shed early each April and grown again in a year, is still not completely understood. While it's believed they may be a vestige from the days when deer had to fight off predators like bear, lynx and wolf, the last of these predators, wolves, were exterminated in the 1740s. But antler growth when the food supply is good has not significantly diminished. Certainly stags use them for occasional jousting, more pushing and shoving matches really, when defending their harems of hinds from other stags in the autumn rutting season, but very often they fight with their forefeet, rearing up into the air to deliver powerful downward jabs or outward kicks. In this way a hummel that does not have to suffer the annual drain of calcium and energy that goes

95

into growing antlers, can often grow to a huge size and finds no trouble becoming a master stag.

One day after writing for some hours I found the hazy sun too tempting and went to watch some red deer on the far ridges above Shoe Bay. The sun was almost behind me and the wind from the west – from them to me – ideal conditions, and I decided to try my first real deer stalk on Shona. Squeezing like a lizard between the heather, crawling crabwise over flat rocks, my hands, knees and elbows were soon wet as I went through gullies. I tried to keep heather or grass before my face and peered slowly after each sequence of movement to see if I'd been spotted before moving on. I came to within forty feet of them before reaching an impossible corrie, a dished hollow between myself and them. They certainly seemed easier to stalk than the British Columbian mountain caribou. Their eyesight seemed poor except for actual movement, as if they could not make my head out from old blackened heather, which no doubt it resembled. But they were now suspicious as a ewe had barked a warning from high above and one large hind, redder than the grey-brown coats of the others, walked round to my right, slightly more windward. There were five hinds and two young staggies with tiny six-inch spikes and as I watched the hind moving through my field glass I thought what knock-kneed grace she had, such slender legs and delicate unfurlings of the foot as she moved. I saw her faintly reptilian head, buff muzzle, black nose and huge hazel eyes like marbles. How I wished then I had my camera back.

Then for the first time the idea struck me – why did I not also *photograph* wildlife in the future, as well as trying to write about it? Surely, I should be *recording* all I saw around me and even a complete novice like myself could have taken good pictures on this day.

Finally I raised myself up on two fists and stared. They did not run but just stared back, then started moving after the hind. Clearly, if you don't look like a man they move around to try and get scent, to find out what you are. The next thing was they began to walk *towards* me, intently curious. The curiosity of deer, if stalked correctly, has often been their undoing. I stood upright very slowly. Still they stayed. Slowly I turned my back and retreated and they followed after me, for almost a hundred yards, so that I began to feel they were actually stalking *me*. To date it was my most unusual experience with wild red deer. Darn that burglar – for I'd heard nothing from the police about my lost possessions. That night I wrote to a photographic firm I'd heard of in London.

Spring was now really under way, the male eiders now cutting off their siren mating calls before the last high note, zooming around and chasing the ducks on the sea's surface in flapping displays. Near Deer Island I saw a pair of ornate shelducks swimming. With their red beaks, green-black heads, bright chestnut chestbands and white necks, backs and bellies, they looked like a couple of carnival tugs steaming along. They often "marked time" in the shallows treading up the sand into billows and upending to grab whatever morsels of food they had stirred up. Britain's biggest ducks, they reminded me of geese and, when they flew, the beats of their black-and-white wings were also regular and slow. Now the little black guillemots, or "tysties", bobbing like burnt corks on the rippling waters, were courting on the loch, swimming round their mates, giving squeaky cries and showing their bright red throats. And if my boat went too near they flew up, hitting the water with feet and wingtips with a noise like heavy pattering rain, until they became airborne and whirred away like mechanical toys. On April 19 I saw the first worker bees humming from flower to flower and a queen wasp, looking for a nest site, landed briefly on my hand. A tortoiseshell butterfly, fresh from winter hibernation, flicked from dust patch to dust patch sunning its wings, and just above me the dark underside of a comma butterfly went past in typical spiral flight, just as they had done over the hazy Sussex ponds of my boyhood.

Iain came halloing over the hills next day in bright sunshine and we found a dead lamb lying behind the old ruined croft. "It was stillborn," he said looking with expert eye at the whitish fluid and blood of the afterbirth. No fox had had it for there was no tell-tale scarlet slash on the throat.

"We'll have to bury it, not through sentiment but if ravens, hoodies, buzzards or black-backed gulls see it they'll be after pecking out its eyes. Once they get the taste they may go after sick or new-born lambs. We don't want any more killers here. I've found four lambs killed by foxes already."

I prevailed upon him to let me lay the lamb out on a grassy patch three hundred yards south-west of the croft, so I could see what bird came down first, and promised to bury it later. Although I kept watch from my desk all afternoon, and one pregnant ewe sniffed it without concern, the only birds that showed interest were a pair of greater black-backed gulls. One looked down, circled twice on its long, black, white-edged wings, alighted near the corpse, stayed still a few seconds then flew away again. Perhaps it was too near the croft. I buried the lamb in the near dark.

Two days later I smelled burning and outside the air was filled with smoke. I rushed out and in a dell a quarter mile away heather and old bracken were ablaze, smoke puthering upwards in great brown clouds. I hurried over to inspect. The fire was creeping in the west wind towards me and the croft! Yet there seemed to be no smoke anywhere else on the island. What on earth was going on?

I ran back to the croft for a bucket then back again and tried vainly to douse the flames with water from a nearby burn but I had to give up as the fire leaped from one heather bush to another. I stood there in the burn, determined to fight it again should it cross the small gorge but the fire finally died on an open green patch a hundred yards away. I threw more bucketfuls along the bank on my side in case it started up again, and went home.

Later, as I was sunbathing, Iain appeared and said *he* had started the fire! "We always burn the heather when it gets too long every few years," he explained. "Young heather is good for sheep, especially in winter but once it's over a foot long they won't go near it. We burn it down and grass grows before the new heather and this is also good for the sheep. Some of the heather wasn't burned even in my uncle's lifetime."

I felt amazed. But what about bird nesting grounds, all the flowers that are needed by valuable insects like bees that pollinate other plants, the eggs and caterpillars of some fine moths, and all the mice, frogs, lizards, insects, beetles and other small wildlife so important in the web of natural life and on which many larger species depend? And what about all the young regenerating trees? What if the fires went out of control? Iain seemed surprised at my questions. Heather burning was traditional in sheep country and on the management of grouse moors in the Highlands. As for control, he always tried to burn only where there was a natural end like an open area, gorge or rock face.

In later years I was to find that unlike Iain some hill burners made little attempt to control the heather fires and often, by accident, whole areas of the Highland hills would go up in flames in April, burning out many square miles at a time.

It seemed an oddly short-sighted policy. Such burning does not, for instance, affect the underground roots of bracken which quickly spreads into new areas, restricting new grass, flowers and slow-growing heather. W. H. Auden's phrase when describing the Scottish mountains came now to my mind – "Hills like slaughtered elephants." Trees and plants are, along with the phyto-plankton of the seas, the lungs of our planet, and the forests and bushes keep the watershed up. When such burning goes out of control all young tree and bush seedlings are destroyed and when too much heather goes also, only sparse grasses and sedges, in brackenless areas, remain to take over. On steep hills exposed to heavy rains and gales, erosion occurs rapidly and then even the earth for growing grass is blown and washed away. Some long heather is useful shelter for sheep and birds like grouse. Heather burning can surely only make sense if done in very small areas at a time and heavily controlled, which means costly manpower, experience and ecological good sense.

Two mornings after the heather burning, I saw an oystercatcher bathing again in four inches of water in the mouth of the burn. And watching the oystercatcher was Harry Heron who was standing right next to a herring-gull on a large flat rock. The two were only about a yard apart. How odd, I thought. Had they formed some kind of friendship? The next thing I knew the oystercatcher was actually *swimming,* something else I'd never seen before. It was then I recalled my vow to get a camera again. But for such small species as birds, wary in the wild, I'd surely need some telescopic device. Well, I'd get a telephoto lens, whatever that was.

Towards the end of April more wildlife was stirring and only the oak and ash trees were not yet sending out new leaf sprouts. Long-horn beetles were out in the sun looking for mates, and the first bumbling black dor beetles, who help bury carrion in which they lay their eggs, were burring past in the air. On a walk down the path, treading down the new snake-like bracken shoots, which like all forms of life are easier to control in infancy, I saw two mating coach-horse beetles. They were joined at the rear and the slightly larger female was towing the male about. He seemed to be trying to help her movement, or possibly to ease his pain, by desperately thrusting backwards with his legs in the direction in which he was being hauled. That seemed to be taking women's lib a bit too far!

Near the beach I saw the first wheatear of the season. Handsome with its blue back, black wings and face mask, chestnut breast and white rump, it seemed to be flying weakly, trailing its wings as if to decoy me away from a nest. But it was far too early for it to have bred and it was probably exhausted after its spring migration flight from wintering in North Africa. It fluttered feebly to between two rocks a hundred and fifty yards away and stayed as still as a statue, watching me with what seemed excellent eyesight. The wheatear has become rare in southern Britain where it was once common, due to the ploughing of downland and the loss of many heathland habitats and I hoped it would be all right.

But winter had not given up yet and three days of hail and darkness came, rendering the landscape barren of activity. Then on April 28 as the sun beamed down I was woken by the loud calls of the cuckoo – so close I thought it must be on the roof but when I peeped through the window it was actually in the ash trees a few yards away. I had never been so near this wary bird before and I was astonished by its beauty – with the sunlight burnishing its slaty-blue back, long, white-spotted tail, grey-and-white barred chest, slightly curved beak and glint in its bright yellow eyes, it reminded me of a sparrowhawk. Again I cursed having no camera.

By now I'd had an answer from the photographic firm in London who said they would give me a discount. Well overdue for a work trip south I drove down to London and came back with the usual goods plus a new 35 mm Pentax camera, standard lens and a cheap make 300 mm telephoto lens but which was all I could afford. For the first time I made it back in one long drive. Using no ferries because it was night, I noted it was 318 miles to the Scots border from Hampstead, another 86 to Glasgow, a total of 476 to Loch Tulla, Argyll, and when I reached the little pier there were 573 new miles on the clock. In a loaded old Land Rover incapable of more than 54 mph, I felt more tired than a rally driver.

As always the sense of loneliness was greater after returning from a trip to civilization. But it was not a jaded hermit's view of "modern society" that saddened me now as a dying energy to actively *look* for a companion who shared my feelings about the wilds. I didn't *like* being alone now any more than when I first left for Canada six years earlier but it seemed I had no other choice. It was a slow, gradual but inexorable process.

But as I used the wet days to work on the Canada book, happily re-creating the wild bear treks, and walked the hills in finer weather, the Highland landscape seemed more than food enough for my heart. That fine writer T. H. White had young King Arthur's tutor Merlin say "The cure for being sad is to learn something new".

Well, after all, I was now not only watching nature but was also a wildlife photographer!

9

DURING THE FOLLOWING MONTHS, indeed years, it was embarrassingly brought home to me time and time again that I was anything *but* a wildlife photographer. By some obscure magic, if not conspiracy, the close glimpses of wild creatures that had happened previously by accident ceased almost completely. The buzzard and kestrel, like a tiny swallow beside the bigger bird, still flew over but seemingly higher up, and it was hard to focus the telephoto lens in mere seconds. The birds *looked* fine enough in the viewer but when the pictures were developed they looked like mosquitos squashed on a window pane, their wing tips or heads being cut off on the edges of the photos. It took a long time to learn the exposure had to be related precisely to the object I was photographing and that I had to sometimes work against the meter reading of the whole view, closing the aperture a stop or two or increasing shutter speed in all sky or sunny day shots so as not to overexpose. I had often taken photos before but only of people or scenery, and now I made every mistake in the book.

When I went back to the heronry on Deer Island I found Harry's low nest had been partly blown out of the tree, and I had to be content with shots of him and other herons flying over. All the other nests were so high I could neither climb up near them nor build the essential tree hide without help. I found a shelduck's nest with ten creamy eggs beneath an old holly stump but though I walked away in a large circle, crept back and hid under camouflage netting in a bush for several hours, the parents did not come near. I did not wait longer in case the eggs grew cold.

Although Charlie Crow and his mate were still using my bay for finding marine prey they did not use their old birch tree nest. Maybe they had an inkling of Iain MacLellan's intentions! One day, after a long search, I found their new one in a tall ash tree fork in a wood to the south-east. It was made of dead twigs as if to make it look ancient and deserted. But now, in the breeding season, Charlie no longer trusted me either. And when I was still a good way off his mate incubating the eggs would slip noiselessly away, dropping down low and swerving through the trees so she could not be easily shot when seen against the sky. But one morning I saw him fly between two large rock folds and not come out again.

I stuck herbage and dried seaweed in the netting of my bush hat and feeling like I had during army sniper training years before, I stalked him, crawling through the wet weed between the rocks. Hooded crows in their distinctive black-and-grey plumage, appear to have poor camouflage for their nefarious hunting methods but I could not see him. Finally I did – he was working through the tide wrack for sand hoppers and tiny crabs and his grey waistcoat matched the rocks while his black back blended perfectly with the dark brown of the seaweeds. I managed one shot of him but as he heard the click he flew away with indignant "*Kaahs*".

Two days later, the fifth "final" version of the Canada book well under way, I took the afternoon off for a long photo trek. More humiliation was ahead. First I walked to Shona House for my mail, saw no wildlife at all, then headed over the highest hills to the north shore, to make a long sweep of the island back to the croft. It was a muggy, clammy day and what little wind there was amid the calm was switching from east to north-east, then north to north-west. From just below a high peak – never show yourself on the skyline – I saw a herd of red deer hinds a good mile away to the west. I stalked them as well as I knew, keeping close to rock faces, through gullies and bogs, coming nearer to their ruddy-brown grazing forms. Setting the telephoto lens at correct aperture and speed I slid round the final rock and took my first deer photo – of the buff, heart-shaped patches of their rumps as they ran away! I learned again, more strongly in these open hills than I had in the wooded mountains of Canada, that on moist days scent carries further and that stalking is often hopeless in changing winds.

From Sgurr an Teintein (High Peak Of The Deer) I traversed the yellow hill of Cruach Buidhe and the four hills to Aonach and Shoe Bay but found only three winter-dead sheep, the carcases ripped apart by foxes and the beaks of predatory birds, with white wool scattered over many yards. I photographed a bloody skull near a rocky den, too shallow for a breeding earth, which may have been used by a fox as a sheltered eating place. High on grass tufts and small rocks foxes had left their usual dark-grey hair-filled "visiting cards" as well as urine to give information on sex, mood and boundary to others of their kind. But

An older lamb leaps across the burn with ease.

only one seemed fresh, filled with blue-black wing cases of beetles the fox had probably taken from beneath a cleaned-out carcase. I approached Shoe Bay stealthily but not one otter did I see.

Back home, perspiring after the five-mile trek, I bathed in buckets of water and learned that in the burn itself I had an ideal washing machine. I could put my clothes into the rushing waters two hundred yards above the croft and they were beaten clean by being tumbled over rocks and little waterfalls. Then I picked them up in my main pool, ready for soaping with warm water! I reckoned natural organic dirt and sweat would do the burn no harm but again drew the line at putting detergent actually into its waters. I just rubbed the clothes in buckets and threw the pollutive remains over the virulent bracken roots.

So my first real wildlife photo trek in Scotland had proved fruitless but when I went indoors I found a compensation in my mail. The American colour magazine that had printed the story of days on the salmon boats in British Columbia now wanted a "philosophical" article about life alone in the wilds, and I could "let it run". At last a fine publication was interested and during the next week I felt the new writing, the synthesis of wilderness experience and action, combined with brief reflections on modern man's problems, the psychic loss from severing our roots to the natural world, and all the wrestling between insight and fact, to be exciting beyond measure. I felt inspired, truly alive, that I was at last starting to *contribute* a little and writing what I wanted to write.

Needing exercise from long desk hours, I dug more stones out of my garden soil and checked the lambs in the area for Iain. One morning I found a hefty one limping badly on its right front foot near the south shore and tried to catch it to check what was wrong. It looked ready to drop but it could run like a deer on three legs. Once I chased it half a mile and was about to throw myself on it when it reached an area of scrub trees and I was too late. On the third day, after sneaking up behind some bushes, I made a mad dash, threw myself down, clutched its thick wool with one hand then struck the side of my face on an embedded rock. The lamb had a small stone wedged between its cloven hoof, the foot sore but not bleeding. I prised the stone out as it panted feverishly in my ear and let it go again. When I got home I found my own wound was worse than the lamb's, blood trickling down my neck. Now I *knew* why Highland shepherds used fleet-footed collies!

A couple of days later I heard high-pitched bleating behind the croft. I went out to find a mothering ewe had leaped the burn and was walking on. But her little late-born lamb was still stranded on the far side, looking helplessly at the yawning chasm separating it from its mother and giving pitiful cries. But as I watched it tried to emulate the ewe, took a jump but landed straight in the burn, *splosh*. Now it was up to its neck in water and couldn't climb the high slippery rocks and it set up a frightful bleating din but its stupid mother, not even watching or apparently hearing it, just carried on grazing a few yards away.

I rushed over and lifted it out, wringing the cold water from its snowy fleece as best I could. It cuddled close in my arms warming up from my body heat and snuggling its head up close to mine, totally trusting. I had to resist the temptation to take it back to the croft as a pet. But the moment I let it go again it ran bleating back for its mother. But next morning the little lamb spied me walking up the slope from the beach and suddenly ran towards me with joyful little *"meh-eh-ehs"*. I picked it up noting it was a little tup and as I stroked its head for a few seconds it closed its eyes blissfully. Then I had a sudden guilty feeling – if Iain spied me he might think I was alienating his sheep from their natural life! When I set it down it ran straight for its mother again, making high, skittish, head-wagging leaps on the way.

That afternoon Iain came across the hills carrying a dead lamb and

A herring gull's nest showing the three stages of hatching. One chick is out, one half out while the third is still hacking the shell.

A fretful Sammy with a front flipper caught in a crevice. After being freed he became the tamest of all the seals.

Buzz, his pinions not yet fully grown, pounces on his food, clutching it with surprising strength.

Harry in unusually lethargic mood; he usually flew away long before I was in camera range.

Seals became used to me and began to follow my boat, somersaulting and splashing.

Young Sebastian roars across the Shona glens to intimidate other stags and keep them away from his 'harem' of hinds.

showed me the tell-tale crimson on its neck. He was angry that the big fox was still around and said the hounds and some terriers were coming back in in two days.

"We were unlucky last time," he said. "I *saw* the vixen go into the den. In went the terriers, got two cubs but didn't bring them out and we had to scrape them out with sticks. And they wouldn't go in again, afraid of the vixen. When terriers have been hurt in fights with many foxes or half killed by a badger by mistake, they're not as keen to work as when they're young and fearless."

I asked him if he thought wanton killing by foxes might be linked to revenge – where a fox had had its mate or cubs killed and tried to get its own back knowing lambs were products of its human persecutors? Iain agreed there might be some truth in the idea but said that foxes often killed like that before hounds or den terriers had been at them.

I told him about the little lamb in the burn and he laughed. "I've known it happen too. I picked one little fellow out of a burn that still had the afterbirth on it. I put it on to the bank but as I was getting out and calling to my dog, blow me if it didn't leap straight back in again. I put it back to its mother but the right smell had gone because of the water and she butted it away so hard she sent it flying from here to there. She was a poor mother anyhow and in the end we had to take the lamb and rear it on the bottle".

Once he found a lamb that had fallen down a crevice. "It was a tup and a good job it was as it had a wide head and its little horns had wedged into a little gap between the rocks. I had to get below and lift it out but the little thing was so far gone, at first it just staggered about and rolled head over heels".

As the soft, soothing notes of cuckoos were now sounding all round the croft, I told Iain of the one that landed so near my window, how it had looked like a sparrowhawk, and he told me an odd tale.

"A sparrowhawk come through our window when we were having lunch a few days ago," he said. "It must have been going sixty miles an hour for it made a circular hole. We heard a crash, then it landed dead on Morag's plate, its skull and ribs shattered, and one piece of glass shot right across the dining room and kitchen and landed in the sink!" He wondered if it had been chasing a small bird which had dodged away at the last moment. I said I doubted that, although I'd heard of sparrow-hawks crashing through glass before, because with its long tail the hawk can dodge as fast as any bird. I knew Iain had a canary and wondered if the hawk had seen it through the glass – or if it had seen another bird outside the kitchen window. "Maybe at speed, not seeing the house, give a quick flip of its wings inside the darker room, then close them when going through the far window to strike the bird".

But Iain said the canary was in the corner behind the wall and the windows were not arranged so the hawk *could* have seen straight through! In the end we decided the hawk must have seen the reflection of the open country *behind* it in the glass and thought the way was clear. At any rate, Iain said, the poor sparrowhawk had been buried by his elder son James with full military honours!

When Iain left I set the dead lamb on a grassy patch by the shore and kept watch from my desk for two days. One hoodie flew over, circled once then kept going. A kestrel hovered over it briefly, decided it wasn't food and flew on. Only a greater black-backed gull showed any real interest, standing for an hour on a nearby rock but at dusk nothing had actually touched it. Not wanting to encourage foxes, I took down my shovel and buried it as I had the first.

Next morning I worked over my garden soil, sieving out the last stones and piling them with the other rocks I'd heaved out into twin windbreaks at each side. But rain poured all day and after digging a drainage ditch too, I went indoors. Suddenly at dusk the air outside was filled with whirring wings. A flock of herring-gulls had come in from the shore and, attracted by the snails that had emerged from hiding and the worms rising to the surface after the rains, were walking among the bright-green bracken stems like stately white ships.

I was even more surprised when a pair of oystercatchers joined them, then saw these gaudy seashore birds probe their three-inch-long beaks into the earth like thrushes, and pull out large worms. For the first time I noticed their eyes were near the top of their heads, giving them virtual all-round vision. Oystercatchers, it seemed, were the woodcocks of the sea. The gulls did not return but on rainy days for almost a month the oystercatcher pair came whinnering around the croft, always at dusk and pleeping shrill penetrating cries if I went outside. Then they landed to probe for soil creatures. Once I had been astonished by an oystercatcher flying alongside the Land Rover, keeping up at 45 mph as I was driving over the high Beattock Summit. It was almost thirty miles from the nearest sea at the mouth of the River Annan, yet it had surely flown up that valley.

It seemed I was witnessing evolution at work. Gulls such as the common, black-headed and herring, have been coming inland for years, attracted first by ploughing on farms near the coast, then to rubbish tips near towns, and in London I'd had flocks of herring-gulls come round my bed-sitter building as some of us tenants had put food out regularly for them. But here it seemed with the coastal seas being heavily fished, more shellfish gathered by humans and seaweed cut for processing, that oystercatchers were also catching onto the new trend and turning to the land for new food supplies. It was the opposite of the hooded crows' graduation to the sea shore to exploit, for them, a new ecological niche.

I knew that many of Britain's twenty to thirty thousand oystercatcher pairs wintered in the north Irish Sea and along the Welsh coast (swelled by birds from Iceland and the Faeroes) fed in the cockle- and mussel-producing areas like Morecambe Bay, the Wash and Burry Inlet (where a campaign to shoot 11,000 over the two winters was launched by fishing interests in the early 1970s) and that they were known to forage in fields as well as mud flats in the winter. But this was the first time I'd known them feed inland in early summer too and as I watched them it was clear they were not only eating worms but performing a useful service by taking many "leatherjackets" (larvae of the cranefly and a pest to plants) too. In later researches into this interesting bird I was to find out that oystercatchers going inland to feed and breed in the Faeroes frequently entangled their legs in sheep wool so they could no longer walk. A vulnerability, perhaps, from not having learned over many years experience to step high and avoid the wool in such new foraging grounds.

By May 10 the "sea swallows", the Arctic terns, were back from their amazing 10,000-mile migration flight from the Antarctic, flipping over the sea with slow but strong down strokes that jerked their slim, little grey bodies a few inches higher with every beat. They often poised in the air, tails expanded like hovering kestrels of the sea, then with beaks pointed downwards, plunged in with a slight twist and half-closed wings to catch tiny, surface-swimming fish. Then they bobbed back up again, took off, shook their wings with little vibrating quivers to spray off the excess water, and carried determinedly onwards. Green-veined white butterflies now filled the air with their flittering forms. There seemed less herons about this spring but Harry still came wafting into the bay most dawns to stand deathly still like a pale, blue-grey ghost, silvery incandescent in the rocky shallows.

As I was digging the garden on May 18, glad that the first midges seemed unable to bite so often or as strongly as the late summer ones, I noticed the tardy ashes were at last catching up with the trees around them, their thickening brown buds sending out their first leaf shoots. It took two more days to get the garden ready for planting. I spread two sacks of sheep droppings which I'd dried and pounded into dust, over the surface then threw on many more sacks of the fertile soil from the new molehills scattered around the croft. A final raking then I planted it all with carrots, cabbage, lettuce and radish. Taking a tip from Iain I put flat stones between the rows – these catch the sun, hold heat long after nightfall and thus act as "radiators" – useful in a cold climate.

Next day I built a preliminary fence round the garden with old sidings from the ruin above, and within nine days the first radish and lettuce shoots were coming through.

Returning from the pier a few days later after a quick trip in the

The seals lying on the rocks.

rubber dinghy to post off the movie book profits, I was just congratulating myself that really *was* the end of all that kind of work, when there was a loud plapping noise like an elephant breaking wind and down went the port side of the boat, dumping me in four feet of water. We had passed too close over a mussel bank and the hidden edge of one protruding shell had ripped a 17-inch gash in the boat's flank.

"The mussels' revenge" I told myself as I waded to haul torn boat and wet supplies to the south shore bay. But as I laboured to carry engine, oars, jerrican and fuel over the ridges to my own bay then carried the rubber boat up to the croft, I remembered. I'd never taken any mussels from that particular bank! These chores took most of the afternoon but at dusk I rectified things – I went down and carefully removed all the offending prominent mussels, the "guilty" ones, and made the best *moules marinière* I'd ever had in compensation. But – a £60 boat ruined and when I saw the rubber was only paper thin anyway, I re-learned an old wilderness lesson: Never buy cheap – you can lose your life trying to save a few pounds.

An attempt to repair the boat with lorry tyre-patches failed when the sun peeled them off again. Finally I bought some liquid polyurethane, shook the two requisite mixtures together in a large plastic bottle and squirted the rapidly expanding and solidifying contents into the hole between the patches. If the other two air compartments also became punctured I'd thus end up with a rubber boat more solid than the main fibreglass one, and totally unsinkable too. Meanwhile I had a boat that was merely one-third solid but it was almost as buoyant and went as well as before. Now if the other two chambers went flat in a sea disaster I at least had something to cling to while getting ashore.

One hot day in May, the first totally cloudless day for a month, I went to take my first photos of the seals who basked in the sun on the rocks just off the mainland peninsula across the mouth of the loch. I rowed over and hauled the boat onto a beach of fine shell sand so blazing white in the sun it hurt my eyes.

The seals had hunched into the sea at my approach so, to let them settle down again, I trekked round the peninsula and saw several herons rise one after another from the flat bowls of peat bogs. Wondering what they were finding I walked over the yielding blanket and examined small pools. Tadpoles! The little black commas wriggled in every patch of water but not a single frog did I see. Perhaps with so many gulls and herons about for years the adult frogs had bred into their instincts to be more devious than usual. After an hour of walking, seeing little more than a huge pair of greater black-backed gulls who flew overhead with deep *"qwuck qwucks"* at the rare intrusion of a human, I went back and stalked through the heather to the small cliff to photograph the seals.

They lay on the rocks with their wedge-shaped flippers sticking out or closely tucked into their sides, like great, fat, shiny moles with snub, up-turned noses. Two of them were very fat as if about to give birth. Their colours varied greatly, the larger ones being blackish or mottled brown, while smaller ones I judged to be eleven months to two years old ranged from light brown, yellowish to grey-white, and there was one marbled with dark grey and cream that with the naked eye looked almost blue. All were common seals (a misnomer because in fact the larger Atlantic grey seals are more common) and reminded me of a tolerant hippy commune – there were certainly no colour problems among this species! Their attitudes and postures as they basked in the sunlight were hilarious. There was a large brown one that lay on its side like a huge sausage flipped from a pan, a black one on its back, eyes tightly closed, velvet brows furrowed like a bloodhound's as a slight bump in the rock pushed its upper neck skin forward. The small, marbled grey seal held one flipper straight up into the air as if saying "Hi, I'm over here". Two had their heads and rear flippers curved upwards as if doing back exercises.

As I took a few shots, peeved that I couldn't go closer because of the open water between the land and their islet, I could hear odd snorts, snuffs and digestive burps that sounded like growls. A noisy lot! After forty minutes I was surprised when two common porpoises came in from the open sea and started their typical undulating surface swimming, comma-ing in and half out of the water between and round the islets and then to see some of the larger seals hump themselves into the water and apparently start to "play" with them. Certainly there were no attacks of any kind and it seemed the porpoises were welcome friends. Two of the larger seals now actually appeared to imitate the porpoises' style of swimming, like a human butterfly stroke without arms, their two rear flippers flailing away on each shallow, downward dive and I managed some photos of this.

I had read that bull seals will perform this "salmon leaping" swim in the mating season but that wouldn't be until late July or early August so it seemed an interesting observation. Common seal pups are born in this area from early June and the females are ready to mate about six weeks later. The pups are born on the haul-out islets or mud- or sandbanks, can swim from birth and suck their mother's rich milk for a month or longer, both above and below water.

After two hours I slid backwards through the heather and went to the boat – to find that on the shallow beach the low tide was now so far out from the mouth of the little inlet the sea had shrunk right out of sight! And the boat and engine were almost immovable on the high friction sand with no wet planks to haul it over. I had brought no lunch with me. Oh well, no time need ever be wasted in the wilderness life and I collected fifty-one cockles for pickling, still leaving plenty behind. I had been worried that my taking cockles would depopulate the local species but it soon became clear only a small proportion came up on the tides and most were left in deeper waters, so really I was only skimming the surface of their numbers.

I collected some mussels too, realizing that day that the best were not necessarily the biggest or those closest to shore but the mid-sized two-inchers that were *always* covered by water, even on the low spring tides. The shore mussels, exposed up to half their existence by the tides, grew more slowly, were often heavily encrusted with barnacles, and because of the action of the waves on the sea bed around them, had to cover with mineral deposits specks of sand and grit that got between their shells. And if you didn't chew such mussels very carefully they broke your teeth. I kept dozens of these "pearls" in a matchbox and once, when I lost a filling this way, I found one that fitted the hole exactly and used it to plug the gap with cotton wool dipped in toothpaste – until I could reach a dentist some months later! But from the day I visited the seals, I dived with a face mask at low tides for the better mussels, a linen "shopping" bag tied round my waist. I had no fears my small needs would decimate populations for I found long beds of thousands of tiny mussels less than a quarter-inch long that with their furry open tips filtering the plant plankton from the water looked like soft, blue-black carpets. Man can live in the wilds without harm – it is always a question of timing and degree. And it requires a humble mind.

I was surprised once to read a news report that heavy conglomerations of mussels were encumbering girders on some of the new North Sea oil rigs. And that to get rid of them the crews had to cut channels through intervening beds of sea anemones, so starfish which prey on mussels could get up to them. Apparently starfish either can't climb over the slippery anemones, or won't because of their stinging tentacles. But why didn't the crews harvest the mussels for their *own* food?

Early June provided some freak weather. Working on the croft's west wall and window, I boated to the cabin site for some timbers when I was hit by a sudden hailstorm that seemed to sweep out of nowhere over the hills from the north-west. I was shivering in my soaked, short-sleeved shirt, glad of the warming exercise of carrying the lumber up to the croft when I saw the oystercatcher pair whirring round the area again. It seemed that when heavy wind made waves pound on shore they found it easier to hunt for worms inland. I realized too that if they fed their young on worms and caterpillars the chicks might thus acquire a taste for them when adult too, and in this way the evolutionary trend would be compounded.

On June 7 I was standing ankle deep in the sea on the west side of my bay counting the first, beautiful, yellow flags that were out in the marshy area by the burn's mouth when I saw three oystercatchers, a curlew and one hoodie were working the tide wrack for food on the far side. Suddenly I was surprised by a large plaice that shot out from just below my feet and went ribboning out to the bluer, deeper waters.

I realized then what a great part the tides themselves played in sustaining many forms of marine life. On every rising tide fish like plaice, dabs, flounders and rocklings came gliding up over crabs trundling along the sea bed, to scavenge whatever food like dead insects, deer flies, bluebottles, gnats, spiders, grubs and beetles had fallen off trees or been left on the beach or had drowned in small pools while the tide was out. Just as foxes, ravens, crows, gulls and other birds came to feed on dead fish, crabs, sand worms, cockles, winkles, whelks and other shellfish and molluscs broken loose by the pounding actions of the waves when the high tides retreated again. It was a two-way swap, twice a day, and played a great part in the whole balance of shore life. Even the size and strength of the shore birds' beaks fitted each into subtly different feeding notches. For instance, curlews with their nebs up to seven inches long can probe for tube, lug and white worms, or razor shells and bivalves that burrow too deeply for birds like oystercatchers or gulls to reach. But the thick powerful bills of the oystercatchers can pluck out the shallower burrowing cockles and stab at the adductor muscles of the filtering mussels, two of their favourite foods. They, along with crows and gulls, can also knock limpets from rocks with a sudden sneaky blow. Most shore birds in fact, including eider and shelducks, guillemots, turnstones too, can also feed on other molluscs, nereid worms, shrimps, young flatfish, sand eels and rocklings. A favourite food too was the sand-hoppers which often leaped in small clouds thousands strong when feeding from the jetsam on the tide wrack at dusk.

Next morning I had a brainwave – to make a plaice trap. I spent a day making one out of a fish box, covering the top with half-inch wire netting and making a hinged fringe of thin wires at one end. Holding it down with rocks on the sand where it would be covered with ten feet of water at high tide, I baited it with meat, bacon rind, worms and mussels. The idea was the flatfish would scent the food and sneak in over the slitted bottom through the inward-hinged wires – and not be able to get out again. A good idea but it caught not a single dab! Tiny crabs nipped in and out of the netting, took all the bait, and the hinged wires were just too roughly made for a flatfish to push against them. For such a trap to work it would need to be machine made with great precision – an ironic admission. But I did manage to catch a few prawns with a funnel-shaped, nylon-mesh trap baited with fish scraps and held on the bottom with a rock, with a float attached so I could haul it up.

One afternoon after being roused from a sunbathing nap by the shrill *"pleep pleeps"* of the oystercatchers, who I presumed were making them for devilment as they had no nest near the croft, I was standing in the deep pool of the burn to photograph the birds when I saw what looked like two branches nodding up and down behind heavy bracken. A large stag with widespread antlers which in early June were not fully grown, was casually grazing sixty yards north of the croft. The antlers were in full velvet and it seemed extraordinary they should have grown to that length since I'd last seen the stag with mere twin knobs back in early April. I raised the camera slowly and took two photos as it stared back at me arrogantly, seeming not at all nervous. I was sure it was the young stag I'd seen for two years near the croft. It was now in its fourth or fifth year and seemed a superb specimen.

I allowed him to walk out of sight before moving myself, then tried to track him over the ridge to the north-east in the hope of stalking for more shots. But with only brief rain in the past four days his slots were shallow, and I lost them on beds of dried old bracken, the grass and rock faces and saw no more sign of him after going down to the south shore.

I need not have bothered for he was back the next two mornings around dawn, exasperatingly when the light was too poor for photos. And by the time the daylight was strong he was away in the hills. I took to regarding him as a wandering itinerant neighbour, the kind who is never there when you want him but who helps himself to whatever he needs of yours. And when I once saw him staring at me with a wedge of

Sebastian the stag, 4–5 years old, in full velvet in June.

herbage sticking from the side of his mouth like a pipe, I nicknamed him Sebastian. Usually he only walked slowly away without showing the panic common to his kind. And every time he stopped he'd turn and look at me as if saying "Don't look at me like that. This is my place as much as yours!"

One day I came out to get a bucket of water and startled Sebastian who took a spectacular flying leap across the burn and galloped away. He had nibbbled all the tender new green shoots from the bramble bushes that supplied my autumn blackberries. Now I knew also where my dock leaf "cabbage" was going.

But when I woke up one morning and saw Sebastian's large backside with its heart-shaped light buff alarm patch and ludicrously short tail a mere three feet from the window, I felt he was taking things too far – his other end was busily cropping away at the cabbage and lettuce plants in my hard-won garden patch.

That morning I boated up the loch for the old sheep netting below the big house that Iain had promised me, and for a large section of blue, nylon, fish netting which I'd seen drifted up on shore opposite Deer Island. With these I made a "stag proof" roof for the garden.

10

KNOWING FROM WILDLIFE TREKS in Canada that 'good luck' comes in the plural as often as bad, I rowed one morning to an islet in the loch's mouth where many sea birds were flying. To keep my camera and lenses from being splashed by spray I wrapped them in plastic bags. I had only walked five yards on the bright-green turf amid the colourful sea pinks and grey-and-white lichened rocks, when a brown eider duck shot upwards from the vegetation and flew away. Her grass nest lined thickly with the soft, brown down she had plucked from her breast and belly – so prized for its heat insulating properties for making eiderdown quilts – contained only three light-green eggs. And one of them was hatching, the egg tooth of the duckling's beak showing through a small hole. Perhaps she had lost the other eggs to crows or foxes – or even otters for there were fish bones on the islet's rocks.

Two herring gulls still had three eggs in their nests but four other pairs had hatched their young out a week or so earlier and the downy-white and grey-speckled chicks squeezed tightly into crevices when they heard their hovering parents making loud "*qwuck qwucks*", a signal for them to hide. When I picked one up it responded with a look of fateful innocence as if thinking, "If I'm to die there's nothing I can do." I also discovered an oystercatcher's nest, a mere scrape containing pebbles the same size as the three eggs as if to help camouflage them better, which were smaller and more darkly blotched than those of the gulls. I had an idea I might find one for the parent birds were flitting round the islet in total silence. They call loudly when one is several yards from the nest as if to warn chicks to hide, but go quiet again when one is very

Herring gull chicks trying to make themselves inconspicuous.

near it. I took my photos quickly, making sure not to disturb any nest or vegetation, then quietly left the islet.

Needing exercise after long writing hours, the boat engine now breaking down frequently, I rowed to the store at the head of the loch to shop and post mail. It was a long ten-mile haul there and back, and while my hands were not blistered, my backside was sore from rocking to and fro on the hard seat. As any distance oarsman knows the rear takes more punishment than the hands once they've hardened.

A few days later I went back to the islet to photo the sitting eider. Remembering the exact spot, I stole quietly near and took a shot of her head and neck in the deep bowl amid the long grasses. She did not move and I backed away to leave her alone but as I stepped sideways another eider on a nest I had not found earlier shot upwards. I looked down – she had covered her eggs with a squirt of thick, greeny-brown liquid that smelled faintly like a fried bacon, liver and mushroom breakfast! This was not her excreta, I found out later, but a special fluid eider ducks emit to camouflage their eggs in an emergency, its scent probably being abhorrent to mammal predators. Usually when leaving the eggs in normal circumstances, she covers them just with the down to keep them warm while she is away.

I looked at the oystercatchers' nest and was surprised to find all three eggs gone and no sign of the shells. But as I stood there a little black-and-white chick with a short, orangey bill moved out of the grasses, as if posing for a photo on the rock above the nest. It's hard to find an oystercatcher chick for it's a master at hiding but as I took photos this one obligingly opened its beak in a wide yawn! I retreated slowly and before leaving took a look at one of the herring-gull nests that had contained eggs earlier. A beautiful picture greeted my eyes – and lens. One chick, wet and bedraggled, was out of its egg, another was half out, while the third was just poking its egg tooth through. The three stages of hatching in just one picture, And the grasses, rocks and bright sea pinks framed the nest with lovely colours. I had been more than lucky on these two short visits and I did not go to the islet again that year.

When I walked over the hills for my mail next day the good luck spell continued. A letter from the American magazine described my article about the wilds as "Fine and magnificent" and they were paying $600 for it. What a victory it seemed – I had at last been given the chance to write what I really believed in and had the work appreciated more than anything I had ever written. My joy increased when I received letters from folk all over America saying I had brought the natural world to them in ways they had not thought of it before. It seemed then I indeed might just be able to repay the wilderness for all it had done for me by sharing the experiences with others, and perhaps continue to earn the little I needed to continue such a life.

In mid-July the mackerel shoals were thick in the shore waters and with greater experience it was easy to catch all I needed in a mere half hour, so I redoubled my summer custom of trying to feed the seals near their favourite haul-out islets. Rounding their rocky shores one morning I noticed that while all the other seals were hunching down like giant caterpillars and flopping heavily into the water, one youngster stayed on the rocks. It seemed to be struggling to go forward as it hunched hard, and as I came closer and it turned to me with fear-filled eyes, I managed to take a photo of it from the moving boat. But it still stayed there. Clearly something was wrong.

I pulled the boat in beside the rock, put its bow rope under a large stone and walked over – his right front flipper had become wedged in an unusual barbed projection in a crevice between the rocks. The harder he tried to get away the worse he became trapped. In fear at this two-footed monster now lumbering down on him, he snapped and tried to bite my hands.

"Come on now, Sammy Seal," I said soothingly, dreaming the name up out of nowhere. "We'll soon have you out of this." By a quick movement I grabbed the loose fur of his thick neck behind his wide head, thankful that owing to the shortness of the neck he had little head manoeuvrability anyway, and then pushing his whole body down and backwards, I freed his flipper. The skin was torn badly but the limb was not broken for it was flapping away every bit as hard as the other.

At that moment I was sorely tempted to try and take Sammy home as young common seals are not hard to keep as pets if they have access to natural food and have water for swimming. I still did not like the solitary life and I now briefly imagined the young seal and me sharing life together, playing and swimming in the crystal-clear summer waters. But my basic belief is that 'friendship' with wild animals should be based solely on giving help when needed, not possessiveness. Taking any youngster from the wild is only justified if one is absolutely sure it has been abandoned, or it is injured beyond self help. Just then I saw a large, dark-brown seal was staying nearer than the others and was anxiously circling the edge of the rock. It was clearly the youngster's mother. I realized too that the pup's flipper would heal as well in the mineral contents of the sea, with its natural salts and iodine, as through any amateur help of mine. So I let him go.

For a second or two he just stayed there, staring at me with total disbelief in his dewy eyes – seals have most expressive faces – then he hunched himself rapidly down to the water and swam out to his mother. It was only then I remembered my camera. I raced back but when I got it from the boat and adjusted the lens there was not a seal in sight! There was ingratitude – after that rescue they might at least have let me take some good pictures. But I came to treasure the one I did take of little Sammy on the rock for I saw him many times later.

It was a far wetter summer than the previous two and one afternoon as I worked the garden I heard hissing then felt I was being pelted by tiny stones. It was a hailstorm – in July! It was strange that all bird song ceased on these wintry days. If such song is only to attract females and mark territories, why don't the birds also sing in rain and storms? They are surely as affected as much as we are by sunshine and fine weather, and there is much *joy* in their singing too.

In the bad weather I made two lobster creels with hazel wands and fish netting and set them out near the islets but when I finally caught a small lobster with only one claw I felt so sorry for the poor creature I let it go. Mostly I only caught crabs or dogfish, small and spotted like leopards. As these scavengers were common I occasionally made a spiced kedgeree from them. Their skins were covered in hard, back-ward-pointing hooks and when dried made an effective substitute for sandpaper.

Gardening on other cold days I now used the thinnings from the young cabbages, lettuce and carrots as salads. I now had battles with slugs that razed away at the vegetables all night. But instead of chemicals I put old wall boards round the edges of the garden. The slugs hid under them all day and I just had to remove them fifty yards. It would take them days to get back and I reckoned they could rasp away at weeds en route and, from my point of view, do some good instead. In the now frequent mists the midges were at their worst, converging in clouds as I worked outside. But I found they were more quickly attracted to a man in a white shirt – that sight played a part in their locating a warm-blooded creature to bite, and I had less trouble in a black shirt. I had no wish to cover myself with costly skin-burning repellent all the time.

But when the weather improved again other insects proved interesting and I made notes of sightings for the British Museum. One morning a loud, whirring noise and the sight of a huge insect made me leap backwards. When it landed on the croft wall I identified it as a drone fly, its thick body just under $1\frac{1}{4}$ inches long. This huge fly is uncommon in the Highlands and it resembles a bee. Its larvae lives in rotting carrion and it is believed this is the 'bee' the ancients saw emerging from the carcases of lions, giving rise to the saying "Out of the strong came forth sweetness". I also found a tiger beetle with bright-green elytra, an alder leaf beetle with brilliant-green thorax, and several pine bark longhorn beetles though there were no pine trees for a good mile. As I worked in the garden buff-tailed humble-bees biffed into foxgloves and honey bee workers landed on white clover flowers. Sometimes they forced their way through thick grass to get to them, sending up dust with their buzzing wings as if making up for time lost during the late cold and rain.

When blazing hot days came again they seemed more precious than before and I took advantage of them too, finding new diversions in the sea. With the cheque from the American magazine I bought a black rubber wet suit and flippers and spent hours snorkelling with a face mask, diving amid the lovely undine caverns and waving tangleweed to watch underwater life. It was a strange and magic world of colour, movement and silence, a dream-like ballet of strange new creatures, with myself the only privileged spectator. Shoals of silvery sand eels darted by only feet away, while afar off the mackerel kept their distance, flashing their striped blues in the green depth of the ocean, and occasionally what looked like salmon smolts swam out from the river for their years in the sea before returning as great silvery salmon to spawn. Bright-red sea anemones waving their soft tentacles dotted the rocks, hermit crabs staggered along under the load of their secondhand homes, and orange, purple and light-brown starfish decorated the crevices of the dark boulders. From the gaps between them streamed flags of red dulse and sea thong, bright-green folds of sea lettuce, furry bladderwrack and banners of tangleweed.

I drifted in this quiet kingdom, body warm in the wet suit, moving buoyantly without effort, suspended in a blue-and-golden mirage.

Great crabs prowled over the bright, white sand for food and I found if I wanted a good laugh I could have fun trying to poke them over on their backs with a bamboo cane. Then they ran sideways fast and when flipped backwards they grasped the stick with a grip like a grapnel hook actually denting it. I could fish for them while actually in the water by lowering a mussel on a weighted line near some weeds, then watch them scent the food and converge on it like packs of dogs. Then I teased them a while by pulling the mussel out of their grips until they really seemed to lose their tempers, clashing their pincers in rage as the mussel danced out of reach. I always rewarded them by letting the mussel go after a while but it was a fine comedy show – and laughs are scarce when one lives alone in the wilds.

One day, however, the laugh was on me and I had a great fright. I was still feeding the seals regularly and when I passed the rocks I often saw Sammy, the little pup whose flipper I had freed, for he seemed to come closer than the others. One morning I decided to try to feed them when I was actually *in* the sea in my wet suit and mask, so I could watch them *under* water.

I caught some mackerel then boated to the islet, dropping a few small pieces offshore. Most of the seals were in the water, Sammy's broad head in the vanguard, while the ones left on the rocks caterpillared their way down with hunches of their forelimbs and thrusts of their hind flippers. I anchored the boat, walked to the far side of the islet in the black wet suit, fitted on my own black flippers, threw more fish out, then edged from a sitting position into the water with my linen bag of fish round my waist. Then I swam quietly out a few yards so I could see them clearly through the face mask.

The seals were transformed from clumsy slow-moving land creatures into dark torpedoes as agile in the water as huge otters. They dived, rolled and twisted, sculling mostly with their rear flippers, sometimes using just one at a time, as they scooped my fish bits up in their mouths, complete masters of their watery world. But as I threw more fish out I realized they were not very hungry for often they just shot past the fish, giving it a playful thrust and sending it spinning off in vortex. One of the two larger seals in the dim distance was hanging perpendicularly in the water and allowing itself to sink down very slowly. It looked as if it had been shot and was sinking dead to the ocean floor far below through inky blue darkness. Although I constantly had to lift my head above the surface for air, some of the seals never came up for a breath at all. Seals can stay under water for over thirty minutes for they have 50% more blood than a land mammal the same size and it is specially adapted for storing oxygen and tolerating carbon dioxide. As I kept watching, Sammy's light-grey and brown form came really close, his large dark eyes staring intently into my face mask so I could see the tightly shut Chinese slits of his nostrils and his long, white whiskers.

But as I turned on my side to reach into my bag for the last of the fish my face mask shipped some water and I couldn't see any more. I had to make fast strokes with the flippers to keep my head well above water while I pulled the mask out slightly, let the water out and set it back into position. As I did this and sank back into the water I was aware of a sudden disturbance and to my horror saw one of the larger mottled black seals, clearly a bull of about four hundred pounds, was boring towards me from the outer edge of the circle of seals at great speed.

There was no mistaking his intentions and I turned, thrashing the water frantically, and just managed to get onto the islet again and scramble up sideways, hampered by the flippers, as he turned back with a swirl, At first I thought he would try to come after me on land too and I wrenched to get the flippers off so I could run for the boat. But it seemed he knew he was at a disadvantage there and he satisfied himself with a somersault, smashing his rear flippers on the surface, then dived and came up among the others again. It was a chastening experience and I climbed into the boat with my heart pounding. Clearly my flailing movements while clearing my mask had enraged him and perhaps as I was clad head-to-toe in the black rubber suit, he had thought me to be a seal too, or at least something that should be driven away.

I thought that was the end of it but as I rowed home there was a commotion on the surface a few yards from the boat, and the bull seal shot half out of the water like a porpoise, somersaulted and again hit the water with a great splash of his rear flippers before boiling down again. It was the last time I tried to watch the seals while actually *in* the water with them myself!

I realized a few days later I had chosen the worst possible time too, for as I rowed past the islet on another fishing trip I looked through the field glass and saw one of the two bulls rolling and turning in close body contact with a brown female and he seemed to be trying to bite her neck with comparatively gentle affection. It was obviously the mating season. But by mid-August the two bulls seemed to have gone elsewhere for I did not see them again that year.

One cloudless morning with a slight westerly breeze I went in the boat to fetch some of the cabin plywood for the croft walls. As I headed in I saw two otters swimming in the sandy lagoon at Shoe Bay. Having no camera with me I made a mental note to go back in a few days' time. When I had the plywood sheets in the boat, the engine, which had been giving increasing trouble, flatly refused to start. And as I'd just polyurethaned the oars and left them in the croft to dry, I couldn't row. So I had the idea to *sail* home. I stood in the boat, held up a sheet of the eight-foot-by-four plywood and used myself as the mast. By changing both its angle and my position in the boat, I managed to sail back round

Mid-February and raging blizzards swept in from the north-west.

After an overnight wait in chilly March, I saw the big tom wildcat, nearly four feet long, return from a hunting trip.

A hind and her calf amid sunlit snow.

Sebastian, with some of his hinds. Aged about ten, he seems to be past his prime and his antlers are 'going-back' – turning inward and with less tines.

the promontories on the wind. Luckily with such an insecure "mast" no strong gusts came to send myself and "sail" flying into the sea.

But as I hauled the sheets up the slope and set them to the west wall, I found none would fit. The croft had sunk slightly at that end over the years and each sheet had to be planed and cut to fit its neighbour. Standing on a saw horse to fit the last one, it suddenly tipped over, the heavy plywood sheet crashed into the burn, and only a last-second, mad, scrabbling hop, step and a jump across the deep rocky pool saved me a broken leg. As I lay on my back the male and female buzzard sailed overhead, the female with her beak wide open yet not making her normal "*Keeyoo*"cry. I had the distinct impression she was laughing at me.

On my next supply trip some of my mainland acquaintances seemed to be enjoying a secret too, for everyone was most affable, greeting me with smiles. The postman stopped me on the road with "How's life over in Paradise?" And the postmistress handed me a great parcel of letters saying "Here's all your fan mail!" *Fan* mail? Me? The story about my search for a wilderness paradise had finally, two years later, come out in the popular magazine and while no address had been published forty folk had written to me that first week. This total finally went up to 367 and I felt it my duty to answer each person who had taken the trouble to set pen to paper, so I did little creative writing the rest of that summer.

The letters came from nature lovers in both big towns and small villages all over the land and I was astonished by the kindness of total strangers for I was sent cakes, sweaters, personal accounts and poems about nature, and recipes galore. I must confess, as I replied l had a naïve hope that I might thus meet the lady with whom to share the wilderness life. I could see now that if I was alone in my mid-forties I had no-one to blame but myself, for my former fast-travelling life had been one of foolishly rejected opportunities rather than a lack of choice. But I still clung to some personal illusions. Possibly some of us, the romantics or the idealists who still believe man is perfectible, or even just the lonely, hold to illusions for without them we are stripped of *hope*. Perhaps if we could really see life in all its stark reality we might instead go mad. Above all, the massive correspondence helped assure me that writing about the last wild places and man's influence and responsibility to them was, for me, the right work to do.

After the first morning of pounding out replies, I took the camera and walked to Shoe Bay hoping to lie in wait for the otters. I was surprised when I arrived to find some campers had been given permission to pitch their tents by the only south-facing, sandy bay and lagoon on the island which was also the otters' main playground. Oh well, that was the end of any otter-watching for a while.

On my next shopping trip Dugald Cameron, my Highland butcher, greeted me with a wide grin. "Are you still looking for a bird?" By now I was a bit embarrassed by the leg-pulling after the article and such English slang words as "bird" for girl seemed out of keeping with his usual demeanour. "No," I said defensively, biting the wrong bait. "I'm not looking for birds. If I was I wouldn't be living way out there."

He laughed then. "No, you said a long time back that if anyone found a young or injured eagle or buzzard to let you know. Well, the new mechanic has a young buzzard the Forestry Commission lads found fallen from its nest. He's living in a caravan, and is working all day – and might just let you have it."

A young buzzard? It had been one of my ambitions to rear a hawk, falcon or buzzard ever since I'd come to Scotland. The memories of the birds I'd kept as a boy came back – a crow, wood-pigeon, jays, magpie, owls, kestrel, and an injured female sparrowhawk. One of the favourite books on my shelves was Tim White's *The Goshawk*. This was my chance. If there was the faintest chance of buying the bird, I wanted it. Thanking Dugald, I dashed round to the wooden shed where motor engineer David Sturrock was starting a new and badly needed garage business in the area – the hard way.

I can't remember what I said but I talked ten to the dozen about rearing birds, how I lived alone on the island, had an empty room overlooking the loch, and a few minutes later Dave stopped work and we drove round to his caravan. The bird was crouching under a cage made from a vegetable rack, trying to avoid the playful attentions of a golden retriever and a young cairn terrier, his feathers wet from standing in his drinking water. But fear seemed not to be in his make-up for, ruffled though he was, he glared in baleful indignation at the excited dogs, ready to fight for his life if they went too far.

Shooing the dogs outside, Dave lifted the rack. Immediately the bird leaped and flew to the safety of a curtain rail, keeping a precarious balance by fanning his beautifully fawn, barred wings, and staring down with intent curiosity at this new intruder. He seemed impossibly small for a buzzard, less than a foot long and despite his similar rufous colouring was far too slimly built. I only knew I wanted to look after this lovely bird whose yellow eyes now glared with luminous ferocity into mine.

I slowly reached up and tickled the bird's underbelly. He quickly stepped onto my fingers, clinging hard with sharp, yellow talons.

"It looks like he's yours," laughed Dave.

"But how much do you want for him?" I asked thinking of my near-zero bank account. Dave thought a brief second then shook his head.

"Ah he cost me nothing at all, so you can have him for nothing too! But I warn you, he eats like a horse. I've been shooting rabbits for him so you'd better take some of these carcases with you. He loves them."

Astonished at his generosity I thanked him profusely and with a jubilant heart carried the bird to my Land Rover. During the jolting two miles back to the little pier he remained perched, struggling to keep his balance, on a board behind my driving seat, and seemed perplexed at the rapidly passing scenery. But the moment I pulled up he dashed and flailed away at the windscreen. My instinct at that moment was to let him free but I dare not. He was far too young and the white down still clinging to his plumage told me he was probably not yet five weeks old and he would have been easy prey for any passing fox, wildcat, stoat or even a group of hooded crows.

But as his wings whirred, spraying me with droplets, and because I still thought he *might* be a buzzard, I knew what I would call him – Buzz. I calmed him down, tied a soft gymshoe lace round one of his legs, then put him into the safety of a linen shopping bag. I loaded my supplies into the boat, cast off, started the outboard and set off on the two-and-a-half-mile journey to my croft on the Atlantic end of the island.

11

IT WAS ONE OF those calm and balmy summer evenings when the air shimmers up from the sea without any wind, and after a quarter mile I let Buzz out on to my hand. He showed no panic but regarded this new world with curious circular motions of his head.

Already he seemed happier. The air, the light, the glimmer from the sea and the trees, rocks and sky, all these were his natural element. At last his eyes could focus on a distant horizon and tattered though he was he responded. His jet black pupils contracted and expanded as he turned his wedge-shaped head and stared with piercing marigold eyes, taking in everything around him.

As we approached the islet near my bay he suddenly stood erect, flapped his wings and cried "*kee kee kee*", perhaps calling for his parents. But as I looked down his little throat and cruel beak, I rejoiced at the sound for now I began to realize what he was. The warm breeze had dried him, revealing the full splendour of his plumage. His back and shoulders were dusty chocolate brown with slight fawn edges to the feathers and wisps of white fledgling down still clung in places. His chest was white and crossed with rich copper bars. His tail feathers, already long though still encased in an inch of wax sheath, were a bright russet, striped with thin bars of dark brown.

Everything, the short rounded wings, the long tail, the brilliant yellow iris, pointed to Buzz being a hawk. Falcons have long stiff scythe-like wings and short tails, specially adapted to hunting down flying birds and small running mammals in open country. They also have dark eyes and notched beaks. As if to remove any lingering doubt, Buzz bobbed his head, lifted his tail and ejected a slashing white but odourless mute into the boat. I was delighted by this final clue – falcons' droppings fall straight down. Buzz was a sparrow-hawk.

The injured female sparrow-hawk I'd reared as a youth in the Sussex countryside had died. Perhaps I could now redress the balance. But I soon realized the enormity of the task. As any falconer knows, the sparrow-hawk is the hardest to train, especially the smaller male known as the "musket". It is delicate, has an intractable nature and must be treated like a spoilt child. If its metabolism sinks too low through poor diet or being overflown, it can develop fits which result in apoplexy, heart failure, and sudden death.

At this sombre thought I looked down. Too late. Buzz ducked, ejected another mute and leaped. My grasp on the gymshoe lace was too slight and he went beating across the sea for the land. I thought "My god, I've lost him already" as he flapped with rapidly weakening wings, ragged and tatterdemalion like an old crow in a storm, and fell into the sea thirty yards off shore.

Scared he would drown, I turned the engine up to full speed, only to have it cut out on to one cylinder. Leaping for the oars, I rowed madly to where he was floundering. Surprisingly he seemed to be making progress, flailing his legs like a duck and "humping" himself forward with his wings as I had once seen a bald eagle do in Canada. Afraid to hit him with the boat, I eased near, scooped him out by hand and put him back into the bag, a scraggy shivering object by now. But as I carried him up to the croft he shook and rattled his wet feathers as if nothing had happened and looked carefully at everything – the row of ash trees, the gurgling burn, the clumps of bracken and the harsh granite boulders – as if memorizing it all.

Inside my large spare room I quickly made a perch by the window from a curved ash twig so that it overlooked the supernal view of trees, islets and sea. He seemed to like it, intently watching birds, butterflies and even moving leaves. Below the perch I made a platform for his water and where he could tear up his prey and meat. Then because I wanted to watch him when he was unconscious of my presence, I sneakily drilled a small hole in the door at crouching height and left him. Half an hour later, shoes off, I stole back – he was now preening himself. Arching his neck high, he thrust his hooked beak into his top breast feathers then wiggled it down towards his legs. Once they were all properly fluffed out, he twisted his head over his back and combed the secondary wing feathers out with little beak quibbles. His primaries seemed too short, barely two inches long, and at first I thought they would not grow. But he smoothed these by stretching each wing out like a fan and raking the feathers with his talons. When he flirted his tail out and rattled it a few times I saw one of the feathers had broken off during the fall into the sea. But his careful toilet now seemed complete.

125

Only then did he look at the rabbit haunch I had left. He glared at it once, relaxed, closed his eyes for a doze, then as if doing a "double take," opened them wide again, looked intently at the haunch and crept down to the platform like a little parrot towards his "prey". Although my back was aching, it was so comical to watch I didn't move. From six inches away he took a sudden leap, struck the haunch a terrific blow with his left foot talons – presumably to "kill" it – stamped on it twice with the other then tore it apart with surprising strength and swallowed the torn morsels. Dave Sturrock had been right – he *was* feeding well.

I knew little about training a hawk except that to "man" one successfully, as falconers do, it had to be trained to sit on the gloved fist or wrist, even learn to feed there. And that when outside and flying free it had to be trained to return to a swung lure of food it recognised even after making a kill of its normal prey. All this takes enormous patience and one technique is to sit up with the hawk for hours at night until man and bird are both exhausted but it finally accepts the fist so naturally it will even roost there.

For the first two nights I tried the first part of this training. Making a special portable perch, I brought him into my room and installed him on my desk. Then I gently stroked his breast with a feather, talking softly to him. But I had to eat too. And when I did he did not sleep or relax at all but crouched on the perch as if about to spring, intently watching every movement of my knife and fork, an expression of outraged query in his eyes. I realized then how the phrase "Watch like a hawk" evolved. His gaze was so penetrating and disconcerting he made me feel foolish. I looked at my knife and fork as if for the first time. What ridiculous implements they *were*!

Shortly after I had put him back in his own room I heard a slight scuffle. I opened the door to find he was not on his perch but on some sacks on the floor. Used to a nest at night, the floor of the cage in which he'd been kept in the caravan, he naturally sought something flat to sleep on. This habit had to be broken for if he ever did it outside, a fox, otter, wildcat or stoat could get him. When I went back in with the paraffin lamp he flew about the room, refused to land on his perch but settled for an old deer antler on the shelf above the hearth. This eventually became his favourite night perch, and before going to sleep he always drew one foot upwards, puffed out his chest feathers, sank the foot into them then smoothed them down again, all snug and warm around his toes. At least *one* foot kept warm that way.

Next morning I sneaked to the peephole – just in time to see him fly from the antler to the window perch, look at the water tin as if seeing it for the first time, then drink copiously, lowering his beak then tipping it up filled with water and swallowing it down. When I went in he glared at me as if he'd never seen a human before, a way of looking right through you. Again I was impressed by his beauty, the penetrating focus of his eyes and his arrogant independence. Then he flew round the room with whirring wings but as I stood hopefully with outstretched gloved arm he suddenly landed on it as if he had been trained for years.

That night when I brought him into my room he again glared at my eating methods. But when I lit a match for my pipe he ducked, sent a mute across the floor then flew wildly around, landed on some sauce pan handles and sent them clattering to the floor.

It was then I felt I was wrong. I knew I did not really want to *tame* him, although I was sure it was possible as I had plenty of time. But such a creature could never be a pet, even if I could get the necessary licence to keep him legally. He would never know feelings of affection, could pay no homage to a human owner. I suddenly realized I had no wish to "man" him in the falconer's sense either, to train him to fly at wild prey, kill to satisfy any hunting instincts I may have then return to the hand. To achieve this the bird has to believe your will is its will for like a cat it remains its own man. But he was not born to be my indoctrinated slave. No, instead I would try and train him to hunt for *himself.* And once I was sure he could do this, and that he would return to a certain place outdoors for food if he failed to catch his natural prey, I would release him. I would help him only to fulfil the destiny for which he was born – to be free.

I caught him again, put him back on the deer antler perch in the far room and retired to think it all out. The sparrow hawk is now comparatively rare in Britain and apart from the extremely rare goshawk, which infrequently visits eastern coasts, it is our only true hawk. It is nearly extinct in twelve counties where it was once common – after years of persecution by gamekeepers, poisoning by toxic pesticides building up in the bodies of its prey and the reduction of its best habitat, varied broadleaf and conifer woodland. But since 1966 when it was given complete legal protection, and the reduction in the use of pesticides, it has slowly fought back to re-colonize many parts of Britain from its strongholds in the west. Clearly Buzz was the son of fine pioneering Argyll stock!

He would never soar effortlessly over the mountains like a golden eagle, or quarter the ground with the incredible long-distance eyesight – eight times finer than a man's – of a buzzard. For sheer speed the falcons would outfly him. He would never match the hurtling downward "stoop" of the rare peregrine which hits with such shattering impact it can decapitate a flying pigeon, nor the flashing flight of the scarce hobby which can fly down a swift, nor emulate the hovering abilities of the common kestrel as it balances in the winds above the fields.

But if I succeeded, he would become the dashing Sir Lancelot of the wood and glen. He would learn to dart arrow-like along hedgerows and woodland glades, spy a finch on some outstanding twig and swoop to pluck it off with one foot and unerring skill. He would be fast enough to snatch a swallow flying from a barn, skilful enough to chase into a bush after his prey without suffering mortal damage. He would learn timing fine enough to pluck a young water bird from a loch surface without a ripple, and to use his long tail for the agile twists and turns in dense woodland of which no other bird is capable.

Next day Buzz's education began. With his primaries still so short I had to first help him learn to fly. I made a pair of light jesses for his legs from the soft tongue of an old shoe. These took an hour to fix on because he hated actually being touched. So that he could fly freely I tied a 400-yard length of thin nylon fishing line to a tiny swivel on the jesses from a spinning reel. This idea worked wonderfully because the line could snake off the reel without any friction. I knew one must never pull a hawk or falcon up in flight during training but if he was about to tangle up in trees or round high rocks I could try to slow him down with a light finger touch so he would turn away. This line was essential in case he escaped to freedom before he had learned to hunt.

On the first day he managed two 100-yard flights. On the second I allowed him three of 150 yards each. On his initial flights he flapped unstably like an old rook and I wondered if his lost tail feather could affect him that much. But it seemed due more to hesitancy because of the newness of the area and the sheer open space around him because by the fourth day he was flying with more determination, deciding where to go before taking off.

There were many problems, partly because man and hawk were learning together. Sparrow hawks hunt mainly in or near woodlands and however long his flights he usually made for the ash trees along the burn. And when he took off again at my approach I had to try and throw the reel over the bough he had perched on and catch it again so he could keep flying. This didn't always work and occasionally I had to regretfully slow him down so he came to earth gently before the line became too entangled. But by the ninth day he could cover three hundred yards at a time and was varying his flight by an act of will. He would fly a little, glide, decide to go elsewhere, hover briefly, then set off in the new direction.

Later, in true hawk fashion, he liked to use the ash trees as "cover" for his flights – and dash through them, drop down low again to the slope of the hill, skirt rocks and bracken clumps, swoop up to avoid some scrub oaks, then disappear at the full length of the line. By this time the line would have passed through the branches of maybe four or five trees and it was a laborious process to get him back. I had to follow the line through the trees until it led to him. Then I'd break it a yard from him, tie him to some flexible bracken, walk back, reel in the loose line, then return to him again and tie him back onto the reel.

Oddly, after each long flight, Buzz was quite wild and obdurate and at my approach reared up with beak agape and wings extended as if I were some would-be attacker he had never seen before. But he never tried to slash me with his beak or talons. Nor, although he'd never worn them before, did he ever try to tug or undo his jesses with his beak, which I thought extraordinary. I had a rule never to get angry with him but as he kept exasperatingly hopping on and off my glove like some little keep-fit maniac after his flights I occasionally muttered cuss words. Strangely, it was always after such little "scraps" he was most hungry.

Buzz had some odd quirks. He reacted strongly to colour. While he *would* perch on my bare hand he absolutely refused a grey or blue glove and was finally happy with an old, tattered brown one. He examined the contrast between my trousers and shirt with intent scrutiny. He did not like white shirts or if, being warm, I went in naked from the waist up. I tried out all my shirts and found he was happiest with a black short-sleeved one.

At first he constantly leaped or "bated" from the glove the moment I opened the outer door when we were too near the ash trees and the croft walls, and for a moment dangled humiliatingly by his legs on a yard of line. After endless coaxings back on to the glove he finally learned not to fly until I either held my hand high or had transferred him to a special ash perch outside my window where I could keep an eye on him.

This perch was most important in Buzz's young life. After his flights I always left him on it, the open reel lying below. I fed and watered him from it during the day and he soon realized he could fly to and from this perch at will. My idea was he would always regard it as "home" when he went free and would return for food there if he failed to catch natural prey and was hungry.

Feeding Buzz proved a big problem. Although he ate rabbit flesh it was not his natural food, being equivalent to what falconers call "washed meat" and was not nourishing enough for a small hawk's high metabolism. A sparrow-hawk's natural prey is small birds, some mice and voles, and a few beetles and small invertebrates. Even so I still needed rabbit for I had to wean him off it gradually. Lean red beef was a good food but again it was unnatural and lacked the fur and small feathers the hawk's digestion needs, but on the fourth day I ran out of both beef and rabbit. As I had been plagued by mice for years, waking me at nights and fouling my stores and once my bed, and because they were common and the hawk was rarer I felt a few would have to be sacrificed to keep Buzz alive.

I had no mousetraps but that night I put some cheese on wire on one edge of a bucket of water, then hinged a small weighted see-saw of thin wood opposite so when the mice ran up a sloping box and along it to get the cheese, they promptly dropped into the water and drowned. Next morning I had three mice – enough to keep Buzz going until I obtained more rabbit and beef.

That day the inlet valve on my boat engine came out and I broke it trying to put it back again at sea. For the next ten days until Reggie Rotheroe, a first-class engineer as well as inventor, repaired it I had to row to and from the pier. Luckily I found a newly squashed rabbit on the road to the store. After scaring away a couple of hoodies, I prised up the rabbit and together with some lean beef from the butcher's I rowed back.

The hardest part now was to teach Buzz to hunt for himself and to do this I decided to make him *work* for most of his meals. I experimented endlessly, trying to arouse his hunting instincts. I tied a dead mouse by its front paws to some nearly invisible line and when Buzz was dozing on one leg on his outside perch, I dropped it near him, walked about twenty yards away and for a minute or two pretended to ignore him. Then I gave a little jerk on the line.

The mouse jumped realistically through the grass. Immediately Buzz went into a crouch, glaring down at the mouse as if about to pounce. But then, to my great chagrin, he looked all the way along the line to me and his expression said clearly "What is that damn fool up to now!"

It was not until I had put him on half rations and partially buried the line in the grass on the fourth day of this new training that the idea worked. I had caught no mice that night and was using a fur covered rabbit leg instead. Hiding behind the big rock, I gave little tugs. Buzz immediately dropped into a crouch and as he saw his "prey" getting away he launched himself, a mad stare on his face. Like an arrow he came, hit the moving leg first time, struck it two lightning blows with his talons, one-footed like a cat, then with his wings mantled over the leg and both feet on it, began to feed. He plucked out the fluff most professionally, tossing it away into the air, then started to eat the raw meat.

As I walked past with the line he ignored me completely, as if intent on his first real "captive". I left him for a while then got him back on his perch by dragging the rabbit leg away from him. He stared with disbelief then half ran, half flew, pouncing repeatedly on his prey, glaring with rage, striking it again and again with his flashing scimitars and mantling over it each time it came to rest and he thought he had finally conquered.

Every day I varied this routine, with mice when I caught them. Sometimes I wound the line right round the croft, using the smooth guttering downpipes to reduce friction on the corners, and came back behind Buzz tugging the mouse. He immediately went after it and it was great fun hauling it all the way round the croft and then see Buzz coming round the last corner towards me, still flailing away at it, striking out with his claws like a little boxer.

When he finally carried his prey up to a branch in the ash trees to eat – thus choosing a "plucking post" all sparrowhawks like to use – I felt we were really making progress.

12

NOW THAT BUZZ HAD learned to catch "running mice" on the ground I had to help him learn the far more difficult skill of catching his principal prey in the wild – small flying birds. At first I tied some small feathers and rabbit fur round a piece of steak and swung it towards him from all angles. Initially he was alarmed, dodging to and fro as the "bird" came near. But after flying him hard on the second day, as the bait swung towards him he followed every movement with glaring eyes then shot out one lightning set of talons and clung determinedly to it while still holding the perch with the other! As I tugged he resisted every attempt of his captive to "escape," pinning it down with great strength for his size. Finally I left him to it and as he ate he swallowed some of the feathers his system needed.

But I soon realized this was a poor method for birds would hardly fly within a few inches of his face in the wild. Indeed, one day the tame chaffinch Little Fat Sergeant, who had already helped raise a brood of youngsters, flew by and landed on the garden fence. Instantly Buzz, who always watched every moving thing around him – blowing leaves, butterflies or soaring dragonflies – with minute interest, dropped into a crouch. But the chaffinch "froze" into total immobility, as if mesmerized by the raptor's eye. This seemed to be a protective device on Sergeant's part because when he did not move again Buzz lost interest and he quickly flew away.

One day my chance for a better way to teach Buzz to fly after birds came in a sad way. Walking down to the south shore I found a wheatear fluttering and hobbling in the grass, too weak to fly. Its legs were entangled in sheep's wool so it could not hop or walk and had been unable to feed. I brought it back to the croft, placed it on its back on a

Buzz bathing in the burn.

cushion – this seems to "hypnotise" small birds so they don't try to fly away – and removed the wool with sewing needles.

But when I fed it a worm it quickly spat it out. That night I caught insects by shining a torch on to a white sheet and fed it those instead. Next day it had perked up enough to flutter at the window so I let it go again. Oddly it stayed nearby and dipped and bobbed uttering a little squeak that sounded like two stones being struck together. But at dusk it hid between two rocks. Fearing the little wheatear would be taken by a predator I brought it back into the croft and fed it, letting it go again next day. But a few days later I found it dead on the path.

As I looked at its pitifully thin body, its bright blue, black, white and chestnut feathers, I realized its death was in fact a blessing in disguise – I could use the body to teach Buzz to fly at birds. I rigged up a "flying run" with nylon line from the roof to Buzz's plucking post branch on the ash tree so that it passed just above his daytime perch. I tied steak to the wheatear's breast, braced its wings open with a thin wire frame and made two little wire loops on its back. Then I tied my thinnest fishing line to it, mounted it on the runway and sent it "flying" down. By jerking the line slightly I gave it a spasmodic realistic flight.

Each time it went past Buzz saw it and crouched. On the fifth run he leaped after it, looped up, missed but pursued his quarry, finally catching it a yard from the ash tree. At first he clung to it flapping, for he couldn't take it off the line. But finally with one foot on the plucking post and one on the bird, he got his meal. Once again I varied the approach, setting the runway from a pole, rocks and small trees near the croft but always ending up on the plucking post. I also collected feathers and tried to imitate the sparrows, finches, pipits, pigeons and starlings which are among the hawk's main prey.

Buzz developed an odd liking for bathes in the burn. Every sunny afternoon about 2.10pm – I always knew the time because it was just after the Radio 2 weather forecast – he flew from his perch to a rocky pool in the burn some thirty yards away. Then, constantly glaring at the sky to make sure he was safe, he waded out to his middle like a duck, fanned out his tail, crouched down and shuffled water over himself with half folded wings. So much for the belief that hawks hate to get their wings wet! Then he flew back to his perch and sat in the warm wind with all his feathers puffed out, looking like a partridge, until he was dry enough for preening.

There were a few mishaps during Buzz's training, of course. Once I had left him on a rock two hundred yards behind the croft so he would become used to being alone. An hour later as I wrote at my desk I heard his high "*kee kee kee*". I traced his line and found him hanging upside down from the ash tree. He was scared but also indignant at the humiliation. Unfortunately he had broken a second tail feather – at the root so I could not mend it. But I managed to straighten out two other bent ones by the old falconer's trick of immersing his tail in hot water. He now had a gap in the centre of his tail and I would have to be careful he lost no more. But as he had ten good feathers left I felt he would not be *too* bothered by this slight lessening of his sail area.

One morning after a meal and when I had left him dozing on his perch, I suddenly heard a raucous squawking. I looked out. Buzz was gone. I felt a stab of fear as I remembered how hawks are sometimes robbed by crows and rushed outside. There in a dell in the glen to the south-west of the croft, three hooded crows were leaping violently up and down. I hastened there and as I looked through the tall bracken I saw Buzz at bay. His beak was agape with rage and resentment but there was little of fear on his face.

Two of the crows were darting at him from above without actually touching him, just forcing his head down, while on the ground another hoodie was launching attacks with its spear of a beak. Each time it went close a flailing stroke from Buzz's rapier claws drove it back, but his movements were hampered because the line from the reel was entangled in the bracken above him. While not actually suspended he was on short tether and the cunning hoodies knew it. But he fought the larger birds off with talons and swift forward snaps of his wings, sideways like a swan strikes for maximum power.

I yelled and leaped up, scaring the hoodies away but if I expected Buzz to be grateful at my timely appearance I was wrong. His blood was up, his feathers shrunken close to his body, and for the first time I saw his long shank feathers as he stood as high as he could to be fast and light on his feet. He reared up as he tried to get away from me too, flapping his growing but still stunted wings, pathetically small but still full of fight. At that moment any living creature would have angered him.

If I had not been on hand that morning, handicapped as he was by the line, he would have been killed. Clearly I could not keep him a prisoner for ever. The longer he became used to me, the harder he would find it to fend for himself in the wilds. Now too, the first winds and rain of early autumn were starting. I had taught him all I could as a mere human and the time was near for his final freedom.

Slowly stroking his belly feathers and making the soothing noises I always used to get him on to my hand, I carried him back to the croft and his indoor perch. Later through the peephole I saw him sleeping fitfully, all his feathers puffed out and swaying slightly, his transparent third eyelids, the nictitating membranes, blinking under the main ones. He was roosting abnormally, on both legs instead of one, and his mutes were now an ominous light-green colour. Both these things are danger signs. Had the shock been too much for his highly strung system?

Then I noticed his water tin. It was on the floor – he must have knocked it over. Quickly I filled it and held it out to him but he took no notice. I nudged his beak into it and tilted up the tin, Instantly he hopped onto my hand and for the first time there began to drink copiously, lowering his bill and tipping it up full of water and swallowing it down, his legs trembling against my fingers. In the drama with the crows I had forgotten one of the three most important rules with hawks – always check they are freshly watered, clear their mutes away for they can cause bacterial infection, and never leave uneaten food near them.

That afternoon as Buzz slept I made the long sea and road journey to the butchers for some raw fillet steak, determined he would not die. As I came back up the steep path I was astonished to see a young sparrowhawk fly past the croft, pause over the garden, then head over the ridges to the east. Had Buzz somehow escaped? I dashed into the croft but he was there, perched on the deer antler on the shelf above the hearth. It seemed an extraordinary coincidence and I wondered if it could possibly have been one of Buzz's own fellow fledglings. By nightfall, after wolfing down a full quarter pound of the steak disguised in rabbit fur, he seemed well recovered.

I gave him a day's rest then trained him intensively for a few last days. By now the sheaths on his ten tail feathers had almost grown out and he stood a full 12¼ inches on the launching pad. He was flying really well now, darting through the trees and gliding down to the shore, looking like a true sparrowhawk with the sun gleaming from the sea upon his burnished pinions. It seemed that flapping against the slight pull of the line had really developed his wing muscles. I just hoped the slight tail gap would not prove too much of a handicap.

Now I deliberately left him alone for longer periods and after his bathes in the burn he rested more in the ash trees than on his perch. Each time I approached him he seemed a little wilder, his feathers sleeking down as I drew near. But when he was hungry he naturally flew back to the perch and looked for the food he had doubtless seen me drop. He still attacked my pulled mice or simulated prey with great gusto, holding them in the grass with amazing strength against my slight tugs.

The day I let Buzz go was fine, warm and cloudy, the kind of day he preferred to bright sunlight or rain. He refused to stand still for his jesses to be removed but flew round and round the room, landing on the deer antler, the window perch, the floor sacks, the firewood pile – the games we had played so often before. But finally the jesses were off and I took him outside and lifted my hand high for the last time.

Away he went, unerringly shooting through the gap in the ash trees, twisting, turning with half closed wings like a huge swallow, and landed in a sessile oak tree three hundred yards away. Two hours later as I typed at my desk, he was still there, the jesses off at last, casually preening his tail feathers through his bill, as if he knew he was now completely free and there was no hurry to go anywhere. But when I looked up later he had gone – and so had a steak "mouse" I'd put near the perch. I felt sorry not to have seen him take it.

As I swept out his room, cleaned up the newspaper sheets with his "mute" testimony, seeing a few wispy downy feathers, symbols of his childhood, still clinging to the ash perch by the window from which he had surveyed the rugged landscape and shimmering ocean that were now his own world, I felt oddly lonely. My mind seemed filled with the memory of his piercing eyes and whirring wings as he'd flown round me before allowing me to attach his 'creance' line for the training flights each day. Yet I was happy that he had survived and was free.

For three days there was no sign of him apart from a brief glimpse of a hawk's form passing swiftly across the garden. But on the fourth there was a flutter of wings outside, a shadow crossed the window and I looked out to see Buzz on his perch, tearing hungrily at the food I had left out. I did not go outside for I didn't want to frighten him.

On my next supply trip I heard that one of the summer visitors had been given permission to shoot the "big stag" that was known to be on the island. I feared then that Sebastian, the friendly stag I had been watching for more than two years might become the recipient of a rifle bullet for he still occasionally came round the croft at dawn. But the stag-stalking season was now open, it was not my land and there was nothing I could do. Two days later I found a dead herring-gull floating in my bay, something I had not found before in two and a half years of walking round the island. Its body was shattered, most of the backbone missing. It seemed it had been shot with a rifle. I felt a pang of fear for Buzz's life then and resolved to try and catch him again next time he returned until I felt the danger was over. That afternoon while I was painting the new west wall of the cottage with an undercoat of light grey, a piece of rabbit disappeared from below the perch – yet I had seen and heard nothing.

On the morning of his ninth day of freedom I was delighted when Buzz returned again. He flew to his perch, dived at some meat scraps I had put out and carried them to his old post on the ash tree branch. He looked more mature now, somewhat lighter in colour. I went out hoping to catch him but found myself staring into the wary eyes of a stranger, and he flew away again.

Next morning the first rain for nearly a week began to fall, and as the wind increased I went into Buzz's room to open the window in the forlorn hope he might seek his old shelter and return to his window perch. Something made me look down - and there he was, lying awfully still on his back just two yards from the croft wall, as if he had been thrown there.

Unbelievingly, I carried him indoors. His body was still warm and his gullet full of blood. In terrible grief I examined him, found no external injury yet I noticed odd differences. The body seemed darker, smaller, and there was a patch of white feathers behind the head I'd never noticed before. The wax sheaths on the tail seemed longer than Buzz's had been on the day of his release, and there were twelve tail feathers when, after Buzz had lost two, I had counted only ten. But with his continual fast movements I could possibly have miscounted earlier.

I looked at the little body on my desk, remembering how he had lain on the ground as if he'd been thrown there. Suddenly in awful doubt and suspicion and then rage, I rushed out and raced round the croft area and the ridges in a huge wide circle, cursing the bracken that tore at my legs, but I heard and saw no-one. Could it possibly have been a different sparrowhawk, I wondered. Then I recalled the young one I had seen fly past when Buzz had been in his room. No, it seemed impossible.

But in those heart-breaking moments I was in no state for balanced reason or any attempt to muster precise memory. And all my photos of Buzz had yet to be developed. I just had to find the truth of what had happened for if any evil had occurred I needed positive evidence before taking action. In despair, I wrote a fast letter, raged across the stormy loch under a steely, raining sky, telephoned SSPCA officers in Glasgow and Oban, then drove the body down to a police station twenty miles away from where the Oban officer had promised he would remove it for autopsy.

For a suspenseful week I waited, going over and over again my weeks with Buzz. Could he have picked up some poison? Or been hit by a stone? Could something have scared him so much he had flown blindly into the side of the house or window? But I had been sitting quietly at my desk at the time, so surely I would have heard something.

Then the autopsy result arrived. ". . . The most significant lesion found was a large bruise, an inch or more in diameter, situated at the "shoulder" at the junction of the left wing and the body...There were no penetrating wounds; no evidence of gunshot. Examination for infectious deseases was negative, and in the circumstances there are no grounds for suspecting poisoning. The site of the external injury is consistent with the bird having flown or dived into a hard object at speed. (Overhead wires? A fence?). The ultimate cause of death was internal haemorrhage, probably hastened by the occlusion of the trachea with blood."

Sadly resigned now to the fact that somewhere, somehow, I had failed, I left for London on a brief but long-delayed work trip, to have my photos developed at a good studio, and to pick up a new 1,000 mm telephoto lens for my work.

It was on the day after my return that the extraordinary dénouement of my life with Buzz occurred. I was on the beach making minor fibre glass repairs to my boat when I heard little finches chittering with terror. A flurry of wings and out from some nearby scrub trees one of the small birds flew with a hawk after it. As it passed over my head the finch looped up backwards, the hawk swooped up after it and as it spread its tail to make the abrupt turn I saw with astonishment the gap in the feathers, and the shortened wings as if the primaries were still not yet quite fully grown. As I stared, my heart beating heavily, the hawk suddenly lost all interest in the bird.

I stayed still as it flew slowly just above me then alighted only a few feet away in a small oak on the side of the cliff. It was the way he landed, with a quick flapping of wings, unlike the silent drop off the curve like mature hawks, that also convinced me. But he looked greyer now, bigger and better feathered.

Suddenly he puffed out all his feathers, gave that little contented wriggle of the neck back into his shoulders, then delicately raised his right foot into his breast feathers, smoothed them down over the foot just as Buzz always did, and *went to sleep*.

Extraordinary though it may sound, it was as if he had been sent to end my tortured doubt. No wild hawk would have done that, land and go to sleep almost within my reach. As if in a dream I stood stupefied for a full minute then said "Buzz" loudly. Instantly he became alert, smoothed down his feathers and as silently as an owl flew close to my head again and then was lost in the trees to the west.

I walked back to the croft with an indescribable feeling of relief. The hawk that had died had been only an extraordinary coincidence; perhaps it had believed the newly painted light grey wall to be part of the sky. Later, as I consulted my diaries, I found items I had forgotten. Apart from the hawk that had crashed through Iain's window months before, I had also found remains of other sparrowhawks earlier in the year, one near Arean and one near Shoe Bay, both upturned on the grass and only a few feathers left. Certainly fast-flying sparrowhawks suffer heavy mortalities, occasionally killing themselves by flying too hard after prey into brambles, thorn bushes and tree branches.

As I walked the woods and mountains in later months I caught occasional glimpses of Buzz, dodging and twisting between the trees like some swift spectre, in full control at last of his real hunting speed. Occasionally he still came back to snatch meat from the front patch. I hoped one day he would find a fine mate, crying *"kek kek kek"* as he courted her through a woodland glade and helped her build their nest in a high conifer. I hoped he would become a good sparrowhawk husband, bringing food to her and the chicks and guarding her attentively when she stood shielding their young from sun and rain with open wings. I liked to think the patient training was not in vain and that at least one human had done a little to redress the careless toll taken of nature's creatures by the interests of the species that believes itself to be the most evolved on earth.

It may occur to some folk why I cared so much about a "cruel" hawk that among its wide range of prey kills small singing birds, forgetting that many of these birds are predators in their own way too. But in our country the hawk is still quite rare and far more damage has been caused to both hawks *and* singing birds by so many aspects of man's civilized interests. No-one can pretend any predator deliberately goes after sick, foolish, unwary and sub-normal birds but these are the ones it most often catches. Thus the hawk's hunting is largely selective and is beneficial to the primary law of the wild kingdoms, the survival of the fittest, to keep a species fit, alert and healthy.

But above all I loved Buzz for his great beauty, his intractable nature and natural courage. Against a more powerful force or being he would have died rather than give in and he epitomised for me what it takes to be truly free. Fear only aroused his natural resistance, became a spur to inflexible will. Tiny though he may have been he was not equipped for compromise and for me he symbolised too what so many of us have lost.

As a boy the sparrowhawk I had laboriously carved over one and a half years of school woodwork lessons, one of the few objects I still retained from years of travel and civilised living, had been a symbol of freedom. Now, thirty years later, Buzz had become a living symbol unifying past and present, giving the future more meaning. I learned as much from him as I was ever able to teach him and he will live for ever in my memory.

13

WHEN IN EARLY AUGUST I heard at the big house that a large stag had indeed been shot by the summer visitor, I felt apprehensive. But later Iain told me that while it had been a good beast its antlers had held only seven points. I felt Sebastian now had a better head than that for even back in early June he had seemed to be growing a really good set. Eilean Shona was a stag sanctuary in winter but in summer the big deer often swam to and from the mainland from the north shore and as I hadn't seen Sebastian for some weeks I wondered if he had been killed on another estate.

But one misty dawn I looked out of the window – to see him standing where he had often grazed before – about two hundred yards south-east of the cottage in a lush grassy patch by an area of high bracken. His antlers were magnificient, still sheathed in the soft velvet which he would soon start to shed and I counted ten good points. I sneaked slowly outside with the new 1,000 mm telephoto lens and tried to focus it on Sebastian. It was a heavy, 12-pound, mirror lens and focusing it was a delicate matter and as often happened in misty early morning Highland light nothing at all registered on the camera's meter – not even at a 30th of a second which would be too slow with a hand-held telephoto lens anyway. But as he moved out of sight I saw from the huge slots made by his hoofs round the muddy perimeter of the roofed garden that he had been trying to get at my vegetables during the night.

By now the garden was in full flourish with seventy-one lettuces, rows of healthy carrots, and fifty-three transplanted cabbages where the radishes, long gone on salads, had grown, and I now evolved a plan to get close to Sebastian with the lesser-powered 300-mm lens which let in more light. As I picked supper vegetables, wearing gloves soaked in

Sebastian grazing in the bracken before dawn.

Sebastian sat down almost next to me in the bracken before dawn.

spruce needle juice – a trick I'd learned in Canada for reducing human scent – I laid many outer leaves in the area where he was now grazing at dawn. For three nights I left him to them and on the last two mornings they were eaten.

On the fourth night about an hour before dawn, wearing spruce-boiled camouflage clothes and dipped boots, I stole outside and lay down in the thick bracken. The wind was coming from the north-east and so ideal, blowing towards me from where Sebastian normally came. I lay there for some forty minutes, totally immobile, and was just thinking I was probably wasting my time when I heard a faint cropping noise. At first I was sure it was made by sheep but I raised my bush-hatted head extremely slowly.

Sebastian was there, only about eight yards from me! He was far too close for the telephoto lens so with agonizing care I unscrewed it and put on the standard lens. To my astonishment he came even nearer, went down on his knees, then with a slight flump sat down right by the edge of the bracken mere feet away. I had never had and probably would never have such a chance again.

Despite the bad light I opened the lens to full aperture, raised up slightly and click – one shot. Click – another. He turned his head towards me but showed no fear and did not leave. Another shot, then he rose to his feet. I was scared then that, knowing something was there but not quite what, he would come to investigate. A stag nearly always runs from man, though fatal attacks have occasionally occurred, and my heart seemed to be pounding loud enough for him to hear. I took another picture then, to clear the bracken fully, raised myself slowly to my knees. He just stared in curiosity, as if wondering what the fool who lived in the old croft and who had never done him any harm, was doing there on his knees in the bracken! Then he trotted off a few paces, turned round - for another photo. Then he walked slowly towards the east. Screwing on the 300-mm lens I followed him slowly taking more shots and he seemed more bewildered than scared but he finally disappeared among the trees along the shore.

Because of the poor dawn light the pictures were not perfect but at least were of a wild stag close to in its own habitat, not a park or "feeder" animal, and conveyed the realism of those exciting moments. Unfortunately I had "blown my cover" and he never came to that precise area again. But I was delighted that the "non-stalking" tech-nique which I'd learned in Canada for bears had also now worked with a wild Highland stag in Scotland.

When a week of gorgeous sunny weather followed the frequent wet days of the summer so far, the purple knapweed and thistle flowers which I had deliberately spared from the bracken scythe so bees would have their nectar, now thronged with many insect species. I was

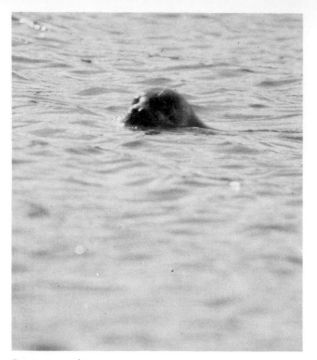

Sammy on the scrounge.

surprised to see, as with the earlier foxgloves, violets, wild parsleys, daisies, speedwell and buttercups which I had also protected, that many bluebottle flies also visited the flowers. It seemed that these pests, from the human viewpoint, also play a part in flower pollination. The butterflies too were now prolific. Green-veined whites were still flying like drifting snowflakes but the flowers were now covered with tortoiseshells, small blues and browns, an occasional comma and magnificient dark-green fritillaries which were not common in the coastal areas of the north-west Highlands.

It is often written that insects are brightly coloured as a warning to predatory birds that they are not good to eat. But as I watched the most brilliant and fast-flying butterflies it seemed the flashing colours as they flew, and the constant opening and shutting of their wings when feeding, helped them locate each other by sight. This is the initial attraction, then scent and behaviour patterns help them mate with the right species.

But once I was surprised to see one of the fritillaries persistently chasing after a tortoiseshell. Time and again the larger fritillary swooped after it but if it suffered from defective vision or felt inclined to mate with the wrong species, the little tortoiseshell clearly did not. It led the fritillary a merry air dance round and above the croft then soared back again, honing straight to the flowers. I even got a picture of this merry chase.

I was now feeding the seals every time I went fishing and it was clear that Sammy was far tamer than the others. As I made the usual soothing crooning sounds that seemed to allay their fears and arouse their curiosity he usually flopped into the water last. But within a minute he'd be up again, only yards from the boat, his snub nose and "bowler hat" pate far in front of the others. And he was usually the first to dive for the fish I threw in – as if showing he had the most right to the easy food. I used his tameness to get several photos but it was difficult from a rocking boat.

As he twisted and turned with bits of fish in his mouth, closing his eyes with that blissful look seals often have when playing in the water, I saw his right flipper had healed completely. There was thicker lighter-coloured tissue where the wound had been.

Through September my garden still provided me with large, succulent lettuces, and the craneflies now laid their eggs round the croft. What powerful instincts they had to perpetuate their species for they risked damage to their soft single wings and flimsy legs, bending them against the stiff grass stems to force their ovipositors deep into the soil so ensuring their eggs would survive. Their "leather jacket" larvae, well-known garden pests, were left alone as I wanted the life around me kept in a natural balance. I had seen the oystercatchers eating them and although it's not commonly known, the adult craneflies are an important food for red grouse, supplementing their usual diet of ling, heather and cranberry shoots, and on long treks round the island I seldom saw more than three or four grouse.

I was reminded of this lack of red grouse in the western Highlands today when I was lent a copy of *A Hundred Years In The Highlands* in which Osgood Mackenzie recorded the prolific wildlife and game in the region in the 1800s. The family game book for 1868 included 314 grouse, 33 black game, 49 partridges, 110 golden plover, 35 wild duck, 53 snipe and 184 hares, without mentioning vital numbers of geese, teal, ptarmigan and roe deer that had also been taken. "In other seasons I sometimes got as many as 96 partridges, 106 snipe and 95 woodcock. Now so many of these good birds and beasts are either quite extinct or on the verge of becoming so," the book lamented.

Perhaps it does not need a scientific sleuth to guess at one of the main causes.

Mackenzie records how he collected 200 gulls' eggs from Loch Maree islands in one afternoon, took osprey eggs as a boy, ("But, alas, the birds have been extinct in the region for at least sixty-five years."), how otters were shot in their dens, how his mother had forty to fifty marten skins brought to her by keepers every year from which "she made the most

145

lovely sable capes and coats for her sisters and lady friends", how he once shot three whooper swans one afternoon and how a foxhound pack killed a mother wildcat and her six kittens.

But the book is a valuable historic document for it clearly shows the fatuous attitudes towards most forms of wildlife that existed in those days, the total lack of a universal view of all life, the poor understanding of the roles of predator and prey species and the complicated food webs that exist in all nature. Such were the attitudes, the arrogant assumptions of mankind towards the natural world that were based purely on tradition which, as in many other parts of the world, is often itself based on stupidity and ignorance. Such an outlook, in the Highlands specifically, led to the near or complete extinction of such creatures as the wildcat, pine marten, polecat, white-tailed sea eagle, kites, and severe decreases in otter, hare, badger, swans, kites, geese and the osprey.

Despite the unintended comedy in some parts of the book I did not feel like laughing for it seemed to me that many of these attitudes towards "non-useful" wildlife still prevailed in the Highlands as well as in the other few wild parts of Britain. But after reading it one afternoon I went on a long hike and was treated to a short comedy show.

As I emerged from the Shona forest I saw a raven chasing a sparrowhawk. At first I thought it was Buzz but then saw it was a larger bird, a female. Suddenly she swerved down, sideways and back up, outmanoeuvring the great black bird by surprise tactics, using her longer tail to turn faster, and then she dived down upon *it*. The raven swerved only slightly then flew on, not at all worried by the apparent reversal of roles. It seemed it had been merely playing a game with the hawk and had had its kicks! And as the hawk glided back into the woods behind me the raven seemed to confirm this by turning almost on its back twice and making a loud "*boing*" sound in its throat, like a spring twanging, then flew out of sight. It was the first time I'd seen a raven fly upside down other than in the spring.

That evening the air was cold round my legs as I sat at the desk – summer was on its way out. Recalling the cold of the last two winters, I insulated the hardboard sheets on the front walls with treble thick-newspaper sheets. When trying to break into London as a country reporter I'd saved money by sleeping out in the big parks – and had found there was no finer cheap insulator against cold than newspapers.

In mid-September after four rainy days, a few hours of blazing sun encouraged a new batch of insects. I actually counted 215 gnats and small flies on the window at night. After just *one* hot afternoon, it seemed, millions of insects hatched but when the heavy rains returned two days later accompanied by cold early autumn gales from the north-east most of them must have perished without breeding. Coming up from the shore I saw some of the weaker butterflies and small moths dying on their backs, pinned to the ground and to rocks by the wet, or washed up on the beach after being blown into the sea.

Nature is ever callous towards the individual life and allows the greatest wastage of all in the insect world. I went indoors and lit the paraffin lamp wondering how long I could hold out *this* year without a fire, when I noticed how the light was shining on to the two largest ash trees outside. A strong wind was stirring them and suddenly the broad heads of the trees looked like a man with a beard kissing a girl, the smaller tree paler as if a blonde! His head was on hers, a branch had become his right arm around her neck and as they swayed he seemed to be pulling her closer. Odd how a little illusion like that can remind one of the isolation of the new winter ahead!

After brief showers on September 21 I was heading down to the beach to sack some seaweed fertiliser before it became too heavy and wet, when I found a huge fat drone fly dopey with the cold on a flag seam as if nearing the end of its life. As I stuffed weed into my sacks I saw a green-veined white butterfly clinging to a single purple knapweed on the shore line. How touching that it had chosen to die clinging to the only beautiful flower left in bloom there. A few large orb spiders had woven their last webs, the brown females with white crosses on their backs in the centres while smaller males waited in the wings, tugging at the lines to signal that they were ready to mate but were not prey.

Next day, anxious to post mail before the weekend, I boated out in increasing winds in the stiff-sided rubber boat when the engine began misfiring, clanked loudly, then broke down totally. I paddled with my hands to the shore below the forest, walked to the big house where the Vanes lent me a $1\frac{1}{2}$ hp engine, carried it back to the boat then made it to the pier. Dave the motor engineer who had given me Buzz took in my engine and lent me a small Seagull outboard. I took the $1\frac{1}{2}$ hp engine back to the big house but on the way back to my bay the Seagull also broke down in the mist and rain, and I had to paddle home with my hands again for the last mile. A fine omen for the new winter, I thought. As I came up the path, arms aching, the poor drone fly was still on the flag stem. I took it into the house to dry in a matchbox.

Two days later the mist lifted, the drizzle ceased and the sun shone so strongly in a blue sky it was like being back in the perspiring days of summer. I put the torpid, unmoving drone fly out in the sun. As the hot rays warmed it up it began to move its head from side to side. This odd-looking, almost peering movement of so large an insect was most disconcerting for it almost seemed to be a *thinking* animal. It began to crawl up a bracken stem then with a sudden brief *buzz* it flew strongly away.

Bees had now appeared again, hover flies had also emerged from hiding and zinged near my face as I sunbathed and played Beethoven's *Pastoral* outside on the little battery player – it *did* sound a little wheezy outside! Later I went fishing, caught some unusually late mackerel and saw the most beautiful sunset I had so far witnessed on Shona. As I walked up the slope with the fish, picking a cabbage from the garden and slooshing it in the burn without a pause in stride, I glimpsed a blue-grey flash in front of the croft. A sparrowhawk, surely Buzz, shot up from the grassy patch by the garden put he kept his tail closed so I could not see any gap from the lost feathers. He had been at some meat scraps hauled off the bird table by the robins, who preferred to eat from the ground if they could.

Next week Dave broke the bad news on my boat engine – big end worn out, crank and one piston ruined. It would take time to get the parts and would be a costly job. Oh well, I had a good food supply and much writing to complete. By now, after working over a quarter of a million words from notebooks, old letters and diaries, I felt the Canadian wilderness book was now coming right.

For some time Dave and I had discussed a possible boat trip up a long, undeveloped fresh-water loch which seemed worth exploring. It was a sunny day with three hours of daylight left. Why not *now*? we drove to it, hired a boat and after four miles of dodging various sandbanks, we were passing long pine and larch forests. Then in the widest part of the loch we came to an island where great snags of dead trees lay against each other like the huge whitened bones of prehistoric animals. The whole scene reminded me so intensely of the wild Canadian inlets I was now writing about, I half expected to see a grizzly saunter out to graze on the marshy grasses! A golden eagle sailed low overhead, black against the sky, her long, broad wings upturned at the tips by the warm southerly winds, and two cormorants winged by like great dark geese to land on the branches of a dead lone spar. As we headed towards a small inlet on the south shore, high conical mountains wreathed in haze seemed to go on for ever, and as we entered the bay, the steep hillsides covered with dark spruce trees, the strange impression increased.

"It's magnificent," I said. "What a place to live! It's as fine as anything I saw in Canada yet somehow more intimate."

Ye'd have a wee job finding an available cottage up here," said realist Dave who had been trying for months himself to find a place of his own and leave the caravan. "What few exist are used once a year for stalkers' shelter or for a month or two by summer home owners." I knew he was right because apart from my frustrating searches before being allowed to live on the island, I had for the past year also been making unsuccessful attempts to buy or lease a cottage with its own land in a wild *forested* area where I could study the wildlife.

As we came out of the inlet again I glanced up the loch. In the distance, illumined by a shaft of sunlight, stood a tiny white cottage flanked by two woods. It was a good three miles further on and with our little engine, the wind increasing, sun dying low, we did not go to look at it. I felt sure it would not be available. On the way back we walked over a little green island that had been a Highland burial ground for centuries. There some of the great Highland chiefs had been laid to rest including John of Islay, one of the Lords of the Isles and the first to be called Chief of the Clanranalds, who had lived at the castle whose ruins still stood gloomy sentinel over the sea loch on which I now lived. With a slight start I recalled my mother's father John Stewart had been born on Islay himself. I suddenly felt quite strange and as we boated back in the gathering dusk I kept seeing the little cottage and the small woods in my mind.

One glorious afternoon in October after several cloudy days, I saw three tortoiseshell butterflies flitting near the outside roof beams of the croft. They were looking for shelter in which to hibernate for the winter. Even on what seemed a perfect summer day the shortage of flower nectar, decreased amount of light, the nip in the air, told their delicate mechanisms that winter was on its way. I left the doors open and when one finally winged into my room and lodged in the corner above the bookshelves it seemed I'd have at least one companion in the harsh months ahead.

On my next visit to the store, then run by Highlander Allan MacColl, I mentioned my feelings on journeying up the fresh water loch. He said I had always seemed someone who wanted to fit in with the area as it *was*, not change it by developmnt and had shown I could live in a primitive place. "There is a wee cottage up there you might get," he added then gave me a few ideas on how to go about it. To my surprise he was referring to the cottage I'd seen. A few days later, although I felt it hopeless, I contacted the land owner. To my further surprise he said while it might be difficult because of forthcoming new leasehold laws in Scotland he would think about it.

Oddly, during this short Indian summer new buttercups and daisies started flowering and humble-bees were working them along with the white bramble flowers which were always the latest blooms of all. I came back from a walk at dusk to find that a wren, looking for a warm roost, had come into the croft and had fallen into the bucket of water I used for cooking. It seemed near death but was still *swimming* feebly with shuffling wings. I dried it out by placing it on a warm cushion then caught some insects for it from those attracted to the window by the lamp light. Every time its beak opened when my hand went near, I popped them in with a pair of tweezers.

I let it spend the night in a hay-lined box and even put the paraffin heater on. By morning it had recovered and was fluttering at the wire netting on the box. When I took it outside it struggled with incredible strength for so small a bird. Like shrews who can eat well over twice their own weight of worms and insects in a day, the wren has a high body metabolism and next to the hummingbird, perhaps, is probably the strongest bird in the world for its size.

There is a fine Gaelic story about the wren. One day in the misty past all the birds assembled in a glen and decided that the one who could fly the highest would be their king. The golden eagle, of course, was sure he would win. But the wee wren shocked them all by challenging the mighty eagle. Up went the great bird of prey, soaring completely out of sight, then he cried "where are you now, silly little wren?" But the wren had secretly perched on the huge bird's back and being fresh he flew up even higher calling out as he went "Fad, fad os do cheann!" ("Far, far above you!"). And in that way the wren became king of all the birds.

By mid-October, although crane flies were still laying their eggs, moths and other insects no longer came to the window. Curlews were again assembling on the beaches for easier pickings than on the cold lands where they had nested and spent most of the summer. They now made curious bubbling calls when alarmed.

One night I went to fetch some water with my lamp in the dark when I was startled by a great, grey, ghostly shape rising like a giant bat in front of me. It was Harry Heron, right by the croft. I kept watch then and found he was flying in close at dusk and landing right in the burn, to catch frogs and other small water creatures. It was clear he could hunt at night and could fly straight home in almost complete darkness. Over the centuries, to escape man's presence and often direct persecution, foxes and otters slowly became more nocturnal creatures, and I wondered if this might be happening with herons too. Or perhaps it was because more small water creatures emerged at night to scavenge for their own food.

Harry was not as wary as most wild herons but he was by no means tame. Although he occasionally swooped over my *moving* boat with hoarse "*kraink kraink*" cries, when I tried to stalk him on foot on the beaches he took off before I was in reasonable camera range. He had also renewed his "friendship" with the lonely lame seagull I had often seen flying on nearby beaches. This was odd for normally gulls and herons exist in a state of mutual suspicion – herons have been known to pluck young gulls from island nests and when a heron catches a fish nearby gulls, especially the greater black backs, will swoop down hoping to make it drop its prey for them to snatch.

It took several days of frustrated stalks before I could get close enough to see what was happening. They often stood close together on windy rocks – with the gull apparently using Harry's much larger body as a windbreak! They also seemed to have evolved an odd "game" for sometimes the gull would leap into the air, circle and then dive over the heron's long-necked head several times, with poor Harry having to "lower the boom" as the gull shot closer and closer. Yet Harry never flew away. Certainly the gull was a loner, not part of the gregarious herring-gull flock, perhaps because it had a twisted foot. Maybe this is what it and Harry had in common.

When the fine weather spell ended a feeling of real winter came. The lamp had to be lit before 6 pm now, rain drummed on the roof, drips from leaky gutters plink-plonked outside, new mice made nightly thumps in the wooden walls as they tried to reach the food stores, the ash trees stooped under the weight of soggy leaves, and the path filled up with slippery ooze. Now the bracken had turned yellow and with the nettles, now spidery brown with seedpods, it fell in swathes before the new gales. Heavy rain really hastens the look of winter upon the landscape by beating everything down physically and drowning the roots of small plants.

One day, with my engine still not repaired, I had to row the five miles to and from the pier for supplies as I had not been out for well over a week. It was a hard trip back for I made barely a yard with each pull of the oars against the wind, and the darkness was almost pitch black. But the sea always gives off a faint luminous light at night and once you know the land and shape of the hills and can just make out their tops in the dimness, you can reach home safely.

14

AFTER HAULING THE BOAT on to its wooden cradle I was walking up the steep muddy path when I was startled out of my wits by a large stag, standing on a low bank in the burn, which suddenly gave a loud roar when I was less than ten yards away. It was not a sound of anger but the long hoarse bellow stags make in the autumn rut and it was the first time I'd heard it that year. I was sure it was Sebastian as I could just make out his form, looking as big as a moose in the twilight against the dark sky. When I neared the croft, heart thumping, I cupped my hands and roared back, and we had quite a contest – until my sore throat gave out. His roars came nearer as if he was actually following me. I dived inside for my torch but only glimpsed the whitish tan of his backside as he was away. I wondered if he had not gathered enough hinds into his "harem" yet and had decided to take no chances with anything else that moved. "Get out of my area" he was perhaps saying.

Next day I helped Iain MacLellan, his wife Morag and three other helpers to gather the island's sheep for sales and winter dipping. They were short-handed. The number of men who would turn out for this hard chore on a mountainous island, involving a double boat trip and hard hill footslogging over a long day for a small standard wage, had dwindled yearly. After that day I was not surprised. We had to drive the sheep in three separate wide arcs up and down the hills, over peat bogs and through the woods and into a large stone-walled fank at the eastern end of the island. After supper at Iain's home I still had to walk the two miles back again to reach home. As I came near the croft in the dark, tired out, I was once more greeted by the rutting roars of Sebastian, but from further away this time.

Early next morning I tried to photograph him with his hinds. I found them almost a mile away in a deep corrie on the Atlantic edge of the island but he only had nine hinds with him. While the island was a stag sanctuary in winter the hind population was never large, perhaps because of the grazing competition from the sheep. Red deer, the largest wild mammals left in Britain, have a mainly matriarchal society. All year the hinds, their young up to three years old and new calves born early June, keep to their own herds. The mature stags, who leave the hind herds at three years old, keep their own company in loose bachelor groups, usually grazing different areas from the hinds who crop closer than they do. But come the rutting season at the end of September and early October, the stag groups break up. One by one, the big "master" stags first, they come down from the higher hills and look for hinds to round up into their breeding "harems".

Sebastian, probably a four-year-old when he had first come around the croft, had carried eight points last year and had ten this. Like all stags, he would have cast his antlers in early April. Almost immediately the new ones had begun to grow under a soft nutrient "velvet" skin covering through spring and summer. From mid August the velvet had slowly peeled off, helped by rubbing on trees and bushes, and his antlers then hardened. At the same time his sex glands became stimulated, his mane grew, his neck thickened and by late September Sebastian, who would have shown no interest in females for some ten months, was ready for the rut.

As I now watched him, safely hidden leeward of a knoll, he walked round his harem but the hinds seemed totally unconcerned by his presence. Now at his most aggressive as he sought to ward off any rivals who came near his "wives", he frequently paused to roar his challenge across the corrie. Sometimes the roars tailed off lamely as if with frustration, and sounded rather like an old man groaning loudly with toothache. These roars seemed less of a challenge than an intimidation, to warn other stags to stay away. There was another smaller, younger stag higher up who had only three hinds and two calves with it. He gazed down at Sebastian's nine as if coveting some of them but he did not venture too far down. Twice Sebastian rushed at hinds as if about to mount but both slipped away easily. Occasionally he trotted round them with short blatting roars "*oh oh oh*," as if he were a large, horned sheepdog rounding up sheep.

The concept of the "Monarch of the Glen" is not true as far as the hinds are concerned for, apart from mating with the stag at the precise time *they* are ready – hinds are only in season about twenty-four hours in a twenty-one-day period at this time - they take little notice of him. In presence of danger, such as the scent of man, it is normally the leading hind, often an old yeld, who barks the alarm and when she runs the

153

other hinds and calves follow her, often leaving the huge amorous swain gazing after them in dismay.

Watching Sebastian and his hinds at dusk on another evening I noticed that he stood quite motionless by one hind, scenting her as if trying to tell when she was precisely ready, and she licked his neck and face with half-closed eyes. Then he trotted round behind her, mounted and served her with one convulsive heave. The hind seemed to hunch too, he slipped down again and it was all over. I wondered if red deer had evolved this swift lovemaking from the days when bears, wolf and lynx – and later man – were their predators and they needed to be alert at all times!

Sebastian seemed to lose interest in that particular hind and an hour later when she moved away from the group he made no effort to stop her. It seemed likely, if she came into a second season, a younger or weaker stag would be able to serve her but by that time the big stag's seed had been securely planted.

Stags, usually hard to approach in summer, are far less wary during the rut and for this reason, *and* because they are now in peak condition after good feeding, this is the time the Scots estate stalkers and their "guests" do the stag stalking which, if done properly, culls the surplus animals from the hills. (The hind shooting and culling is performed by estate staff between October 21 and February 16 and until the late 1970s when venison rose in price had been regarded more as a work chore than a revenue-producing sport) although of course, as with the stags, the carcases are sold.

To allow red deer to become too numerous on the Highland hills is poor conservation because after several mild winters their numbers burgeon – populations in fact increased from some 180,000 in the mid 1960s to some 270,000 in 1979 - they outgrow their feeding ranges, and control is necessary. Man has wiped out the deer's natural predators and if he does not assume the predator role himself, the herds carry many old and runty animals prone to disease and death through cold and starvation and winter mortality is then tragically high. Also, when grazing and browsing thus become scarce, red deer invade agricultural land and young forests, break through fences, browse the growth tips off young trees, strip bark, and inflict great damage. And not only to man's artificial commercial forests for, along with sheep and *uncontrolled* heather burning, they also prevent the natural regeneration of the few wild forests left and new young trees on the hills.

Watching Sebastian with his hinds at this time I found he initially showed curiosity and aggression toward any source of disturbance, and would sometimes trot closer, just as he did if I imitated his roars. Poachers can use such tactics, just as they use powerful torches and vehicle lights at night – for red deer are less afraid of vehicles than a man on foot – to blind the animals before shooting. Rightly, there are heavy penalties for such knavery. Many deer escape with fearful wounds from poor shots by poachers, just as they do from the occasional incompetent stalker, and die lingering agonizing deaths in the hills.

Once during a dawn walk I came across Sebastian having a wallow in a peat bog where he seemed to have trodden the peat and mud into a blackish cream. It seemed he did this to rid himself of flies, keds and other pests but he emerged looking dark and fearsome and perhaps he did it also to look more intimidating to other stags for deer are more scared of dark objects than light. Again he just *walked* away showing no sign of aggression or great fear. It surprised me that he had so far not been shot but perhaps he knew me as a harmless individual. Anyway I strengthened my garden roof as the cabbages were in top shape now and many lettuces were still left, as were the carrots I had yet to store in a clamp.

By mid-October, with natural food harder to find, Little Fat Sergeant came back to the bird table with his family but his hen and two youngsters disappeared after two more days, probably migrating to the village area at the head of the loch. As I painted six more sections of the tin roof in a dry spell bees were still working the brambles and a big blue Aeshna dragonfly was hawking along the burn for insect prey but its wings were now brittle and rattled with apparent old age.

Now the north-west winds began to blow, bringing heavier rain and churning up the seas. I lit the paraffin stove on October 19, having lasted without it only one day more than last year. Curlews were clustered on the sandbanks, all facing the winds, a sure sign of stormy weather but by the 21st Dave had my boat engine repaired and so thankful was I to get the 7-hp outboard back on to my boat the £60 bill seemed not so bad. As I came back, no longer having to row, a flock of fieldfares with dark bodies and whirring wings flew over the boat, heading for the rich farmlands to the east. I counted fifty-one oyster-catchers, all bunched miserably together on a grassy island above the main sandbank near the pier. They all faced the same way, into the gales, and a few days later had flown south, probably to the mussel and cockle areas of the Welsh coastline.

By now the insect life above ground seemed to have ceased. Finding a last humble-bee hanging as if dead on a faded knapweed flower, I touched its furry back and it moved slightly. When I brought it into my warm room it recovered a little and began to stumble across the desk, towards the light where it could *work*. I put it on another flower and its first instinct was to lower its tongue and with its last dying energy try to find nectar for the nest. But it was too weak now and as the natural cold enveloped it once more it fell off from weakness and clung to the underside of a leaf, waiting patiently for death.

A winter storm sweeps in from the Atlantic.

At the end of the month with the brief spans of most insects over, only a few spiders, beetles and flies crouched beneath leaves, in rock crevices, under tree bark and in the croft eaves, as if hoping for just one more try at life in the sun. The eggs, larvae or pupae of their myriad species were now ready to over-winter and of these only the strongest and most securely placed would survive. I picked the last of the blackberries, having culled nine pounds from just four bushes, but I left many for the small birds whose purple droppings showed how much they needed such food.

The long aching winter silences once more lay ahead, the hours of slogging away on the typewriter. Fending off loneliness and the depressing fact that after six years' work I had still not sold either of the two books I really cared about, I went for twice-weekly treks. I ran or half-walked across the hills to Shona House for my mail. Coming back once, the sky a metallic blue-grey and shot with orange and a crimson underlay from a vanished sun, I felt I was walking in a Celtic or Greek legend. I seemed to see the forge of Vulcan in the sky, leaden, horrible, glowing to the west with an air of latent doom and death as in the north-east wind I strode, leaping across brown bracken that twisted and snarled at the feet. A huge stag, almost certainly Sebastian, now finished with the rut and pinch-bellied with semi-starvation, leaped with a flash of his light rump patch, stamped on a twig and vanished into the forest gloom. With what ponderous lightness he moved, his clean heavy bulk moving like a dancer. But as always after a trek, when I reached home I felt better. One is always more creative and alive spiritually and mentally after physical exercise than from just sitting down all day and *thinking*. Never more than in a wilderness life is one reminded again and again that the human body and soul are, in this existence at least, really interdependent.

Through the gales and hailstorms of November, finance dwindling, the Canadian book rejected yet again, I kept writing. I decided to aim for a wider audience and sent two stories to *Reader's Digest*, plus some notes I'd made when training sparrowhawk Buzz to be free in the wild. A lifeline was thrown by the popular English magazine who had received such reader response from the earlier article about living in the wilds that they commissioned another, this time to be written by me. At least I now had some photos to go with it. I felt like an ageing fighter saved from defeat by the bell.

By the end of the month the constant onslaught of the newly swollen burn had carved a new path on the shore, filling the usual boat parking area with rocks, gravel and banks of debris. It took two days with a crowbar to clear a new landing deck. Shopping trips were only twice a month now. Each time I would come back to another fortnight's total isolation, the outboard burbling away, driving me through an unreal

The storm breaks.

liquid world of almost complete darkness, the inky oily sea slipping by, the stars above in patches between the hail clouds, the brightest far away to the west over the horizon, and hard granite rocks waiting to hole the boat if one made a mistake. Once I was rewarded when Sammy Seal came really close. It seemed he had not migrated to the warmer bays further south like some of the other seals but I had no fish to give him now. By early December even the gulls were fewer, the smaller common gulls had gone south to work for livings round harbours, fields or even city dumps. Just a few curlew, greater black backs and herring-gulls still cruised widely.

On one supply trip I saw a small flock of seventeen white-fronted geese flying high and heading south-east. "They're away south," said someone at the store. "It'll be a hard winter." But at dawn next day exactly the same sized flock headed over the croft, this time flying *north*. In fact white fronts spent all the winter in the area, just migrating ten or twelve miles some days to other favourite grazings. Although many of these have been whittled away by development, as there are far less geese than a hundred years ago the birds still have a choice of pastures. And certainly that winter proved no worse than the previous two.

With increasing rains, hail and a few days of whirling snow the ground round the croft became waterlogged and I had to dig a drainage ditch into the burn to drain the mountain run-off from my foundations. The garden carrots were now sprouting little white roots so out they all came, along with much of the cabbage, for a two-day clamping and brining session and then I dug over the whole garden, turning in the seaweed and compost. As I worked, Little Fat Sergeant, two robins and a blackbird who were now using the bird table landed in the newly turned soil for the worms and grubs. I noticed no matter how much rain fell the birds' feathers were always dry. It is not only ducks, gulls and other water birds who have oiled feathers – *all* birds have to some extent and even little "dicky birds" have at least showerproof suits. Only when a bird is old or in poor condition do the feathers admit the wet, hastening their deaths in winter. A few days later a hedge-sparrow began coming to the table but the little wrens never did.

One snowy day, my feet cold despite three pairs of socks and hill boots, I was working away yet again on the Canadian book, wondering if I ought not to just give it up and head south to warmer climes and easier work for a few weeks when something made me look out of the window.

There, creeping along like a little winged mouse through the brown bracken stubs, searching for insects and seeds, was a tiny wren. As it explored the frosty crevices between bracken and grass tufts, it shook little snow showers over itself. Once it caught an old spider's web over its head and cleaned it off with its toes like a cat, moving its foot so fast it was a blur. Then on it went again, refusing to give up. At that moment I decided if the little wren could stick it out so could I. If Robert the Bruce could be inspired by a spider then I could learn a lesson in courage from a wren, and I kept on with my work.

Each Christmas alone I worked out some new little philosophy to help me keep going. And that year I invented a good new one. I imagined I had been sentenced to death and that on the last morning the priest came in and said "The governor says your sentence has been commuted to life imprisonment". I realized how grateful I would be in such a situation, although facing long years cooped up in a jail cell, just to be still alive! Well, I'm alive now, I told myself. And I'm not cooped up. I'm free. So what the hell am I worrying about! And the depression passed.

On Boxing Day afternoon Harry Heron passed like a great cloud by the window and landed in the burn. I hastened for the camera but before I could reach the door he was away again, his broken toe sticking out clearly. I went to see what he had been after but saw only a dipper flying, white rump flashing from its dark brown body, straight up the burn with a faint "*chink*" cry.

I looked towards Shoe Bay – to see a buzzard hovering some fifty yards above the ground, then it dropped straight down like a huge kestrel. I tried to stalk it with the camera but the ground was bitterly cold and wet so I did not crawl, and from nearer than I had judged it to be the big bird flew off. I secured only a brown blur on the film. There was a dead ewe there and she had been ripped about by a fox, buzzards and ravens. That afternoon I built a hide some thirty yards away. Two days later I went into it but despite a shivering four-hour wait nothing came down. I learned then that working a hide with such a sharp-sighted bird as the buzzard requires at least two people to walk in. Then the bird sees someone walking away, thinks the coast is clear and comes down. She could have been high in the sky and seen me coming from two miles away. I was learning but slowly.

So the third winter on Shona passed but the main breakthrough in my wish to write solely about the natural world came in January. *Reader's Digest* sent back the written stories but were interested in a new one about training the young sparrowhawk to fly and hunt for itself. They warned it was highly unlikely a newcomer would be able to meet their criterion of short but densely focused articles but were prepared to guarantee me a basic fee to have a try.

No experience in the Highlands had been so complete as the weeks with Buzz. After nearly seven years of mainly wilderness living I was coming up to forty-five. This would have to be the best thing I had ever written or maybe I had no chance. For days I slaved away, taking temporary respites in hikes, jotting down little phrases that came as I walked, my mind filled with the hawk's piercing eyes, his indomitable will, trying to encapsulate the little innuendos I wanted to make comparing hawk and man and all the wild creatures with whom we share the web of life, the chains of time and the splendours of our earth. Yet the words constantly escaped. Writing, cutting, discarding, re-writing, I had it finished after twelve long working days and posted it off.

I now felt I should really intensify the efforts of the last two years to obtain my own wild place to study, in a far larger undisturbed area. I loved Shona but while the Vanes would let me stay on *ad infinitum* I had no real security of tenure. Also, in summers, the sandy lagoon which was the otters' main playground and was the best place to watch and photograph them was often filled with visitors who had not slogged through the winters in the area, and football, barking dogs and bonfires replaced the otters. The one summer morning when I thought I had obtained a fine film of otters swimming and of one chewing a fish on a rock ended in disaster. I did not have the film developed until after summer was over and it came out totally black. In my excited haste I had not wound it correctly on to the take-up reel, the film had not gone through although the numbers had mounted up on the dial. From such failures, and the foolish belief *one* film was enough on such a subject, the amateur learns hard lessons.

But my efforts to buy or lease my own place proved frustrating. Offered seventeen acres at a good price I spent days reconnoitering where and how I would build, only to be told by a lawyer in the nick of time to forget it - it was common grazing land. One owner said if I could find an old ruin to repair on a bay I liked we could talk about a twenty-year lease. I stumbled over the rocky wooded hills for two days and found a ruined croft hidden in the trees, but was finally offered only a five-year lease. No-one with his brains intact is going to build a new home in such terrain when it could revert to the owner in five years. I heard of an idyllic spot at the head of a sea loch eighty miles away and drove to see it. Perfect little cottage with a gravel beach only yards away. Then I met some forestry workers. "The place crawls with hikers and campers in summer and the rock slabs above the cottage are used by a climbing club." Good for them, bad for me, and that was the end of that. Once I even drove down to Wales to see an isolated cottage in the rare red kite country. But the hills in that particular part of Wales did not compare with the Highlands and the price was beyond what I had any hopes of raising anyway.

When I received yet another put-off letter from a large estate to the north I felt increasingly annoyed with absentee landlords who own vast unused tracts, spent little time in the Highlands except to use them as a sporting playground to kill fish or deer, yet would not part with a single acre or allow one to rebuild a ruined cottage. Yet in all this, I was now glimpsing, lies the greatest dilemma of the natural world of the Highlands - without such unused tracts wildlife would be more disturbed and decimated than it is. Nationalisation would be the answer, said some folks. But only if it set aside vast areas as wildlife reserves, where all development under the guise of progress and "economic viability" was severely restricted, would nationalisation work to preserve these finest areas of the natural world left in Britain. In one critical Highland reserve in the Speyside area where the rare ospreys were returning to nest after their persecution last century, the R.S.P.B. have shown that temporarily high human density and a sensitive wild species *can* co-exist but only after extreme vigilance and expensive intelligent wardening. Nationalisation seemed an unlikely candidate for the ecological understanding and sensitivity needed to achieve this over far larger areas throughout the year.

I was now totally fascinated not only by wildlife itself but the complicated interacting roles of man, wildlife and the whole natural world. Two million folk visit the Highlands annually and most of them, often subconsciously, come to this vast natural heritage *for* its wildness, its rugged beauty, the possible glimpse of a peregrine falcon arcing across the sky like an arrow from the gods, a golden eagle soaring the misty peaks, a fox in the gloaming, a badger rooting in the woodland debris at dusk, a red deer stag roaring across the glens. It seemed to me now, too, that to preach conservation of wildlife for merely its own sake was no longer enough because an important value of wildlife and the natural world is also what they can do *for* man. As I was now writing in the Canadian book the last wilderness places not only filtered our water, regulated climate and produced oxygen but were a last fine source of spiritual inspiration for city flayed souls, places to take stock and develop awareness of oneself, to contemplate, to become more in tune with the great universe beyond man, be inspired by nature's wonders, and become more spiritually complete.

The wilderness had helped me during a critical period in my life and I now wanted to communicate its great value *for* man in several books, and the only way to achieve this was to try and write accurately in the deepest detail, to impart any insights gained, from total involvement and personal experience. Above all I wanted a place with trees for woodland combined with open glen and hill, gives the best habitat for wildlife. And I needed a large, wild, uninhabited area behind it too through which I could trek the year round with camera and notebook. Perhaps then, with luck and surrendering totally to the wilds for some more years, I might be able to write with understanding.

For days now the memory of the tiny cottage set in its own little woods nine miles up the fresh-water loch returned to my mind. By now

I'd heard from the landowner that while he would not sell the cottage freehold he might grant me a lease if the leasehold law changes could be overcome. It seemed there might be a chance! When I told this news to Allan MacColl at the store one early February day, he said "Why don't you go up there when it's fine in the spring and take a good look at it. You'll not find a wilder place in all the Highlands."

But when I returned to the little pier the thought struck me: "No, I will go and see it *now*, in the winter when it's at its worst. I'll camp out there in the cold, pay the price, get the feel of the place." That evening I visited the estate's keeper who said I could use the deerstalking boat which had been left in a small inlet in a pine wood some six and a half miles from the cottage. I had just shopped so I had enough food. I had no tent but there were a couple of sheets of plastic in the Land Rover which would do. I had a mug, a lighter, two pots and a sleeping bag in the truck too. What more did I need? I removed the engine from my boat, stowed it below the vehicle and with hailstones banging on the metal roof slept the night by the pier.

Wraiths of mist covered the gunmetal sea next morning and dark clouds drifted overhead but I was determined to go. I filled my pack with the pans, plastic sheets, camera, lentils, rice, two hard-boiled eggs, mince, raisins, bread and three onions then drove up a dirt track-road past a farm and found the wooden stalkers' boat half full of rainwater resting on the sandy bottom of a small burn mouth. I bailed it out with a pan, fitted my engine, loaded in the pack and extra jerrican of fuel and set off up the loch with a strong westerly wind at my back. It was an eerie, ghostly trip in the near dark and I didn't see another human being or boat in the full six and a half miles.

The huge old pine snags, remnants of the original forest which had been uprooted by gales on the island and which had gleamed like whitened bones on the sunny, early autumn trip with Dave now looked different. Stark and grey reminders of a primeval age, dark peat showed between their blackened roots. A lone merganser fluttered from the rough water before me into the wind, circled over the boat with odd harsh croaks then sped downwind, its white wing patches twinkling before it vanished into the misty gloom ahead. The force of the wind increased and I nearly went aground on a long gravelly spit but I fought my way off sideways with an oar before the waves filled the stern and carried on, rolling with the troughs past a long wood of leafless oaks and birches that clothed the steep slopes below the grey and tawny hills. The further I went the darker it became so that it was occasionally hard to make out where the dark grey of the loch waters met the threatening dank blackness of the sky. Once I had the feeling that while I would reach my destination I might not get back and my gloved hands were so cold that I had to grip them in the crook behind my knees for warmth.

The loch level was high and as I neared the shore below the cottage I saw the waves were falling onto a green, grassy bank. I swung the prow into the waves so it would divide rather than ship the rough water, leaped out and hauled the stern as far as I could up the bank. Even on that dark day the place seemed idyllic. The small L-shaped cottage stood above a forty-yard area of land covered with brown bracken and rushes and between two small woods. As I walked round them counting twenty-one different kinds of trees and eighty-four windfalls, ideal for building lumber and firewood, I found an unusual situation. The four-acre west wood was mostly coniferous with silver and Douglas firs, spruce and several kinds of pine, while the larger east wood which flanked the main burn and a spectacular waterfall had mainly deciduous trees with feathery larch, spreading oaks, ash, birch, holly, rowan and tall, stately beech trees predominating. Here were two separate woodland environments. Clumps of nut-bearing hazel bushes abounded everywhere and I was just thinking how ideal the whole area seemed to be for wildlife when I saw a red squirrel scampering over a ruined wall. The cottage itself, its windows and roof intact, was protected from both the east and west by the woods, from the north by high mountains whose first hills began a few yards behind a small dilapidated woodshed, and was screened from the loch by a fringe of ash, hazel and alder trees which ran along the shore.

Right then I went for a six-mile trek to a large river, back up a steep killer of a hill to nearly 1,800 feet, so sheer in places I had to hold onto jutting rocks or small trees, then returned over the tussock-filled plateaus along the tops and down again to the cottage. I found wildcat tracks in an open patch of sandy ooze by the river and a pair of buzzards spiralled above in the dark sky, the larger female higher and scanning the long view for carrion while the male floated along the rockfaces like a shadow, A single red grouse shot from near my feet and whirred over a ridge, a kestrel beat past way below, a flickering copper light against the black loch, and two red deer hinds trotted away in a half circle, halted as if to make sure they had really seen a man, their long ears coming forward tardily as I took a picture knowing the light was really too poor.

Before dusk I made camp out of the wind in the east wood, gathering wet brown bracken for bedding below one of the plastic sheets. The ideal flat spot was under a huge oak tree but first I eyed it carefully for dead branches above, then jumped up to pull one spike off as I had no wish to be skewered during the night. Then I staked the other plastic sheet down with twigs over three bent hazel wands to make a low "tent".

As I wandered through the quiet woods again, the waterfall spouting its white and tawny waters over three forks, the burn tinkling and gurgling through rocky pools so that it was as if I could hear friendly voices amid the music, the wind sighing through the branches above, there seemed an aura of magic about the place. New and old images were coming together strangely in my mind, the great conifers and deep gorge above the falls reminded me of Canada, the hazel bushes fused into the Sussex woodlands of my boyhood, but those images faded and my Highland blood stirred as I realized a feeling of love for this wild, lonely, beautiful place had already put down roots into my heart.

I wondered if this was the final destination, was this the end of the long search? I do not know if I spoke aloud or just thought the words but as the old Scots-Indian Tihoni had taught me in Canada, I walked to the trees touching each one, the oaks, the rowans who are the guardians of lonely homes in Gaelic lore, the beeches and larches. Like the Indians of North America the real old Highlanders had a mystic feeling and reverence for their land, reflected in the poetic Gaelic names for the burns, waterfalls, bays and hills. And Tihoni, with Highland blood himself, who had taught me some of the ancient arts of tracking animals, had told me how the Indians invested every mountain, fall and river with its own deity, good or evil, linked to the great god of all, the Great Spirit. I recalled how his words had made more sense to me than the concept of a single impersonal God, religions that dismissed all animal creation, and the meaningless litanies, chants and catechisms of the churches, and now I asked the trees, the whole wild place and its spirits of the past, if they wanted me there. It was eerie, misty, and strange, wonderful feelings were coming. My heart was pounding as if I were speaking first words to an admired woman and I think I said "If you do want me here, help me".

It was a hard task to get a fire going as I broke off dry wood from dead branches below the canopy of a huge spruce and packed the twigs with half-dry bracken from below the biggest clumps. But eventually I got it going between a square of small rocks and cooked a supper of broth mix, onions and mince, using an old piece of fencing wire for a grille. It began to drizzle and it was hard getting to sleep at first. What with my excitement and the noise made by great splats of water falling from the oak branches above on to the plastic that kept me dry. Once I heard a strange thumping and snuffling. The treads sounded heavy and I thought it must be a deer but as I poked my head out I was just in time to see a large boar badger veer off and trundle away through the gloom.

As I hauled myself out on my elbows at dawn I was scared by a loud hoffing bark - a small herd of red deer hinds, my scent obscured by the "tent", had been grazing nearby and the leading hind had given the alarm. As they cantered away up into the hills a small tribe of bullfinches came along, peeping mournfully as they investigated a few

164

old fruit trees lost among the hazel growth for early buds. As I ate my usual trekking breakfast of cheese, fruitcake and cereal, they were followed by a flock of tiny long-tailed tits, filling the damp air with high-pitched "*zee zee zees*" as they flitted like flying musical crochets through the twigs above.

Striking camp and putting everything back into the pack, I hiked through the long woods that lay to the west, finding several old nests of hoodies and buzzards in the bare trees. Then I boated right up to the far end of the loch below the high conical mountains and in the strong following winds until I saw the village at its head. When I turned back the waves hit the boat with great force and the engine began to sputter and cut out as it still often did in stormy water. For the first time I realized why – water was slapping up through the slightly broken lid and was shorting out the plug wiring. How strange that I should solve that mystery in this new place.

Sitting in the centre of the boat to keep the stern up I turned the engine down to its lowest speed where the spark seemed strongest and rowed in that fashion for ten miles until I was near the long gravelly spit of land. Making headway was a real battle in the foaming waters, the troughs shorter and deeper than in the sea because of the narrowness of the loch. But I felt the strange wonderful surge of total solitude for the loch and hills were totally devoid of human life, as if there was only myself left in the world. Sweat poured down as I heaved at the oars, mingling with the rain on my brow. One man against nature - get there, get there or die, but all you know is to keep battling. It was now getting dusk so I pulled into the lee of some small cliffs on which stood a dark conifer wood just across the water from the island with the giant snag trees. I felt as I had on my first boat trek up a wild British Columbian inlet but I hadn't made that in the dead of winter and I'd also had my old wild dog Booto with me. Now I was totally alone. Dear old Booto, I thought, as I heaved the boat up. How I wish he were with me now. But I knew he was still well for friends still wrote to me of how he went visiting various folks in their cabins on that coast.

I camped for the second night in the arbour of the pines and firs, woken up from damp, fitful sleep by a branch thumping down twenty-five yards from my inert form. After breakfast I went for another long walk in the bare hills before boating back to the Land Rover parked in the woods. I paid a visit to the green island with its Highland burial ground. On its summit stood the ruins of a tiny church built to the memory of a local saint, and on the stone slab of the altar, washed by centuries of rain, hail and snows, stood an ancient brass bell, green with age. I held the bell reverently, thought again of the little cottage and its woods and silently asked if my work might prove of value then I wanted to live there.

Then quivering with the cold, wet and fatigue, I hauled the wooden boat out onto the mainland shore, drove to my own boat at the little sea pier, loaded up and once more fighting the waves, beat my way back to the croft.

Nothing will ever convince me that those three hard days, with thirty-six stormy water miles covered by boat, nineteen miles on foot in the mountains, and two primitive nights out in that lonely wilderness at winter's height had no bearing on the events that followed.

Within a week the *Reader's Digest* informed me the sparrowhawk story was fine and I need not re-write a single word. And when I renewed negotiations to acquire the cottage and wooded area I later came to call Wildernesse, everything flowed smoothly. They took several months but by the end of summer Wildernesse became mine - on a lease of twenty years - before the end of which time I realized with a shock I would be an old age pensioner.

But it seemed my prayer had been answered.

15

SPRING CAME EARLY TO Ballindona that year and by March 7 the daffodils thrashing back and forth in the high winds with which winter announces its arrival in late autumn and tries to delay its departure, had grown the long, green cases in which intricately folded saffron petals waited their chance to surround the croft once more in a blaze of yellow bugles. In sheltered nooks along the burn banks above the danger line of sudden spates, their main rivals the primroses had begun to thrust out wan lemon faces for the first blessing of the springtime sun. Missel-thrushes dipped and dived above the croft in the winds and now filled the dawn air with ringing song, one cock again fluting defiance at the weather from the top sprig of the little spruce high on the cliff north-west of the croft. He clung and sang, flashing his white underwing patches as if he was sure the heavy February snows that had tried to turn my home into a dripping igloo would not now return. The silvery songs of robins came from the thickets sounding like tiny coins being tipped on to glass, Little Fat Sergeant was back on the bird table and the pied wagtail pair homed in from the east. Next morning saw the start of five days' calm and glorious sunshine and on a walk to the Shona forest I saw the male courting his mate, his wings hung low and long black-and-white tail spread out, among the bright pussy willows that lined the south-shore burn.

Inside the forest a red squirrel chased his mate up giant fir trunks and along branches in the curious "slow-motion" chase which is a prelude to mating for these now uncommon sprites of the northern conifer woods. I tried to photograph them but the heavy 1,000-mm mirror lens had too fine a focus and branches cut off a head or a tail. Slow chase maybe but it was still too fast for me to use such a lens and I now realized it was not suited to such work. The squirrels were dark brown rather than red, probably descendants of the darker continental varieties that were introduced into Scotland when the red squirrel verged on extinction in the early 1800s after many of the original forests had been destroyed for timber, fuel and to make grazing lands.

Three days later with the first queen humble-bees burring through the air looking for nest sites and newly hatched bluebottles buzzing about the compost heap, I boated out in brilliant sunshine for supplies. At the store Allan MacColl told me he had seen a huge wildcat early that very morning in the fields above the pier where I left my boat.

It seemed an impossible hope for few humans have ever photographed a wildcat actually *in* the wild, and I only had my cheap 300-mm lens with me. But I dutifully prowled around below a huge rockslide under some towering cliffs in which a pair of ravens were now nesting. And there, in a marshy part among the winter-battered old grasses, I found two unmistakable four-toed tracks of a cat, too circular for a fox and too large for a wandering domestic cat. Through the grasses there was a flattened track, too narrow to be a badger's trail, showing no slots from deer hoofs, and although I went on all fours to play bloodhound I could discern no taint of fox.

Hopefully I hid at the edge of a small wood downwind of the area but after a fruitless and cold half-hour my attention was distracted by the ravens. One had flown out when I'd reached the cliff but now I was out of sight it came back with food in its beak, and through my field glass it seemed to be a chunk of deer meat with some grey hairs still on it. The great black bird hopped onto the nest, a blue-black bill emerged from its depths, certainly the female on her eggs, for ravens are Britain's earliest nesters, and took it from her mate. But instead of flying away again he hopped ponderously on to a nearby stunted rowan growing at right angles to the cliff, sidled along it in an oddly undignified way then started bowing and calling "*krok*" to her as if still trying to court her, his throat feathers so far distended he looked as if he were swallowing a large plum.

He was too far away for a photo and it was now too dark anyway. His little courting show seemed to have no effect on the female for she stayed deep in the well of the thick stick nest on the ledge, and he soon flew away again beating towards Ardnamurchan peninsula.

Only then did I see the animal in front of me, a mere thirty yards away. It looked almost as big as a roe deer, its legs hidden between the deep grassy tussocks. A heavy, thick-bodied creature with a dark, tawny-grey coat, surely too large for any cat. Now it was slipping along through some patches of heather and it paused, lifted its head and then I saw the short muzzle, the broadly spaced pointed ears. It *was* a wildcat, a huge tom I judged, and it kept low as it headed for some small willow bushes growing in a bog beyond which were open fields where rabbits had their burrows. It was away hunting and now and again it paused to sniff the air, as if stalking as much by scent as by sight.

Despite the dusk I tried to take a photo but it heard the shutter's click, turned, but too briefly for me to take another, then slipped away like a ghost. I stayed unmoving for half an hour in the increasing cold, knowing that while I was fully camouflaged in bush jacket and hat any movement would give away my exact position. But I didn't see it again. I noted where it had come from, sure it *was* using the slight trail from the rock slide, but I refrained from going over to check or look for its lair as I didn't want to leave my human scent there.

Overnight I camped in the Land Rover down by the pier, hoping I might get a shot of it at dawn in the open area *if* it used that trail again.

Forcing myself out of the bag in the new, early twilight, I slid back one of the steamed-up windows to look at the weather - and saw a large otter, its sleek coat dripping water, carrying a youngster across the road in its mouth and just a few yards to the side of the vehicle! But as soon as she heard the sound she dived into the undergrowth. Then I heard a loud, plaintive squeak like a loud hedgesparrow call. I thought she might have been calling another youngster over but nothing moved.

Without breakfast I stole through the woods east of the little road again and hid myself overlooking the open boggy patch, ready for a long cold wait. As the light improved I heard for the first time that year a cock chaffinch give its tripping song. Then a pair of tawny owls began calling to each other in the woods behind me. I'd never heard owls hooting and kwicking in the morning before.

To my surprise I'd only waited about forty freezing minutes when I caught a brief glimpse of the wildcat. It appeared between two large tussocks west of the single-track road, turned south and vanished. I hadn't moved nor did I try to take a picture for it was still too dark and there was no point in scaring it. I waited five minutes, ten, half an hour. Suddenly I saw it again. It was coming back!

Quivering with excitement and cold, I watched fascinated as it stalked along, its head low but moving up and down slightly with every second stride. Occasionally it stopped to peer about and sniff the air, with one paw upraised. It was indeed a huge animal and my heart pounded. Slowly I checked the meter switch. At a thirtieth of a second the needle barely quivered. Treading carefully and yet somehow ponderously it came slowly nearer, ran across the little road in a crouching run like a soldier does when scared of air attack, then sneaked along through the grass and heather again.

As it reached the open area before me I tried a shot. Even at that distance it again heard the click. I cursed silently. But it moved on, mounted a big slab of rock then stopped and turned round. Perfect!

Click. It was glaring straight towards me with magnificent green-gold eyes, its huge, thick, striped tail resting on the ground. Risk a 60th. *Click.* Then it disappeared over a grassy ridge and into the rocky cairns of the slide.

It was the kind of miraculous luck that only comes to a beginner. Later, I used the photo to measure the wildcat's image over the actual ground – that big tom must have been nearly four feet long,

Knowing it would be useless to stalk such a wary, keen-sensed creature, I put the camera and lens into their plastic bags in my pack and boated back to the croft with yesterday's supplies. As I headed north through the narrow channel at medium tide, ready to swing west after avoiding the big sandbanks, I saw what looked like a floating tree in the sea. To my chagrin it was a red deer stag swimming and I recalled the one I'd seen in my first November on the island and how I'd wished then that I'd had a camera. Well, I had a camera now but it was in the pack! As the stag flailed away from the boat, breath blasting from its nostrils in near snorts, I grabbed the pack. But by the time I had undone it, hauled the lens and camera from their bags, fumbled to find the screw thread properly, whipped off the lens hood, set the exposure and shutter speed, made sure the boat was not heading aground and had raised the camera and focused it, the stag had gained the land. Shaking itself vigorously, its barrel body and coat colour reminding me of a lion's, it set off at a gallop for the forest below the great Dorlin cliffs. I got a picture all right – of a brown dot with spikes, barely discernible from the gloom of the woods.

Thirteen has never been "unlucky" for me but on March 13 I was reminded yet again of what an amateur wildlife photographer I really was. I had seen the brilliant black, white and orange oystercatchers in their odd beak-low, loudly pleeping, courtship dashes along the sand and had decided to take pictures of them. I put up a makeshift hide of hazel hoops and fish netting with herbage stuffed in the sides among the deep bracken clumps and after a two-hour wait had focused the bulky 1,000-mm lens on a pair actually in the act of mating.

Suddenly a whoosh of wings and a loud, raucous "*Kaah kaah*" right over my head made me jump just as I pressed the button! And away flew the oystercatchers. A hoodie crow, almost surely Charlie, had perceived my inert human form through the inadequate herbage on the hide's roof and with the devilish sense of humour some crows have had dived down and given the loud alarm calls no wild creature ignores. Furious, I leaped to my feet, clapped my cupped hands loudly and he turned so fast in terror, thinking it was maybe a gunshot, he almost de-feathered himself. Right then I could happily have put a charge of No 5 or 6 shot into him myself.

By now three pairs of chaffinches were visiting the bird table, squabbling with robins and each other. Sergeant seemed no longer the dominant cock and was having to back down to a new, fat cock, perhaps one of his own sons. As usual, with the new grass growing, red deer hinds and last year's calves were coming round the croft at dusk and just before dawn to vie with the sheep for grazing. I noticed, however, that the deer did not crop as closely as the sheep who could still find some food from ground the deer passed over. The hinds were hungry, stalking was easier as they were weak from winter and once I was able to photograph nine of them outlined against the dawn sky their heads gleaming like soft golden velvet and wreathed in mist. I also saw a yearling, or, rather, a nine-monthling, still getting suck from its mother.

On a mid-March Sunday I hiked to the big house for mail but seeing no deer on the low forested route in, I headed back over the high tops to see how far the stags were keeping from the hinds on the lower ground. Spotting a bachelor herd of seven from Shona's highest peak, I decided not to stalk them as mist was smirring and it would also have meant a long, circuitous stalk because if you're moving downwards deer see you easily against the skyline. But as I walked on and the herd took off I almost stumbled on a couple of stags right below me in a small grassy dell between the rocks. These two, in a small zone of silence, had not seen or sensed the running of the others. They went a few paces then stopped as if deciding to stand their ground, and stared back insolently, literally posing for portraits. This frequent habit of stopping for a second look at any source of danger has long been stags' undoing.

As I looked at these beasts, too close to get even one wholly in the picture, I had a slight feeling of unease for they were big, a good 250 to 300 lbs each but with poor 8-point heads as their antlers were "going back" with advancing age. By now some local folk knew I was trying to acquire Wildernesse and one had told me that week of how a man had actually been attacked by a big stag up there in the rutting season fifteen years before. Apparently he had just been walking along unarmed when the stag had launched an attack, driving him under a small wooden culvert. The beast had half destroyed the culvert with antlers and powerful blows of its forefeet but just as it had been getting through the man had managed to slash its throat with his dirk.

I had laughed the story off as a good yarn., I knew that red deer stags have killed humans but extremely rarely, and usually in parks where they had lost heir natural fear of man. But as these two huge beasts glared at me I had a queasy moment. I took two shots anyway and as usual they turned and sped away, floating along and light on their feet as boxers. I went easily on the hill that day and realized I had had no lunch. It was worth remembering – you travel better when light in the gut.

Towards the end of March the sheep were coming closer and with the lamb season starting, were baahing noisily about the croft. At times, until one got used to it each year, it was as bad as being back in the city. At least this barracking racket (each sheep made a different noise and I swear one had a throat of broken brass) was no worse than I heard on the only radio programme my set was capable of receiving, where there seemed a total obsession with pop music, pop stars, showbiz and football, and whose hosts apparently believed Britain ended somewhere just north of Barnet. But while I would move to Wildernesse if negotiations were successful, I was still repairing the croft. That had been the deal after all. So during the early hours each morning, before the sheep went higher to graze, I used the noisy time to make more repairs.

Unfortunately good intentions are not necessarily rewarded and after one long boat and truck journey to the inland town for more hardboard, paint and guttering, I almost failed to get home. The engine dunked beneath the waves in the loaded boat and I had to dry it with cloths under a plastic sheet while rain poured and we drifted in rough seas. One day, nailing a sheet up on the rear room wall, I heard a high-pitched bleating. A newborn lamb trying to follow its mother had fallen into the burn and was cold, wet and terrified. I rushed out, rescued it, then as I got back indoors a very old ewe started licking it all over. I thought this odd as the lamb fed from a younger ewe which was clearly its mother. The young ewe seemed to tolerate the older one's attentions to her bairn but butted her rather symbolically once.

At that moment there was a knock on the door. Iain MacLellan was there and he'd hauled up a sheet of hardboard for me. He was starting his most intensive spring work and was out checking the new lambs. He told me the older sheep would be the young ewe's mother and that 'granny' sheep often supervised the way their daughters brought up their own lambs!

After three years we had come to know each other better and when I'd helped with the sheep gathering Iain had finally decided to call me by my Christian name, which I preferred to the deadly polite Highland "Mr Tomkies". He told me some more sheep problems.

"If the old ewes aren't sold off each year in the autumn, and they mate with a tup, they often die. If not during the hard winter then after it in March or April, before or during or after giving birth – they're weak from the birth, having to make milk, and the poor winter grazing. The new grass growth also upsets the digestive system. We had a poor gathering last year and we lost about ten older ewes this winter, some with lambs in them, which means about £50 less from the sheep." I felt few men worked harder for a £50 estate gain than the conscientious Highland shepherd.

After Iain had gone I was painting the inner walls and roof white (to increase indoor light) when a large dollop of paint fell straight into my left eye. The pain! But I swiftly made an eye bath from a wine glass brimming with water and eventually floated the paint out.

By now I thought I knew the way of the seas well but on March 31, with an urgent story to post, I ran into the worst boat trip of all my time on Shona. Setting off in west by south-west winds and hail squalls, I reached the pier without mishap. But on the way back the gales had increased to Force Nine, the boat had dragged its anchors and was banging against the side stones of the pier. In that violent sea there was no way to re-set it so I either *had* to go or watch the boat be destroyed.

Banging off against the waves I hugged the south shore of the loch to gain the slight lee of islets and small land spits but after a quarter mile the boat had shipped a lot of water. A foot-long gash had been made in the hull where the pier stones had torn off the fibre glass patching along the starboard chines. This had not shown up when the boat was empty but with my weight, fuel tank and shopping, water was now coming in fast. Twice I had to pull into small bays to pump out the water, my frenzied efforts wrenching the little plastic pump from its fastenings. Hit by a squall of hail, unable to see properly, I was forced to dash into the small inlet right opposite the croft. As I waited for over an hour, with no overhanging trees or shelter anywhere, I suddenly realized where I was. This was the inlet that the infamous seventeenth-century smuggler Black Ranald of Eigg had pulled into when chased by the revenue cutter from the open sea. He had run into the inlet, pulled in behind a screen of high rock and immediately lowered his sails. The revenue crew, believing he had gone up the loch past Castle Tioram, had swept past. And once they were far enough away Ranald had rehoisted masts and sails and scudded back out to Ardnamurchan Point. But this was no time for recalling history. Wet through and bitterly cold, I was shivering, and as I could see no tail to the storm I decided to chance rushing across.

Kneeling in the centre of the boat to keep the stern high with both knees braced and reaching back with one arm to control the engine, I prayed to the simple god of my childhood – just as I had when in a similar position in a small boat in Canada, only then I had been among a pod of killer whales and at the time still believed the legends about them. Now the waves were six feet high, and short so more dangerous, their tops lashing off in spray from the shrieking wind. The boat bounced up and down and twisted like a cork as I tried to ride them sideways yet still go slightly *with* them. If the engine had been swamped again it would have been the end but it held out long enough for me to reach the lee of the island just outside my bay. A near mile of pure hell. When we limped into the beach and I hauled the boat out on to its wooden runners my knees trembled and I was shaking with cold and

173

shock. And all just to post a story and fetch some stores! I hung my wet clothes to dry in the spare room, it took two hours to re-patch the boat again in the next dry period, and I really had to gird myself up mentally before my next trip out in it.

The big spring tides were here now, beating the rocks, weed and sands lower down then throwing the jetsam higher up the beach as they came in, and on April 5 I saw a motley crew of sea birds working the wrack together. Two oystercatchers, a first-year lesser black-backed gull with a speckled brown back, two herring-gulls and a hooded crow I felt was Charlie, were all spaced out. Standing on the edge of the incoming sea they watched as the waves pounded into the loose seaweed, turning it over and over. And each time the waves receded the birds dashed forward to pick up struggling sand eels, rocklings, butterfish or sand-hoppers. Only once was there any friction between them - when an oystercatcher clearly felt Charlie had come too close, for it leaped into the air then dived on the hoodie actually making him flutter further away.

One fine evening Harry Heron flew close to the croft from high up the burn and glided down to the beach. Through my glass I watched him for nearly half an hour – not a movement or stab did he make. I felt sure he was able to live on little but fresh air. I was about to turn away when he made a swift dart and pulled his beak out of the sea with a tiny flounder in it. So he didn't actually stab or *spear* fish with that great beak – he grabbed them *between* his long mandibles. Surely, if he stabbed *any* fish it would be a dab, flounder or small plaice. If a heron stabs a fish he can't open his beak and would have to shake it off – when it could still have enough life left to escape – or scrape it off with a foot which I had never seen happen. Though, of course, herons will stab fish to kill them once landed. But what timing!

Next morning I was emptying sacks of molehill soil into the compost heap of seaweed and lime for the garden, when Iain arrived with his collie. He looked concerned.

"I think there's a big, mangy old fox here," he said. "I have found two lovely big ewe lambs with their faces torn off." He had one in a bag over his shoulder, its head a gory mess. "Just born and a few hours later this happens. Such a fox kills badly, wantonly, drinking the blood from the throat to cure its mange. I've tried all day but can't find its den."

By now after years of isolated thought and writing the first wilderness book about Canada – where my research proved too many of the now rare grizzly bears were being shot for sport in their last strongholds – my general wildlife views seemed set. I felt we must do *far* more to preserve the dwindling natural world, not just for its own sake but also because of its intangible values *for* man, and try to completely understand all wild creatures and their roles.

But I had now seen the shepherd's life in the hard Scottish hills was far removed from the idyllic myth of man sitting on a mountain, crook over his arm, smoking his pipe, peacefully whiling away the sunlit hours. I felt if I were a sheep farmer I could forgive a fox or eagle taking the odd lamb or two, especially when so many sheep die in winter and lambs suffer accidental death anyway from various causes in these harsh hills. But wanton killing by an individual fox – where many lambs were slain and often just left lying about uneaten – was a serious matter. Men's livelihoods were at stake.

I could see the genuine worry on Iain's face. I agreed again to watch over lambs in my area, and said that if he had trouble getting the killer fox I'd try and help him do so.

16

IT WAS ON A pertinent date, Friday April 13, that an avuncular and belligerent co-tenant moved into the croft. A sudden knocking startled me as I was painting an indoor wall. At first I thought it was just the usual sheep rubbing its horns against the porch, but breathless on the doorstep was the island's young schoolteacher. Something bumped spasmodically in a rucksack on her back.

"I found it on the rocks at Shoe Bay" she gasped. "Do you think it will live? I heard you liked animals. Can you do anything for it?"

She opened the rucksack on the floor and out stumbled the largest and most indignant herring-gull I'd ever seen. Hampered by a dangling right wing it struggled to its feet, glared, then stalked into a corner and registered its disapproval by relieving itself, whitely and massively, on the wooden floor.

Ominous clouds were gathering to the west and after the teacher had left for home at the other side of the island, I took a look at the gull. His right wing was so badly twisted that the long flight feathers, covered with dirt, tripped him up when he walked. Yet his huge yellow eyes glared at me with jaundiced disdain, like an ageing uncle who had been forced at last into an old folks' home. He had seen a few places, this old bird, had weathered many a stormy sky. He looked at me without affection, hope or even fear, just belligerent suspicion.

I spread an old sheet over my desk so I could examine him but as I went to pick him up he plap-plapped over the floor on his webbed feet and screeched an ear-splitting "*Hiaow, hiaow!*" It sounded so much like Harold I almost called him that – until I remembered we already had a Harry about the place. I don't know why but herring-gulls always look like "Berts" to me but I'd had a Bert in Canada and had named the crippled gull who frequented the sea shore here "Bert" too. I couldn't have a third Bert. Well, *Gil*bert would do!

As I turned him upside down he pecked one of my fingers hard. I pulled my hand away forgetting the edges of a gull's beak, below the red patch at which youngsters pick to make their parents regurgitate food, are like razors, and the blood flowed.

Quickly I covered his head with a cloth to keep him quiet and inspected his wing. Holding both wings out to compare the bad one's joint with the good I was surprised to find the flight pinions overlapped the edges of my desk. Gilbert had a wingspread of four feet, eight inches. He was a magnificent specimen which made me determined to nurse him back to health and let him go.

No bones seemed broken but there was a slight dislocation, probably due to strained ligaments. The last bad storms had been on April 5 and I felt the injury had possibly occurred then. But how had he escaped the mangy, hungry fox that had torn the faces of at least two lambs? Highland foxes often tour the seashore just before dawn to pick up any wounded, sick or young sea bird or dead fish they can find. But Gilbert was old and could probably match the fox in cunning by hiding at night.

I settled for the old classic remedy of binding the wing up, immobilizing it and giving the ligaments time to mend. Taking the one and only bandage from my medical kit, I safety-pinned the wing close to his body, ensuring the pinions were above the tail. Gulls have smooth streamlined bodies so binding a wing is difficult for the legs must also be left free. Not until I put a coil round his breast too could I make the bandage stay on. As soon as I let him go he tried to walk off but kept falling over and it took him two days to learn to balance with one wing tied up. I let him have the spare room and for a roost place I tipped a large box on its side, filled it with grass and bracken, and left a bowl of water nearby.

Gilbert ate just about anything – bread, milk and egg and meat scraps the first day, then I put him back on to his natural sea diet. He ate like a wolf and his digestive system was extraordinarily efficient, able to process anything from stale bread to small bones, and I had to spread newspapers everywhere.

During the first night I was woken up by a loud clonking. I hurried in and found Gilbert on his back, and with one wing out of commission he was banging on the floor with his heavy beak as he desperately tried to get up again.

Next day, after checking the nesting herons on Deer Island – Harry's old nest had not been rebuilt and I did not see him – I tried to catch Gilbert some fish. But it was cold, windy and too early in the year for

Gilbert bathes in the burn in spite of his injured wing.

the mackerel to be in. I had no luck but when I returned to my beach I collected a pail of mussels, whelks and winkles.

When I went in Gilbert was parading round the room, the bandage flowing loose from his neck like the garland of a seaside beauty contest winner. But when I put two mussels before him he nibbled at them then looked round helplessly. I soon realized what was wrong. Mussels were far too strong and unstable in a loose state to be pecked or prised open and normally to weaken them gulls fly high above rocks and drop them from a fair height. Gilbert could not do this now. So I steamed them until they opened slightly and he soon avidly swallowed half a dozen.

After his meal I took him on to the desk to replace the bandage. But as he pecked ferociously at my fingers again, I had a brainwave. Bending a pipe cleaner into a double coil, I popped it over his beak as a muzzle. That would protect my hands, I thought.

But as I was winding the bandage Gilbert was in trouble. His throat was distended and he started choking. I removed the pipe cleaner – and he promptly regurgitated his entire lunch over my writing papers.

I had learned another lesson. When scared, gulls always regurgitate their food. This makes them lighter so they can escape enemies more quickly. The great skuas know this and often chase gulls to make them regurgitate their catch in midair – then down swoops the skua to scoop up the easy food. Naturally, my ministrations scared Gilbert. From then on I never fed him at all until after his sessions in the "casualty ward".

With the bandage back on I stood Gilbert on the desk. To my surprise he shot forward and gulped all his lunch up again then looked at me quizzically with his bright eye as if to say "Didn't you know? Food's just as good the second time around!" I recalled then that gulls also often swallow all the food they can before competitors reach it, then fly off alone, regurgitate the lot, then break up and eat it again at leisure.

On the third day I took Gilbert out for a walk as I felt just sitting down in a room all day was doing him little good. He waddled off down the path but kept tripping and falling over. Gamely he hauled himself back onto his feet with his beak. Looking after an injured gull is like looking after a baby but you can't put nappies on birds. After twenty-one years as a newspaperman I now had to buy them to mop up after a gull.

He showed no gratitude of course and at times I wondered if my care was worth while. Herring-gulls are the commonest in Europe, so successful a species they have been known to almost double their populations in ten years. They have learned not only how to live with man but to *use* him. They have become as much at home on inland rubbish tips, reservoirs, behind the farmer's plough or on airfields – where they are a hazard to plane jet engines – as they are on lonely sea cliffs. They are almost becoming pests.

But then I'd look into those amazing yellow eyes. Like huge glass beads they were, amazingly mobile. He could squint at the tip of his beak, look forward with the stereoscopic sight of a falcon, or sideways with just one eye at a time like most other birds. I just didn't want to see that light in them fade and die.

It was not until the end of the first week that I really began to *like* him. By now the primaries of his injured wing were messy and tattered. Reluctantly I had to clip them just a few inches. Then I took him to the burn to see if he felt fit enough to bathe.

He became totally transformed and as he paddled off into the deep pool like a river steamer, joy now suffused his being. He plunged his head in and out with great abandon, throwing water over his back and shuffling his wings. Twirling about like a rubber duck in a bath, he dipped and shook his beak, hunched his shoulders and wiggled his tail, all the while performing a quaint little jig with his kicking feet. He looked so comical I laughed. He wiped his dirty face feathers against his wings, scratched his head with his webbed feet and with his feathers wet he climbed out and up on to the bank.

There he tried pathetically to flap the water from his wings but kept overbalancing because of the unequal weight and the fact that the right wing had almost no movement in it.

But heavens, he was trying hard. He preened himself, stroking the water from his breast feathers and shaking it off his beak. In two hours he was completely dry. He looked a different bird, sparkling white like some advert for soap powder and his bristly tail was now blanched and stiff. From the back he looked as wide as a duck, a small paddleboat.

If he could make such an effort, ill though he still was, it behove me to do likewise. I tidied up his room, burnt all the dirty papers, scrubbed the floor with disinfectant, gave him fresh bracken and spread out new papers. Then I boiled him an egg as a special reward.

Gilbert I fear, was becoming an opportunist. Like some overpaid unionized worker he'd now had a taste of the good life and wanted more. And if he could obtain more without an increase in effort, it troubled his conscience not at all. He ate up all the yolk, looked at the egg white with distaste and turned his back.

Next day I left him in his room and met the factor of the estate that would lease me Wildernesse. We boated there, walked the boundaries of the land I wanted, finally settled on a few acres with access to other woods but it was dark when I set out across the sea again for Shona.

Entering the croft I switched on a torch – no Gilbert. I looked everywhere. How could he possibly have escaped? Then I heard a faint movement behind some cardboard boxes. There, upside down and wedged tightly between them lay Gilbert. He must have climbed up, slipped and with one wing immobilized, had been unable to climb back out. When I put him on his feet he was dizzy and stumbled about in half circles but he soon recovered and gulped down a few mussels before squatting down to sleep. Clearly a human room was not the best place for him. If I wanted to return him to the wild the closer I kept him to the wild state the better.

Next day I took him down to a rock on the shore. As they saw me carrying him down other gulls swooped overhead with the odd "*qwuck qwuck*" duck-like sounds they utter when slightly alarmed or curious. I feared they would attack Gilbert for like many birds gulls will often kill their sick or injured brethren – part of the harsh wilderness code to eliminate unfit individuals from the race.

But as I watched him through binoculars from my window only one gull landed near him, perhaps curious at the bandage, as others flew above. None made any attack on Gilbert – maybe because of his great size. Encouraged, I went up the loch on a supply trip and when I returned he was still on the rock. He had made no attempt to find food but somehow he had tugged his bandage off again and it was merrily floating away on the outgoing tide. As it was the only one I had I shot out again in the boat and retrieved it. But his wing which had always stuck out to the side like a man carrying a plank seemed much higher now. The exercises in the burn had done him good.

Next morning I caught him tugging the hated bandage off again. "All right Gilbert," I said as he padded with protesting qwucks round the room. "If that's the way you want it, no more bandage." It was the first time I'd actually spoken to him and it had an oddly calming effect, so I kept talking. Gilbert looked up in query, his head turning from side to side like a dog's.

After his bath in the burn next day he climbed on to the bank and as he flapped to dry himself I saw with delight that the bad wing now had the right kind of movement in it. As he preened in the sun I left him to do some writing. A couple of hours later I went out - he had gone. I walked round the croft in widening circles but there was no sign of him.

Up early, I used the post-dawn search for Gilbert for a photo safari with the hefty 1,000-mm lens, trying to picture the seals on the rocks and a beautiful little roebuck on the edge of Shona forest. Near the shore I found a dead lamb with the fox's bloody marks on its throat despite a recent visit by the local foxhounds. Clearly the fox had not been scared off the island either and was still killing more lambs than it needed to eat or for its cubs. I just hoped white-plumaged Gilbert really did have sense to hide himself at night.

Searching again after lunch among the thickets of birch, alder and willows along the burns, it seemed that every outcrop of white quartz and lichen on the huge boulders amid the heather looked like a gull. Finally, almost a mile away as I returned along the rocky shore line from the west, I found him. He cried out "*Hiaow hiaow*" in alarm at my approach and led me a hard chase, leaping from rock to rock and spreading out his bad wing with the other to lessen his falls. At least he was in good shape. I eventually caught him when he tripped on seaweed within inches of the sea and escape by paddling, and brought him home for a whelk and mussel supper.

Next day, to keep him outdoors yet within checking distance, I made some thick leather jesses for his legs and put him out on a long line as I had with the sparrowhawk Buzz. But Gilbert was no hawk, could not learn to ignore what he could not change, and tugged persistently at them. Then he walked to the burn but during his usual spectacular bath he twisted the line around his legs half a dozen times. When he saw me coming he tried to run but, hampered by the lines, ended up performing an undignified nose dive into a mud patch.

He shook his beak furiously – gulls hate getting dirty – and when I picked him up he pecked so viciously I was forced to fetch gloves and his pipecleaner "muzzle". Finally I snipped off the offending line and jesses and Gilbert waddled disgustedly down to the beach. He found a rock crevice filled with moss and grasses and settled down for the night.

Each time I looked through the field glass until dusk his white head was peeping out just above the rock like a white golf ball as he kept a good eye on me too. By now I felt sure that if the fox left delectable young lambs lying about it would hardly bother with a tough old gull like Gilbert, who could inflict some damaging pecks before he succumbed, so I decided to leave him alone for two days.

On the morning of April 24 I saw him standing at the edge of the incoming tide. As each wave rolled in it nudged the loose seaweed a little further up the shore and Gilbert darted forward to grab sand-hoppers and small sea creatures. Each night I looked for him to make sure he had a shellfish supper and it became clear that he *knew* he had to hide for I always found him deep in some "bed" in clumps of new bracken, thick rushes or beds of yellow flags.

The sun beamed so strongly through the window next morning I took down the plastic "tent" around my desk and stowed it away. Outside Gilbert had disappeared but I didn't look for him in such good weather – instead I sieved all my garden earth and was busy planting vegetable seeds when Iain appeared. He had his shotgun and two little bedraggled terriers, a cairn and a Highland, which he had borrowed from a mainland friend. He said the big mangy fox was still killing and they had lost twenty-three lambs to it this year and he was now going after it himself. The cairn terrier was on a lead – Iain explained it wasn't safe with lambs about! I looked at the other terrier, such a tiny scrap of a canine it seemed, with watery doe eyes and a woebegone expression, that I suggested it could hardly be a match for a rat never mind a fox.

"Aye it is," Iain protested. "It's accounted for a score of foxes already." And he lifted the terrier's lip – to expose canine teeth almost an inch long! This tiny sweet-looking creature had in fact ripped Morag's cairn bitch when he had brought the duo over in the boat the previous day, making a deep, two-inch-long gash in its back from which it took many days to recover. I felt there was reproach in Iain's eyes at this semi-Sassenach's apparent pacifist attitude to foxes. I fought a losing battle with myself for I knew two guns were better than one when after foxes at the den.

"Have you got a spare gun?"

"Ay."

"Right. I'll come with you tomorrow."

To my surprise, far from showing gratitude, Iain seemed worried about my handling of a gun, that I might shoot one of the terriers in mistake for the fox! It was easily done, he explained, the cairn being of a similar colour, the fox bolting suddenly, the heat of the moment. . . . One of his own co-workers had shot a fine terrier only a few years back. As Iain talked, memories of my younger days when I had lived with guns and shooting came flooding back, the years with a fine Sussex gamekeeper and my father, both superb shots, on a 4,000 acre estate – years of ferrets and nets, long netting in the fields, pheasant drives, rough shoots, deer culling . . . the times I had hit running rabbits with *rifle* bullets, and had once taken two partridges out of a covey, both through the head, with a .22 bullet for a bet. I recalled the weeks of marksman's training in the Guards, the Canadian wilderness years, trekking through bear country when one had to shoot a deer or two, purely for sustenance. But I said little of this to Iain for I was no longer interested in shooting animals and after such a long gap was by no means sure my performance next day would match any past skills I may have possessed. Instead I assured him I could handle a gun. I also pointed out it was correct to always break a shotgun when crossing any obstacle, that one should never put one's thumbs over the barrels and that when one left a shotgun leaning against a cottage wall it was a good idea to remove the cartridges first!

Next day I boated to Shona pier, picked up the spare 12 bore and was told to join Iain on the high hill north of the main forest. Sure enough he was waiting there, right at the top. I hurried up so as not to keep him waiting and as soon as I arrived, puffing, off he went like a rested deer!

But it was a great day on the hill as we traversed the island, working the corries, the major rockslide cairns and the dens Iain knew. Usually we stationed ourselves forty yards apart covering wide arcs each side. Only at one den with many exits on a precipitous 500-ft slope that ran almost sheer down to the shore near Deer Point did the terriers hole up for a while. First there was silence, then the sound of little running feet below, then silence again. Twenty minutes after this both terriers emerged. Iain thought the vixen was away but they had probably killed some cubs.

As we paused for lunch on the leeward side of a hill, the spring sun lighting up the greens of new grass growth against the grey and tawny winter drabness, Iain told interesting yarns of his battles to keep foxes down before the use of both the gin trap and leaving poisoned carcases on the hill had been banned.

"We used strychnine in a dead cormorant or hens' eggs. It had to be in the right amount – too much and the fox would vomit immediately and the poison wouldn't work. For the eggs, I broke off a bracken twig, dipped it into the strychnine and then stirred it briefly into the yolk – just enough. As soon as the fox feels the poison he rushes to water to clear his insides. But the water expands and helps kill him quickly, like rat poison. Now, one winter I put a cormorant's body on a rocky islet just off Deer Point, with two eggs by the side of it.

"That year we had a tup we could not catch in the autumn gathering and the following April I went back there with Morag, found the tup on the Point and decided to drive him to the old schoolhouse on the north shore so we could fetch him by boat the next day. I had to get above him so I could work him down, because if he got in front of me he'd take off over the hill. But he wouldn't keep to the path – he ran down west and on to the cliffs. Then I could only come at him from below for he was on a tiny ledge. I climbed up but my only handhold was a clump of heather. I grabbed his horn with my right hand, scared if he jumped he'd pull me down too. Well, he slipped, and then he was dangling from my hand by the horn. It just showed how starved and thin he was, just a bag of bones, if I could hold him up by just one horn. I lowered him slowly so Morag could get hold of his backside and we got him down the rocks without injury.

"As we herded the tup along Morag suddenly pointed to the islet off shore – and there was a strange sight. The fox had got there, eaten part of the cormorant and had then felt the poison. He had just made it across to a small burn, drunk water and had died right there. His skeleton was on the bank, his big tusks showing white even at that distance."

Iain told me of a young keeper who tried new ways to catch foxes. "Once, to save cost, he made a snare from hay bailing wire and we all laughed at him. One day he came in and dropped a fox in that snare at our feet. We laughed no more. The fox had got its head and paws through but was caught round its middle, and in its efforts to escape had torn its insides. The snare looked like the same wire the fence was made of – and the fox was not suspicious of it."

Iain paused, a sandwich in one hand as he smiled at another memory. "The same keeper made a big cube cage from wire netting and fencing stobs. Then he made a hole at grass level in one corner and baited inside with a dead lamb, pieces of venison, fish and a dead bird. He left it several nights but once he found the fox had been in and eaten some meat, he set a snare over the hole. He was as clever as a fox himself. Instead of first setting a snare and making the fox suspicious, he let it think it could get in and out easily for free meals, *then* set the snare. He caught nine foxes that way."

I asked Iain if he agreed folks who did not lock their hens up at night in a properly secure poultry house really deserved all they got?

Iain laughed. "But what do you do when a tree falls on your hen house? That happened to my mother's ducks and hens and until we could repair it we put them into a shed which had housed the dry toilet. The door was kept shut but we made a small hole in the bottom so the hens and ducks could get in at night. One morning there was chaos. Nine hens and ducks had been killed and the fox had buried the ducks and covered them up with leaves. But the odd thing was he buried them all upside down so nothing showed through but the bottoms of their webbed feet. These pairs of little webbed feet were sticking up everywhere, as if the fox had left them as markers for his return!"

It was back at his house after our tiring and foxless fifteen-mile trek, and after Morag had cooked us a fine supper, that Iain handed me a good dram and told me the oddest fox story of all.

"Did I tell you about the den we found through a dream? We caught an old vixen in a snare once and she was in milk, her teats full, so we knew she had cubs but *where* were they? Two nights later I had an odd dream – no-one believes this but it's true. I saw a sand hole I knew of and in the dream the vixen came over the hill, a lamb thrown over her shoulder, and went into the sand hole.

"Next day I went straight there. In fact there were now three holes and one of them was scraped out new. I put the terrier in the top one and he came out of the second, went back in and came out of the bottom hole. Naturally I thought there was nothing in there but then I saw something way down in the hole. I cut off a small forked branch for a rake, and the first thing I scraped out was a *heron*! And it still had seaweed round its feet from where the fox had caught and dragged it. Then one by one out came six lambs, all had their rich milky entrails taken out for the cubs.

"Then we found a dead cub buried a few yards from the hole. I scraped away and out came two more, also dead. The funny thing was *all* the cubs had bloody scrape marks round the ribs. One rib was stripped bare on each side, almost all round the body. We couldn't understand it but after talks with friends we decided what had happened. The cubs, hungry for milk after their mother failed to return, kept wandering outside. And each time the dog fox had carried them back to the den. He was killing for them – a heron, lambs and so on. But they were too young to eat, they needed a drink of milk. And each time they went out looking for their mother, so he carried them back. Foxes have long canine teeth and after hours of this his teeth must have worn a girdle round the cubs' chests for all were bloodied in the same place. Finally he must have buried the cubs himself."

As I finally walked and clambered the two miles home in the now cold darkness I knew I'd had a fascinating day. I felt a little guilty knowing that with Iain's critical eye upon me, if a fox had made a bolt I would have shot it. He worked hard to preserve lambs in these harsh hills and if he said twenty-three lambs had been killed by an unusually "wanton" fox I could believe it. To remove from future generations the genetic strain of such a killer made sense. What I could not believe was that *all* foxes kill in such a manner, and how would we know we had killed the right fox? And I still wondered if after such disturbances as the hound pack there might not have been an element of revenge in the killings. At the time, however, I knew little of such matters from the Highland shepherd's point of view, and I was not too sorry I had not shot a fox.

17

WHEN I HAD NOT seen Gilbert the gull for three days I started tramping the rocky cliffs and beaches to look for him. I was over a mile from home when I heard the quivering bleat of a tiny lamb. It was lying alone by some ruined walls and there was not a ewe in sight. As I drew near it staggered to its feet and tottered away from the huge giant it had never seen before. It was pinch-bellied, hump-backed, so it had probably not been fed much since birth, if at all.

I rounded up the nearest ewes and drove them towards the lamb. Bleating pitifully it staggered towards them but as it hopefully sought the teats of one ewe she swung round and bunted it off its feet. It was apparently not the mother and the other ewes ignored it.

I could do nothing but bottle feed the lamb and when it regained its strength, try to put it back to its real mother or a foster parent. I slipped the thin, shivering mite into the backpack and walked home. But who should be walking up the path – Gilbert!

He looked frayed about the head, his eyes sunken, and he was hungry. The sea had been calm despite a mixture of hail, snow and sunshine for two days and had not helped him by turning over the seaweed. I was delighted he had walked all the way up to the croft when things were going badly. As I fed him meat scraps and cheese – which he loved – he kept away from me. He was warier now after his freedom, stretching his neck out for the food but looking at me as if to say "Keep your distance. You may feed me because you have been appointed to do so by the Great Sky Spirit but don't assault my dignity by picking me up!"

For three days I struggled to keep the lamb alive, handling it with gloves because if I did succeed in finding its mother she would identify it as her own by scent. Iain came by once and assured me I had done the right thing by taking the lamb. "It's always a dilemma. You leave it and when you go back the next day it's dead. It probably had a young, inexperienced mother and never got a suck of milk." He shook his head when he saw the milk had to be forced into the lamb's throat by squeezing the plastic bottle. "That's a bad sign. If it took to the teat after tasting the first milk you'd be all right. But remember, if it survives it will be like a little dog and once it has your scent it will follow you everywhere. You'll be stuck with it for three months!"

Oddly, Gilbert stayed near the croft each morning now, as if he was jealous, for he had never done so before. Sometimes he woke me by turning the debris of my compost pile or rooting among my box of old tins. He even acted as an unwitting decoy for other gulls and some mornings I woke to see flashing white pinions outside the window as a small flock joined him at the heap. But as soon as I fed him he sneaked off down to the shore again, sidling along under the herbage, his head low, like a furtive white rat. Once fed, it seemed he wanted to keep out of my sight in case I caught him and took him back *into* the house. Usually he stumbled over the stones for a drink of sea water, a swim or a refreshing bath at the foot of the burn. At night he'd come back up again, find a hidden grassy patch in the lee of a rock so the wind would not blow up his feathers and freeze him, then settle down to sleep.

I admit I neglected Gilbert a little at this time. The lamb was delicate and hard to keep alive. Sometimes it recovered enough to climb into my waste paper box or into the chimney and look up the chimney. It sniffed at my shoes like a dog and at all things under the bed. When it scented objects its top lip curled upwards like a black bear cub's. Occasionally it scratched in my seed box of tomatoes and ate the fine earth as lambs do, or followed me from room to room, its tiny black trotters going "*donka donka donka*" over the wooden floor. But then I'd find it lying down, eyes closed and jerking or coughing convulsively. I put the fire on for it but it seemed I had arrived too late. The cold April nights combined with lack of mother's milk had given it no real start in life and on May 3 it died.

As I sadly buried it I realized I hadn't seen Gilbert for a while. When the other gulls fluttered up from the garden tip around dawn no earth-bound gull remained. Had they chased him away? I looked down to the beach and saw the tide was up so I decided to search for him by boat.

Half a mile away, where the island reached out into the open Atlantic, I found him sitting on a huge domed rock, his feathers fluffed up and his eyes sunken again. But when I went to catch him his plumage sleeked down and he fluttered away, actually flying a few yards before plopping down heavily into the water. Clearly his bad wing was stronger now but he was still handicapped by it being shorter than the other.

187

Gilbert stands on his good leg to preen and dry himself.

The trouble now was that he did not look well. He paddled round the boat as I tried to get near him with a curious zig-zag movement, as if one webbed foot was pushing harder than the other. He made it to a sloping rock but he could not get out of the water and as he flapped, trying to scale the rock's wet surface, his left foot hardly seemed to be working at all.

He pecked hard when I picked him up but when I turned him over I was shocked – one of the toes on that foot had been almost severed and was bleeding. The next one was badly cut and the "dew" claw further up the leg was missing. He must have been in pain and, almost unable to walk, had found it hard to get food. It seemed the fox may have caught up with him after all, with Gilbert only escaping into the sea literally by the skin of his foot.

That was the end of Gilbert's "freedom". He couldn't look after himself now and I clipped on his beak pipecleaner and carried him home. Now it would take as long again to get him back to health.

As I walked up the path with him tucked under one arm, passing the profusion of primroses lining the burn, I saw the rowan trees were the first to bud and throw out tiny silvery leaves, followed by birch, alder and hazel but the sap in the oaks and ashes was taking longer to stir and they seemed to be still in winter's grey grip. The first crane-fly flew uncertainly by, tangling itself briefly in new bracken heads. A black dor burying beetle just out from hibernation burred clumsily by and three humble-bees dosily worked the daffodils and primroses. From afar came the soft call of the first cuckoo.

Just as we entered the croft a swallow came homing in from the south. Twisting and turning as if with joy at being home again it shot past us and headed on north and, as it flashed above, Gilbert's bright eye followed it all the way. I thought he had an almost wistful look, for he too had once been a master of the sky.

Indoors I put Gilbert on his back, bathed his injured feet with hot water and diluted Dettol then put antibiotic cream on the wounds. After a treat feed of raw steak and mussels I left him to sit back in his old room. He seemed glad of its security and was far tamer as if he now realized I was really the only friend he had. There was a softer look in his eye and for the first time he let me stroke his snow-white neck and sleek grey wing feathers, which he still insisted on cleaning though he could now only stand on one foot. It was a marvel to me that no matter how ill he was Gilbert was fastidious about his toilet. Perhaps keeping himself spruce was the only morale booster he had left.

Four days later, however, his foot and knee joints had swollen to twice normal size. In the burn for daily bathes he made great efforts to clean himself but the bad leg stopped him climbing out again. I had to set him on the bank where, hopping on one foot with the swollen leg raised, he still tried to preen, constantly being blown off balance by the breezes.

Trying to prevent the poison spreading I fed him luxury foods – egg yolks, steak, whelks, mussels, cheese and even a few prawns I caught in the small baited funnel trap. I also put vitamin C in his water. I didn't want him to lose all movement in the bad leg so for a time I herded him round outside like a sheep as he "*qwuck qwucked*" in protest but before long he just sat tight and faced me with open beak. One morning despite the rain which had swollen the burn, Gilbert was so dirty and woebegone through loss of morale and lack of exercise, I found a quiet place in the deepest pool and left him there. I felt the flow of the water would force him to swim, keep him exercised and keep the leg muscles working.

Foolishly, busy at my desk, I left him alone too long. Suddenly something white caught my eye through the window. Gilbert had somehow swum into the mainstream and was being washed over the little falls. I rushed out as he tumbled like a frayed wrap-tangle of old rags, and I thought he'd be dashed to pieces but he somehow recovered his footing twenty yards downstream and was flutter-staggering out, bedraggled and wing-heavy, as I reached him. I had clearly overestimated his strength for he was now very weak and shivering with shock. Tenderly I carried him to his room and fed him. Too weak now to stand at all, he *still* tried to preen and dry himself sitting down.

Over a few days of rest the swellings began to shrink but when I turned him on his back, although he pushed up indignantly with his good leg the other had lost all power and two of the toes were inert. It was serious for I felt gangrene could set in. I tried taping up his good foot so he'd have to use the other to move. But he just sat, pecked at my efforts to move him and finally ripped off the tapes with his beak.

I now had to supervise short sessions in the burn, scaring him round in the water to try and get the bad leg working. At night I held bits of his meal away from him so he *had* to come to me for them, but he only raised his wings like an old plane trying to take off and hopped on one leg. There seemed only one hope left – physiotherapy. For the next few days, a quarter-hour at a time, I laid him on his back and exercised and massaged his foot with my hands. Anyone peeping in the window and seeing me talking to and playing "footsie" with a gull may well have concluded I was a suitable case for some kind of different medical treatment myself!

To keep his wing muscles toned I walked and trotted through the nearby pastures holding Gilbert's body high in one hand like a model aeroplane. Soon he was flapping away with those regular jerky downward beats that gulls use when effortlessly keeping up with boats and watching for thrown scraps from the passengers. He really seemed to enjoy these sessions.

One day Iain came round while I was exercising Gilbert, watched me a while then thrust his hand deep into a bag and handed me a fine two-pound sea trout for which he said there was not room in the deep freeze! As I thanked him he looked round, his blue eyes shining brightly.

"You've made a good life here Mike," he said. "I sometimes wish I had this place out here, just to sit and do some thinking, away from everything."

I looked round the croft, seeing it again as if for the first time, noting I still had not properly repaired the porch door.

"I haven't done as much with it as I should have," I said. "But I'll fix that door before I leave."

"Ah,"said Iain, paying me a compliment which coming from him was one I will never forget. "You've brought the old place to life again, Mike."

It was five weeks to the day since coming to the croft that Gilbert's bad leg showed signs of returning to life. To perk up his appetite I had put him in the burn for a bathe. When he had had enough he reached the side but he still could not scale the steep bank so he just clung there with one foot, his outstretched wings propping him up. Cruelly, I just left

Gilbert free again.

him and dangled his favourite raw steak above. Finally he struggled up again – then I saw it. The bad left leg went down and *pushed*. Then he was up on the bank and eating the steak. And later when he preened himself, he put the bad foot down tentatively for balance. The crisis, it seemed, was over.

During the next few days I kept Gilbert to strict "play" periods, chivvying him over the sunlit grass and daisies outside and making him flap and run after long squatting periods. I tempted him with titbits, threw him a few feet into the air so he had to fly and land on his own, but always rewarding him with food. He rarely pecked now, as if he faintly realized I was only doing it for his own good.

Towards the end of May, the buds finally breaking open on the ash trees lining the burn, it was clear there had been a good surviving lamb crop despite the earlier predations of the old fox. The sheep near me grazed on an oval daily migration, starting from their sleeping spots high in the hills and working down westwards to the beach. By midday they were all round the croft and at that time of the year I was treated to a real "lambs-and-ewes" chorus as each had a voice of slightly differing timbre.

One day I was watching Gilbert have a good preen after his dip when a baby lamb with a fine, wide face and long black "boots" went up, sniffing cautiously like a dog and intently curious about this great white bird. Gilbert, scared, jumped up and flapped his wings. The lamb leaped about five feet into the air and came down on the wrong side of my garden fence. It dashed over my new lettuce plants to escape this frightening feathered creature, and as it could have damaged itself against the wire netting I rushed out to rescue it. Off it went shaking its head and doing a high skittish leap every so often, until it found its mother's reassuring teats. Then it banged her up and down like a boat as she stood there looking at me with happy, silly-looking chewing smiles.

I soon found most of the lambs liked to come and sniff Gilbert. Sometimes they stood in small groups, heads close together, as if discussing what prank to play on him next. Then up they'd come, Gilbert would leap wildly, terrified, and away they would flee, hugely enjoying *their* little fright. As the lambs liked to frolic in and chew the fine earth from my seed boxes, I put Gilbert on duty beside them like a guard dog. That I had any onions at all that year was largely due to Gilbert's success as a sentry.

The scrub oak trees were at last in leaf on the day I decide to give Gilbert his freedom. I carried him down to the sea and, facing the warm southerly breeze, gently threw him into the air. He spread his wings and flapping harder than gulls normally do because his wing tip was still short, he flew round my head.

The sun shone through his pinions giving them a beautifully transparent look, and as he passed above me his white head turned to look down. "*Qwuck qwuck qwuck*" he intoned softly almost as if saying thanks, then away he went out to the far rock of the bay. There he landed in the water and began happily paddling around.

He occasionally came near the croft on the first few days snapping up food I left for him, and sometimes at dawn I saw him down on the beach, hurling over small piles of seaweed with great gusto as he searched for breakfast. By late August new primaries were growing to replace the few I had been forced to clip so that he could then soar and wheel almost as well as the other gulls. Sometimes he came over my head as if allowing me to take photos of him back in possession of his full flying powers.

He no longer allowed me close enough to pick him up but as the weeks passed by and I looked out in the mornings and saw he was still using my bay, where most of his battle for a return to health had taken place, well, that seemed reward enough.

18

FOR THE REST OF my last spring and summer on Shona I tried to intensify wildlife observations and spent many cold nights out in uncomfortable places. Watching wildlife is difficult enough but successful *photography* in the real wilds when major mammals are most active at dusk and before dawn, is harder still. And in these open hills the glens, rockfaces, long ridges and low corries so changed the course of ground winds they often blew in the opposite direction to the movements of the clouds.

My first target in May was the big fox which I felt was hunting mainly among the rockslides, meadows and a huge half-mile-long corrie between the high hills and seaward bluffs on the west edge of the island. Whether the terriers had killed a cub or two in the steep slide by Deer Point or not, I was sure the vixen had taken any surviving cubs elsewhere and that the foxes would be using other temporary dens in the area now. This idea seemed confirmed when Iain appeared by the croft on May 21 and said he'd been on a foot hunt with the foxhounds. They had found a warm, freshly killed tup lamb above Baramore on the north edge of the island, its innards taken, possibly by the vixen for a cub or two. The hounds had followed scent to various small corries and slides near Deer Point but had not been successful.

I told Iain I would set baits out for the foxes and sit out overnight to keep watch but I felt he was right when he suggested baits only really worked in a harsh winter when foxes were starving. I said there was probably too much natural prey about now.

"Ay," said Iain with feeling. "Too many defenceless young lambs about now!"

Still, I felt it worth a try. I made a hide of hazel wands, bamboo and camouflage netting stuffed with bracken and grasses, and after boating for supplies and a pile of meat bones and sheep ribs from the butcher, I rowed to Shoe Bay and carried everything over the hills to the big corrie. Choosing an open spot near some large boulders so the fox would feel safer, and wearing gloves dipped in spruce-needle juice I set the meat and bones out, pegging them down with ash twigs and obscuring these with scattered earth and grass tufts. Then downwind and about ninety yards above, I set the hide up between three five-foot-tall granite slabs. Sure the fox would not approach the bait the first night, I went home.

Up before dawn two days later I trekked back to check. On the way as I slipped between rocks on the western shore I saw an otter swimming in the sea, rolling and playing among the fronds of brown kelp that washed to and fro on the ocean swell. Although the light was poor – I could barely see the otter through the dark mirror lens – I banged off two shots – hopelessly as it turned out – and as it didn't reappear for twenty minutes I carried on and into the hide above the baits.

I watched as the light grew stronger – no fox. But it seemed the baits were now in different positions. When I went down in full light it seemed the fox *had* been there. The bones had been torn from their fastenings, most of the meat eaten and when I bent low I could detect a musky scent. I reset the red ribcage plus a juicy new bone and left.

Returning well before dusk I found the bones had again been ripped away, ravens were pecking at the empty ribcage, and the smaller bone had disappeared completely. So the fox had come to the bait in daylight? I resolved to wait out all night and after re-setting new bones, now slightly "off" as I had no fridge but for the cold tin in the burn, I retired to the hide. Hours went by as dusk turned to almost total blackness and only the miserable discomfort of my sitting position, the cold of the night increased by the cooling sweat in my clothes, kept me awake. Both camera and my field glass were tied in position to the hide, supported by one of the rocks. It is an eerie business, sitting over two miles from the nearest human habitation, shrouded by darkness in a gloomy glen, the huge hunched shapes of the hills brooding all round you in the land of the fox, eagle, wildcat and stag. The eyes play tricks in the dark, images form and pass across the retina of your mind and you have to constantly move focus, blink and look away and back to see things at all. The whitened bones were all that could be seen through the field glass, hardly at all through the camera, and at times appeared to be moving on their own. Many times I *imagined* I could see the form of a fox but when the pre-dawn twilight came it was clear the bones were exactly where they had been and were untouched.

Then the ravens came in, first a loud "*krok krok*" above me then down swept the first huge black bird. It landed with a sinister bat-like folding of its long broad wings, kept deadly still for a few seconds, head and powerful wedge-shaped beak held upwards, then it stalked sideways round the bones. Its first pecks were attended by brief jumps backward and scared looks around, as if it anticipated a trap. Presently others came down and all began tugging at the meat on the bones.

It was the first time I had been really close to so many ravens and I was amazed at the different sounds they made. I tried to divine the meanings of some of them during the next two hours and compared them with other raven noises I'd heard over the years. The loud *"prruk prruk"* seemed to be a light warning call in flight, a loud *"roawr"* is a serious warning to others, often made by a flying raven or one perched on a rock when its mates are feeding below. There was an oddly metallic *"poop poop"* sound, rather like a loud cuckoo, seemingly to inform a mate that it was in the same vicinity, an amusing *"gloop"* made when performing aerobatics and flying along on its back, plus an even more hilarious metallic *"boing"* which it makes when turning on its side in flight, going into momentary free fall, and uttered just as it rights itself again. As they fed now they hustled each other out of the way and made a variety of soft sounds – *"glogs"*, *"whows"*, *"crucks"* and *"pops"* but what each of these meant I had little idea. That ravens "talk" to each other and have a large vocal litany was obvious. But why should such a variety of sounds have evolved in a bird that is not, after all, as gregarious or a social nester as the rook or jackdaw? At any rate the sun was over the hill and the ravens had all gone again by the time I roused my stiff body and went home for some brief sleep.

As I had much writing to complete, I decided to have only one more try at seeing the fox and was back at the big corrie with the last meat bones at 8 pm. This time the old ones had not been pulled about but had been heavily pecked by the ravens so there was little meat left on them. Just in case any fox was actually watching and to obscure my scent, I kept some yards away, threw the new bones by the old then walked on over the hill towards the shore. Then I doubled back upwards and crept down to the hide, keeping low between the rocks by following the course of a freshet.

It was an even colder night for it had been a gorgeously hot day, the first of summer really, and the sky was clear, At least the stars shed a wee bit more light on the scene though it was still extremely dark. At about 2 am I roused from a brief doze to look through the eyepiece of the camera – I distinctly saw something move across the grey image of the bones. I stretched up to the field glass which had better light-gathering power and blinked with excitement. The fox was there! At least I thought it was for there was a dark shadow, doglike but slimmer and longer legged, moving by the bones. It moved slowly, as if floating, and I constantly had to shift my gaze slightly to make its shape out against the dark background. Certainly it was a fox, a big one, and I could see now its huge brush, almost as long as itself, thin at the base and swelling out like a black banana before thinning down to a point at the tip. As I watched fascinated, hoping it would not hear the banging of my heart, it seemed to grip the last big bone with its mouth, sink down until its belly was nearly on the grass, then it tugged with great jumping jerks, its forefeet braced far forward. The bone must have tangled up with some herbage or the ash stakes. Occasionally it stopped pulling and its front changed shape as if it were moving its head, watching and listening. Then back it went to attack again, pulling with strong jerks. I slid down to look through the camera but could not make it out against the general gloom through the lens. Back to the field glass. Within a minute or two it had worked the bone loose and knowing it would run off with it, I took a chance knowing the light was far too poor, and pushed the camera button hopefully at an eighth of a second.

Instantly the fox stopped, froze dead still, and suddenly was no longer there. Even at ninety yards, upwind, it had heard the metallic click of the shutter and was away. That was that. I knew it wouldn't come back that morning, probably never. But I kept waiting. Once again as light came so did the ravens. One by one they swooped down like monstrous black bats and again the corrie was filled with their strange echoing voices. This time I was treated to an odd little spectacle. Two of the birds started walking alongside each other, their throat and head feathers all fluffed out. Then they turned and bowed to each other like contestants in a Judo contest, one bird gave a peculiar "*chrraw*" croak deep in its throat, its head feathers flattened down except at the sides where two distinct crests like little horns appeared, then it jumped at the other with its claws extended. The second bird immediately flew to the far side of the group.

As I neared Shoe Bay later on my way home I again saw an otter so two days later when I took the fox hide down, I set it up again forty feet from where an otter had left fish scales and bones near a fresh-water pool. I spent two more early-morning vigils there but not another otter did I see. It was a long time before I learned one never used hides for mammals like foxes, otters, badgers or wildcats. Hides are mandatory for birds but are useless for animals with keen sight *and* sense of smell and higher reasoning powers. With mammals one is far better off arriving surreptitiously downwind in camouflaged clothing and just waiting amid trees, bushes, bracken, long grass or between rocks.

But there were minor compensations during this tiring period. Once I came back to find a merganser drake and duck preening themselves in brilliant sunlight on a rock just above the sea, and took some pictures. Another time I saw a mother eider fly up from heather near the shore.

She had seen me coming from a fair distance and had covered her seven dull-green eggs with her dark-brown down. I set the hide up but spent a fruitless afternoon – with her eggs covered in this way on such a hot afternoon she had no need to return for several hours. I was about to give up when a hooded crow flew to a rock near the nest. "This will be interesting," I thought. "A picture of a crow actually taking an eider's egg." Suddenly, with a great wooshing noise, the eider mother swept in, landed with a loud crash in the heather by the rock, scaring the crow out of its wits for it leaped into the air and flew off almost as fast as a hawk, squawking with fear. Clearly it hadn't seen the eider coming and it wasn't going to argue the toss! None of this did I photograph. I was focused on the nest alone.

I also found that if I kept a sharp eye on the ground there could be extra bonuses to every foot trek. On a sultry walk to the east I found a huge blue-black beetle, the like of which I'd never seen before. It had tiny, short elytra, or wingcases, but no wings at all and as I picked it up it released pools of clear orange-coloured oil from its joints. I popped it into a specimen box and consulting my insect book at home found it was a rare oil beetle, which could measure anything from 13 to 32 mm long. This one then, was a giant for it measured a fraction over two inches! Its life history was more fascinating – the female lays batches of tiny eggs in holes in the ground. When the little bristly larvae hatch they climb to the tops of flowers to hitch a ride from a bee! Once attached, they cling on until they arrive at the bee's nest where they turn into fat little grubs and eat the honey the bee has stored up for its own young. I photographed it then let it go amid grasses and bird's foot trefoil below the croft. It immediately clambered in an ungainly manner under some plantain leaves out of the sunlight and seemed to start eating the trefoil.

From interest I sent a photo to Bob Pope, a beetle expert at the British Museum of Natural History, London, whom I had known from many years ago in Sussex. Bob's reply was even more interesting. ". . . it seems to be an example of *Meloe violacetis,* Marsham. This species is less common than *Meloe proscarabaeus* (the common oil beetle), is rare in Scotland but has been taken from the Argyll area. . . . The common species occurs even further north, as far as Moray Firth." So I had made a first discovery of an important and interesting insect in Inverness-shire! I was delighted and ever since have taken specimens or photos of rare insects, butterflies and moths to the British Museum, registering a small number of first sightings for the region.

One blazing hot day, feeling guilty that I'd sunbathed all afternoon, I set off for a long trek over the hills to Deer Point and back along the hard way, among boulders which dwarfed the mere human along the western shore, still hoping I might find one of the dens the foxes were currently using. As I ascended the final hill, below a vast flat, almost circular area filled with peat bog and floating banks of mosses which formed the main rain-collecting area that fed my burn and three others, I saw a cuckoo behaving oddly. As I hid in the bracken it flew waveringly like a sparrowhawk might if it was dying of old age, fluttering low over the grasses as if checking nests in which to lay her eggs.

Suddenly a pair of meadow-pipits flew up, circled round her, looping and swooping excitedly but not actually buffeting the bigger bird. Then as they flew away again the cuckoo landed on a large mossy rock fifty yards away and sank down low as if not wishing to be seen. A female cuckoo "spies" on potential victims for when laying she has an egg ready to deposit roughly every 48 hours and she has to keep in her memory precise knowledge of the exact *condition* of several nests at a time. If she lays before the foster parents have laid their first egg, they may throw hers out or desert the nest. If she lays after the mother bird has started to incubate her own full clutch the other youngsters may hatch out faster and beat the young cuckoo in the competition for food So, to find all the nests in which she may lay up to a dozen eggs in a season the female cuckoo does not waste time and energy searching the terrain on wing or foot – she perches in a tree and keeps watch on her victims. Once she has located a nest that way she flies down to inspect it. But here there were no trees and this cuckoo was using the mossy *rock* as a spy perch.

She waited there about ten minutes as I took photos, then as if unable to hold back any longer she flew direct to the place where the meadow-pipits had risen, vanished in the grasses for a few seconds then flew off again, disappearing behind a small ridge to the right. Keeping my eye on the exact place I walked over and found the pipit's nest – with four of their own reddish blotched eggs plus a slightly larger, rounder, paler and warmer egg – certainly the cuckoo's. Noting its position with an impromptu "Treasure Island" map, excited that I might later take photos of a young cuckoo ejecting its foster brethren or being fed, I went on my way.

As I turned west between the high hills above Deer Point the strong breeze from the sea turning my perspiration into the effective body cooler it's meant to be, I heard a spitting snarl, saw a flurry of reddish-brown and had a glimpse of blackened hairs at the tip of a thick brush as a big fox disappeared back into the gloom of a recess in the rocks. Just then the pungent sweet-ammoniac scent of the fox hit my nostrils.

Cursing myself for not going slower, at the sun being in my eyes and for my slow reaction because for once I actually had the camera and lens in my hand, I went over to look. It didn't appear to be a regular den, just a hole between the rocks of a small slide which vanished in a dark bend no more than a foot high. There were no scats about, no prey remains or signs of an oft-used trail so it was probably just one of many resting and watching places the fox used. Certainly there were some vole runs in the grassy edges of the crater-like area of bogs, and many frogs hopping round the pools, some of which were black with tadpoles.

I was sure now the fox used this area for hunting, maybe more often than the big corrie above the western shore, and I tried the baiting technique once more. But though I waited out two more nights the meat bones remained untouched. Had I seen Iain at this time I would have told him of the "den" I'd found but it was some weeks before we met again and by then the lambs were bigger and the killings had stopped – possibly also due to the increase in natural prey. But when I returned in ten days to photograph the young cuckoo in the meadow-pipits' nest I was doomed to disappointment. Everything had gone, nest and all and I was sure the fox had found it, probably using the nest as a convenient "carrier bag" to take away the eggs or youngsters.

Another small tragedy occurred a few days later. I woke up one rainy morning to guttural croaks – four ravens had discovered a dead lamb caught up on some rocks lower down the burn and were making a meal of it. They appeared to be of one family, two adults and two youngsters, bulkier and loose plumaged with smaller heads and softer looking about the eyes. Standing on the bank they watched their parents with rapt attention as one stood on the lamb's body and appeared to lift its tail while the other pecked hard until it was able to tug some of the entrails out of the rectum. There was much croaking and I had no doubt as I peered from my window – one movement of the door and the ravens would have flown – that the parents were actually *teaching* their young this technique, which allows ravens to secure their carrion meal without having to puncture the dead animal's hide first. Once they have broken their fast on tender innards, the big birds can relax more and spend time attacking through the flank skin or through the front of the neck, which they are perfectly able to do. It was not the most pleasant sight in nature perhaps but interesting.

After a couple of hours the ravens flew away and I went to examine the lamb. It was not injured but was heavily swollen and as it had not come from the flock around the croft and was small for the time of the year, I concluded it had been late born, had not received much suck and had fallen into the water from the steep rock faces higher in the hills and had drowned. Then it had been washed down in the spates following recent rains. Oddly its eyes were still in place. I decided to leave it to see what other predators might come to the feast.

The torrential downpour accompanied by driving south-west gales continued throughout that day and the next night and it became so cold I had to light the paraffin stove. Even spiders and beetles were sneaking into the house to avoid the weather. Next morning the burn, now swelled to winter height, had washed the dead lamb a hundred yards out to sea but when the wind switched to slightly warmer southerlies it drifted on shore again, this time on the east side of the bay and behind some rocks. Nothing went near it all day but at about 7 pm the ravens arrived again, the original family plus three others. Failing to find the lamb where they had left it in the burn they flew to the shore, a few pacing about, and from the occasional croaks that came through my slightly open window they seemed to be "talking" to each other.

Presently one bird flew out over the waves, circled round the west side of the bay and went down again. I could not see the lamb from the window and wondered if it had been moved out to sea again, or had sunk. But then another adult raven flew out, this time in an easterly circle, baulked suddenly, gave a loud "*krok krok*" call and wheeled straight down to vanish behind some rocks. The other ravens, including the two young, needed no second bidding and flew to join in. It seemed the birds had worked out that if they sat on the rocks and just let *one* search for the lamb at a time, they would find it without all tiring themselves any more than they had to. Not until the following morning when, strangely, the ravens didn't return, did a cruising greater black-backed gull find the carcase and after this big bird's visit I found the eyes *had* been taken. Not once had I seen a hooded crow near the lamb, though of course I had not watched it every minute of the day.

In mid June large sunny patches of blue appeared in the sky, the winds dropped and summer was upon us once more. Within three days the bird life appeared to have doubled about the croft. Nesting willow-warblers sang sweet diminutive songs from above their young in the boggy thickets, the chaffinches, robins and wrens, also nesting, sang in their small territories, and a pair of yellow-hammers, rare for the area, had moved in from the south. One sang from a garden post for two mornings, his usual "bread and no cheese" song ending here with a definite Highland accent so it sounded like "we'll let the de'il take ye". Once even a bright yellow-green siskin appeared, a long way from its favourite conifer habitat. Perhaps it was after insects for its young as it competed with some fly-catching grey wagtails in fluttering gamboge dances near the cliff walls of my bay which, now the winds had dropped, was a trap of halcyon calm for thousands of insects. Butterflies such as small fritillaries, tortoiseshells and green-veined whites hopped and dropped through the warm humid air – infinitely preferable to the clouds of midges that had begun to bite in late May.

Now one of the buzzard pair whose nest I could not find, and more often the male than the female, sailed over each morning announcing its arrival with clear ringing "*keeyoos*" which allowed me time to grab my camera. After lunch one day I was at my desk when a flash of barred feathers made me look out. A superb little sparrowhawk with glaring eyes had landed on the garden post nearest the bird table, briefly stared in at me and in a trice was off again. But not before I'd seen its tail feathers were now perfectly grown, for I was sure it was Buzz.

No doubt he had wintered in Shona forest, keeping to the shelter of the glades where small woodland birds lived and sheltered too, until the better weather allowed him to hunt more in the open again. It was wonderful to know he had survived, that perhaps the time of year, the summer foliage, the sunlight and whole look of the place where he had learned to fly and hunt, had drawn him back so that this was now an integral part of his summer hunting area. Down on the shore Gilbert Gull was still occasionally flying to a rock to be fed a mussel or two, though he no longer allowed a close approach either.

As I thought of these old "friends", I remembered Harry Heron and how his old nest had been empty in the spring. I decided to check the whole heronry and see if he *had* mated this year after all. I boated to Deer Island and as I tramped beneath the trees, young herons squawked harshly *"ar ar..quarr.r.r. quarre"*, their necks stretched up like thin, grey bottles with button eyes near the tops. There seemed to be seven new nests yet a few of the older ones of the original thirty-eight appeared to have been abandoned. Some of the adult herons were more wary than others and just kept sailing high over the treetops but a few flew in, landed heavily, spotted me and took off again, while others, with perhaps slightly younger young, came sailing in sneakily low and alighted gently. But one heron sitting in the topmost twigs slightly to the side of a new nest stayed where it was, refusing to budge as I passed an open patch below, and as I put the glass up the unmistakable broken toe stood out clearly. Certainly there were young in the nest but without climbing irons there was no way I could get up the tall fir. Besides, I consoled myself, it was far too late to start trying to build treetop hides!

On the nearby islets I took a few photos of young common gulls as they crouched in the grass. Four of the nests contained eggs in which half-formed young had died, some, it seemed, in the act of hacking their way out with the egg teeth on the tops of their little beaks. Five other eggs had not hatched at all. Out of a total of fourteen nests this seemed a high mortality, probably due in part to marine pollution in the parents' food, for in the world's oceans pollution does not stay only in the areas where it is released but permeates in diluted form, theoretically, right around the globe. Perhaps the wildcat or a fox had kept the parents off the nests all night in the recent bad weather and the chicks in unhatched eggs had died of cold. Oddly the terns had not nested on the islets at all this year though a few desultory individuals were flopping into the water off shore for fish. Perhaps it had been a bad winter in the Antarctic for them.

As I rowed home in the late sunlight Sammy the seal and two others sported and dipped near the brightly flashing oars, allowing the closest photos ever, and when I hauled the boat up they came close into my bay, treating me to a fine diving display as they constantly broke surface and sounded again with hissing snorts, the water falling and gleaming from their black polished pates.

There was an added bonus to that golden day for no sooner had I stepped into the croft than Little Fat Sergeant and his new family were back on the bird table. His wife was sitting on a twig weaving her tail sideways and he exchanged loving "kisses" with her, their beaks together and gently plucking at each other's plumage, as if to help their summer moult. He not only fed the young, I noticed, but also popped the odd morsel of bread into her mouth as well. It made me feel quite lonesome.

19

THE THOUGHT THAT I would soon have to leave Shona for the even wilder place up the fresh-water loch began to weigh on my mind. Certainly with its woodlands, far higher mountains where golden eagles soared and miles of uninhabited glens and rivers, it was a wonderful wildlife area. But could I really bear to live away from the sea? I would be going to far greater isolation for even with the Land Rover parked in the pine wood I still faced a thirteen-mile return boat trip – easy enough in summer but hard in winter when the loch would often be a mass of seething foam.

But one cloudy afternoon when such doubts assailed me I happened to look to the east – the only patch of blue sky in sight was now hovering over where Wildernesse lay tucked below the hills! It was the first time I had ever seen that for usually my croft was bathed in sunlight while the cloud cover started a mile inland. How odd! In an isolated life such "signs" assume a strange importance.

Next morning dawned in a dull calm and realizing I would need good cut lumber at my new home I decided to go and take the partly built cabin apart. As I set off down to the boat I thought I caught a glimpse of Buzz again – so I put a small chunk of steak near his old perch. At the site I dismantled the two walls with both sledge and claw hammers, jemmied up the 12-ft floor joists, removed all the nails and carried everything down to the rocks above high tide level. It was hard, sweaty work and when I rowed home at teatime I felt ready for a good soapy bath in bowls outside before the sun went down.

As I walked up past the garden and plucked a lettuce I saw the steak had disappeared. Surely it had been taken by Buzz for Gilbert never came up to the croft any more and it was too heavy for any small bird to remove. After my late lunch I looked outside again – still calm and in an hour it would be high tide. To hell with a bath then. I went out, put engine and tank on the boat, went round to the site, loaded up, made a huge "boom" of the biggest timbers with a couple of timber-hitched ropes, and towed the whole lot back to my bay in one go. There I carried all the timber up ready tor the big move. As I had my belated "bath" by the side of the burn I felt pleased, I had moved most of a whole 12-ft cabin in one day – the hardest work since I first arrived on Shona and had struggled to make one room livable, so long ago now, it seemed.

Next day on a trek in hot sunlight I saw Harry Heron gliding into a small inlet near a disused log dump two miles along the south shore. As he did not associate my human figure emerging from the forest with the one he knew on *my* beach, I stalked him like a deer. As I peeped through bushes, quietly clearing a way for the lens between the leaves, the sun streamed upon him through a gap in the trees. He was bathed in light, his light blue uniform, smokey dark blue epaulettes and long black plumes transforming him into His Excellency as he stood there on his stilts, haughty and aware. Two shots, two clicks and he heard them and was winging away, his body moving up and down with the effort.

On the way home again I walked back over the hills and saw not a single deer which didn't surprise me for at summer's height many of Shona's deer forded the narrow shallows on the north shore during the night at low tide and went up to the high tops on the mainland where they could still find good pasture and escape the biting flies. As I approached the croft in the dusk I saw a strange form moving to and fro just above the ground in the evening mist. Sometimes I could see it, sometimes not, and it swung like a pendulum swinging from an invisible cord. It was a ghost moth, one of the swift family, the males of which fly like this when trying to locate a female. Its chrysalis is an oddity too, for when the imago is ready to emerge it wriggles up through the soil to the surface to let it out.

One evening as terns flopped in and out of the water with little fish in their beaks, I was out fishing when I met Iain and Morag in one of the island's smaller boats. They came up for a drink and when I showed him my stacked lumber on the shore and wondered aloud how I was going to move it and all my gear to Wildernesse, Iain said he would give up a Sunday to help me.

"How much pay will you want?" I asked.

"Och, I'll leave that to your good self!" he said. "Helping folk move is part of my work!" I thanked him with relief for alone it would have been a two to three-day task.

On July 2 I began hauling the cabin timbers and a few spare fish boxes (for furniture at Wildernesse) over to a boathouse on the mainland. The move had started. When I returned the chaffinch family were tucking into the food I'd left on the bird table but now the hen was doing all the feeding. Little Fat Sergeant was now showing no interest in his youngsters who were soliciting both parents madly, weaving from side to side with tails and wings splayed and making odd little *"creeop"* notes. Instead he ignored them totally, eating his own fill and looking about him with an air that said "I've done my share for this year. It's up to you now, missus!"

In mid-July, I paid a quick trip to London and after seeing all the year's films developed, managed to part-exchange the unwieldy 1000-mm mirror lens for a new 640-mm Novoflex which was far lighter, had a larger aperture, pistol grip focusing and was ideal for wildlife work. Knowing I'd need a more powerful engine and better boat for the winter gales at my new home I bought a 20-hp Johnson outboard and also ordered, via a Mallaig firm, a 15 ft 6 ins WITH 450 fibreglass boat which had a small semi-cabin up front. My finances took a dive back to well below zero but it was better than suffering premature death. I was assured the double-hulled boat would still float even when full of water, which no boat I'd used on seas during my life on lonely beaches in the past seven years would have done. As I drove home to the Highlands again I couldn't help reflecting this playing safe possibly indicated advancing age!

One day in early August I found a dying lamb, its feet sticking out straight and its eyes turned inwards. It lay in the bracken below a small ruined croft in which a pair of swallows now had four young ready to fly. I was about to go and fetch Iain while collecting my post from the big house when I saw him on the hill above the croft. He had brought not only my mail but a gift of twelve eggs from his hens plus a mighty lettuce that put my own plants to shame. He looked at the lamb, now dead, and diagnosed "pulpy liver". It was not a contagious disease but if not found until the late stages one could do nothing about it, he said. As we went back into the croft for a beer Iain sat down on the bed, the only other perch apart from my old desk chair, and voiced what he had on his mind.

"Now you have a new engine, what will you do with the old one?" I said I'd probably use it for fishing in the old small boat at Wildernesse, and as a spare. He was silent for a while, then "Will ye be needing a 'fridge up there? You'll not be making many trips to the store from that place?" I said I had not possessed a fridge or had the use of electricity for over seven years and as always I would use a "cold box" for meat and suchlike in the new burn.

Iain coughed. "Well it's just that I have this calor gas fridge we'll not be needing any more. We're getting a new deep freezer to put on to the generator. I was thinking. . . ." he paused a moment, wondering how to put it. "Now, your engine is worth fifty, sixty pounds and the fridge only about thirty. Would you take our fridge for your engine plus an adjustment in cash?" He looked at me intently, a slight smile on his face.

I looked at him sitting there cross-legged, a man I'd misjudged on earlier meetings. He may have regarded himself as a servant but to me he was a man of uncommon skills – bi-lingual for he had the Gaelic, skilful fisherman, deer stalker, tree feller, sawmill operator, ferryman, gardener and shepherd. He was also a fine enough piper to have earned his living at the pipes alone. Although I had not wanted casual walk-in company while writing in the lonely croft, I had come to enjoy his occasional visits and lively talk in the lambing seasons. I could see he wanted my 7-hp engine badly.

"No," I said. His face fell.

"We'll do an Indian trade," I said.

"What's that?"

"You want engine. I need fridge. Your need. My need. Straight exchange. No cash adjustment. That's it."

Iain found it hard to believe but that was the final arrangement.

After he'd gone I carried the dead lamb down to the shore a quarter mile from the croft, set up a small hide in the bracken two hundred yards away and entered it before dawn. I still wanted to see which predator came first. Within an hour and just after first light a pair of greater black-backed gulls sailed in and for the two hours I watched had the carcase to themselves. No ravens or hooded crows came near. When I went down to bury the lamb the upper eye was missing and the powerful beaks of the gulls had hacked a hole below the ribs where they had feasted deep on lungs and heart. This again did not vindicate the crow completely, especially on inland hill farms where there are few black-backs.

The wildlife adventures during my remaining time on Shona now became fragmentary for I was working on yet another "final" version of the Canadian wilderness book and still repairing the croft, to fulfil my end of the deal before I left. On August 8 I was installing new front guttering when Gilbert the gull came circling and "*qwuck qwucking*" with another herring-gull that kept at a greater distance. It seemed he might have found a mate though I doubted if they would stay together until the following year. He had grown most of his new wing feathers by now and I raced indoors for my camera, managing a good picture of him in flight. At dusk Harry Heron flew into the bay accompanied by two youngsters. They kept together on the dry beach with their heads hunched into their shoulders but watching intently as he stalked and waited, stalked and waited, in the shallows. It seemed certain he was actually teaching them how to fish. Why in heck didn't he ever come back in photographable daylight!

Next day as I boated back with a huge scythe borrowed from Iain for cutting the bracken, I saw a red deer hind actually *climbing* a fence. One stob had snapped off so the fence was leaning away from her. She climbed slowly up it like a long-legged monkey, her long neck and almost reptilian head extended, put one foot carefully above the other, seemed to hook the wires under the two upper rear claws, then sprang off and away. Later, after cutting a quarter acre of bracken, I started sharpening the scythe while standing on the steep slope. Flailing away with the carborundum stone in most professional manner, feeling pleased I was carrying out my policy for wilderness living – live quietly, enhance the *natural* beauties, pay the place back for what it has given you, leave no permanent fixtures and, like a nomadic Indian, depart without trace – when I felt a sudden sharp pain. Careless in self-congratulation, I had nearly severed my right index finger on the curved blade of the scythe and the blood spurted. Scared I'd need stitches I raced indoors for my animal medical supplies. I sucked more blood out hard, forced the top of the finger back down, ringed it with antibiotic cream, wrapped a bandage round and let the blood congeal inside it, so forming a hard protective cast. Luckily the flesh knitted back together but typing was impossible for over a week. I didn't like that scythe after that and found by swinging an old saw flatways I could hack the bracken just as well, for that way I cut it on both the back and forward swings.

Two days of gales followed, raging so hard that leafy twigs snapped off the ash trees and were plastered against the wet windows, reminding me that autumn was not far away. But when the third morning came in a cloudless blue sky I boated for supplies to the village at the head of the loch five miles away so I could fish on the way. I was just trolling along when suddenly the rod felt strange, lighter, and the line was right up in the air by my side. My heart chilled for I was just passing Castle Tioram and I first thought that someone, maybe a ghost of the Clanranald chiefs, was sitting behind me and holding it up.

But when I looked back I saw a *tern* had taken the lure and was flying at the end of the line like a kite, diving and swooping as it tried to get off but it weighed so little it did not undo the rachet on the reel. I had been going a bit too fast for the weight I was using on the line, the artificial lure had been travelling near the surface and the tern, believing it to be a fish, had dived upon it. I slowed the engine, reeled in and the poor bird hit the water by the side of the boat. Luckily the hook was only in the side of its beak and there were no flesh wounds. I removed it as the tern pecked hard with its sharp bill and let it go, none the worse for its odd adventure.

That evening as I cooked supper I heard the rutting roar of a stag behind the croft. I slipped out in camouflage jacket and stalked near as it

208

roared again, I was sure it was Sebastian back from his summer on the mainland but while his antlers were magnificent they still only had ten points. I roared back but after a few paces forward he turned and ran off up the hill. It was strange he should be making his rutting roars as early as mid-August, especially when there were apparently no hinds near, a fact I confirmed after an early trek next day. Maybe he was just asserting himself back in his old rutting territory.

When I returned from the walk two glowing garden tiger moths, just hatched out, were resting in the sun on one of my garden posts. A new hawker dragonfly, the black and yellow ringed species of the Aeshnas, which a hasty look at my insect books told me was "not found in Scotland," was now working above the burn for insects to snap up in flight.

Now I checked the few bramble bushes for blackberries hoping some would be ready in time for bottling and taking to Wildernesse. But as yet the fruits were green and red. The second-year shoots of the big bush nearest the croft that had borne such luscious berries last year had all died off and were brown and sere, and the few new shoots growing through them had no flowers. Yet further up the burn the smaller bush which had yielded a poor harvest last year was now filled with unripe berries. It was interesting that brambles thus stagger their fruiting peaks, being more prolific every second year, as well as each bush having ripe *and* unripe berries from early September to mid-November. Thus both humans and birds had a constant supply over at least a two-month period, and with birds scattering seeds via their droppings, more new bushes could take root. But I kept the brambles trimmed, not only so the strength of the thick probing leaders would go into the fruit but because they were dangerous to weakened sheep in winter.

It was a hot day and after lunch I sunbathed on the green sward below the croft. Now the yellow stinging-nettle flowers were exploding with little puffs of pollen into the warm air like cannonfire, providing their own miniature Waterloo before my half-closed eyes. When the sun went lower I spent the rest of the day forking all rocks and large stones from a fifty-yard strip of beach. On this cleared shingle I would berth my new boat in a special rope and plank "cradle" I had made for her.

Towards the end of August she arrived at the little pier and she looked a beautiful creature. Digby Vane and Iain and some of the other islanders and mainland friends were also there and we lowered her into the sea. She sat like a swan, high, light and buoyant as if basking in the admiring compliments. But I was in a hurry to get her home at the peak of the high tide for I had to haul her out alone and she weighed 400 lbs without the engine. As I towed her back to my bay, curlews with a few young were back on the sandbanks from breeding further inland and several cormorants passed across the bows bobbing their heads in and out of the water as they tried to paddle out of range before making a frantic last-second dive.

I hauled the first boat out as usual but found I was hardly able to budge the new one. Only by splashing water to make the planks slippery and by hauling her at a rush from the sea did I manage to get her onto the cradle. Even then I had a slightly pulled back. When I looked down from the slope they both lay as if talking to each other. It's just as well boats *can't* talk, I thought, or the old one would tell the newcomer yarns about the Highland storms to frighten her out of her wits.

During three drizzly days I pounded away at my book but when sun blazed on the fourth I decided to try out the new boat. I carried down and screwed on the new engine which with full tank brought the total weight of the craft beneath me to well over 500 lbs. She moved superbly, solid but easy in the water, and when I turned up the throttle and she planed at twenty-two knots I soon slowed down – scared stiff at the unaccustomed speed. I always try to go quietly in a boat but it was good to know the power was there if needed up the long loch that was soon to be my home water.

I was so delighted I went further than intended so decided to burble on slowly past Deer Island. To my chagrin there were forty-eight herons sitting on the rocks below the great nests. The dark slabs were thick with both adults and youngsters all sitting hunched like flecks of snow in the dying sunshine, and I had no camera with me! By the time I returned the tide was well past the ebb and the boat plus engine were now too heavy for me to haul up the steep banks of shingle. So, laying down planks and putting rocks on their ends to hold them down when the tide rose, I bent a long branch of the nearest alder tree down about eight feet and tied the boat painter to it. As the tide came up and floated the boat the spring-back of the branch would constantly haul it inch by inch out of the sea's reach. The idea worked too, as I found when I went down at midnight and made the final heave to safety myself.

On the last day of August the worst gale since winter came blasting in from the south-west but anxious to fetch supplies so I could spend a final week on the Canadian book before the move to Wildernesse, I set off in the new boat. After a mile I was overtaken by pounding rain, the gale force increased and I had to anchor in the lee of Castle Tioram rather than at the pier which was a mass of raging foam. On the way back the boat performed feats of which the old dinghy would have been incapable. Her bow drove deep into each crashing wave and reared again easily, the semi-cabin diverting water to each side with cleaving thrusts so I no longer had to contend with drenching spray *and* rain, just the rain alone. Even so I had to dash into the lee of the little inlet opposite Ballindona. My experience told me the gales would now increase for several hours before lessening and after waiting several minutes I made a dash for it. Although we shipped a little water from the high waves the powerful new engine thrust us home in minutes, smashing the way ahead. With the tide now low I left her on the sand with the double disc anchors out from her stern then tied her to the alder with over a hundred yards of new, steam-tarred nylon rope.

I was just in time for within minutes of being back in the croft I could hardly even see the land opposite and the sea had turned into a mass of raging white. Crags and grey prominences appeared occasionally through the swathes of hissing rain and mist, while the wind howled through the ash trees, tearing off branches, rattling my roof, and on the slopes below bent bushes almost double. Despite the comparative shelter of the cliff-walled bay the rising tide came in with great crashing waves so that the new boat dragged its anchors and the bow rope became snagged round several weed-covered boulders. It was now impossible to haul it in straight and as I fought for footing up to my waist in the waves, trying to free the rope again, the boat pounded up and down at the edge of the tide.

Somehow I got the engine off and the fuel tank and oars out before the boat began hitting the small rocks of the middle beach. But terrified it might yet be damaged I made superhuman efforts and managed to haul her out over planks. I was down there for three hours and August or not, found myself trembling with fatigue and cold. It was just like the day I had lost my boat below the clifftop cabin in Canada and I really felt that some strange wilderness nemesis, which appeared whenever I was about to leave a place had again overtaken me. That too had been a summer storm. After seven years of living with small boats and the sea it seemed I could still make mistakes and misjudge the weather.

Up the slope the swollen burn had burst its banks, flattening and tearing off some nettles. Several tortoiseshell butterfly caterpillars lay half drowned in the ooze. I warmed them up in my hands then put them on new nettles in the shelter of the big rock below my window. In a minute they all recovered and with their great rounded clasper feet set firmly they clipped away at the leaves like little machines thrust into high gear.

This sudden touch of harsh weather seemed to remind the birds that winter was no longer far away and many began flocking to the bird table – young robins, hedge-sparrows, chaffinches, blackbirds, all with one parent or the other. Wren families flitted in the bracken and once a young wren landed on the bird table and squared up to the hen chaffinch – who ignored it. Harry and his two youngsters came to the bay nearly every evening now, even when I was collecting cockles and mussels to bottle for sea food at Wildernesse. On September 4 a young buzzard landed on the rock outside the window. I had never seen one so

Harry on a rock near the croft early in the morning.

close and it looked like a small eagle but with brown eyes and a softer expression. When it flew away I put a piece of meat on the rock hoping it would return. Within the hour there was a flash across the window, the sound of rushing air, but it was not the buzzard – sparrowhawk Buzz snaffled the meat and was away again so fast I was up in time to see only his long tail vanishing into the cliff bushes to the south-east. His speed was now dazzling but it was good to know he was still alive.

I finished the new Canadian book on September 12, determined if it failed again it would also go on to the shelf with the novel's various manuscripts which had also taken up exactly three-and-a-half years of my working life.

Brilliant sunshine blazed during the last three days as I carried gear down to the beach – fishbox cupboards, pictures, sea-scoured "ornaments" from the roots of trees, ten times more books than I had first brought with me, the wooden scaffold for painting the roof, and tools, boots, tinned foods and clothes – covering all with plastic sheets held down by rocks in case the weather changed again. I dug up all the onions, carrots and cabbages, bagging some and brining others.

One evening as I returned from stowing two more loads into the boatshed on the mainland and came up the slope in the dusk, the leading hind of a group of nine grazing behind the croft barked at me like a bear. I stayed still and waited. Sure enough, Sebastian was with the hinds and later I heard him roaring. A real master stag now, he was having first choice of the hinds and would keep all young rivals away until he'd had his fill of rutting.

Two days before leaving Harry Heron came floating alone into the bay early in the morning making his familiar harsh *"kraink kraink"* calls, sounding like someone tearing a heavy sail. I went out with the camera to actually call to him, wondering if he would take any notice. By constricting my throat I made a passable imitation. To my surprise he immediately wheeled round and flew towards me. It is quite a frightening sight to see such a huge bird, dagger beak extended, coming straight for you but I kept still and darned if he didn't land on a large rock just a few yards from the croft. I took his picture then he flew away again. It was perhaps the most astonishing experience I had with him in his maturity.

On the last day I tore up the old blue carpet and hauled it with the last items down to the beach – more books, the ancient paraffin heater, the desk contents, clothes, tape recorder, little battery record player, containers, cold box, and the old fish net to protect my *new* garden patch. I took down everything but my bedding, cooker and the big mahogany desk I had grown to love and was now loth to leave behind.

As I worked a lovely red admiral butterfly, the first I had seen at Ballindona, landed on some white bramble flowers. Dandelion seeds were blowing in the wind on their tiny parasols, crane-flies were laying eggs in the earth and the first blackberries had ripened on the bushes, moving slightly in the wind like farewell offerings.

In late afternoon Iain came round with the island's largest dinghy. We loaded the three boats and took everything over to the mainland woodshed. There my big boat and new engine were lifted on to the trailer of a friend who would leave them on the new lochside where the little farm track ran out six-and-a-half miles from Wildernesse. Personal items were loaded into my Land Rover and everything else on to a flatbed coal lorry which Iain was to drive on the morrow and which had been lent me by Allan MacColl.

On the way back to Ballindona for the last time I called at Shona House for a farewell drink with the Vanes. I had dreaded this moment most of all, and as I sat in their lovely lounge, my hand none too steady on the huge dram of whisky Digby handed over, I tried to thank them for letting me live on their island and for the loan of the radio, the disc anchors and the fine mahogany desk which I had grown to love as if it were an animate thing and which seemed to have been "lucky" for my writings.

Suddenly Kay Vane said "You'll need that desk now, Mike, so you had better keep it, with our good wishes."

Reggie Rotheroe coughed lightly and referring to the radio which he had made himself, pointed out that as everyone on the island had his little radio mine was now surplus to requirements, so I had better keep that too.

"Don't bother about returning the anchors or the calor gas regulator," said Digby. "You'll need them up there, and you'd better take this along as well." He reached behind his chair and produced a new five-gallon water container with a tap. "We never use it and it may come in useful for your drinking water in a winter freeze-up."

"Don't worry if life doesn't work out too well up there," said Kay. "We've talked things over and you can come back here any time you wish. We'll keep Ballindona free for you to return to for at least two years."

As I looked at them, scarcely able to stammer out my thanks for these new kindnesses, I think I hid my emotions rather well. They had been more than good to me, these people.

It was dark when I boated back to the little beach and walked up the steep slope for the last awful night. I recalled then the last day at my clifftop home in Canada, when useful objects had floated by on the evening tide as if begging me not to go, and I'd had to find a new home for my only companion of those years, dear wild dog Booto, because I could not condemn him in his old age to months of jail in British quarantine kennels. How lonely *that* last night in British Columbia had seemed, but no sadder or more lonesome than this night for I knew I was now saying farewell to this wild, beautiful place with the same reluctance.

As the last hours ticked away, with everything gone, I sat staring into space. The washing mirror gleamed its bleak emptiness on the wall, reflecting the empty shelves, the bare wooden floor, my stew simmering on the little stove. I felt a strange emptiness and everything sounded louder, as if I were sitting in a drum, a void. Everything I possessed, nothing much more than a boat, engine and the old Land Rover, plus a few personal documents and photos, were now in the boatshed or on that lorry two-and-a-half miles across the sea. A few house flies, small and flying silently, swung to and fro in the still air as if they had moved in for the wake. It was hard to sleep for the last time in the little bed on the fishboxes.

Early next morning, with the weather finally broken and rain teeming down, I said my goodbyes to Ballindona, to the burn, the ash trees, the heathered hills, to the room where Buzz had spent his nights during the weeks of training, where Gilbert the gull had recovered his health, and to the croft itself. As I walked down the path with the final load, oblivious to the tears of the sky, and set sail in the old boat for the last time sparrowhawk Buzz appeared from nowhere and flew low over my head as if assuring me he was well and would still survive all right. And before I had gone half a mile Harry Heron, looking immense against the dark and raining sky, also flew over with terrible harsh cries. Herons carry away the souls of the departed, the ancient Highlanders believed, but as he came really close I felt that he sensed I was leaving, was even saying goodbye.

I hated to go yet leave I must, to follow the lonely star of my fate, to even greater isolation and deeper Highland wilderness experience. It was not fear I felt, for loneliness had for me become a liberation, but there was more than rain upon my cheeks as Ballindona receded in the mist for I knew now that while Canada had been a step aside – a rebirth of a kind – on Shona I had found a personal meaning to life itself.